ORGANISATIONAL BEHAVIOUR

The Business Briefings series consists of short and authoritative introductory textbooks in core business topics. Written by leading academics, they take a no-nonsense, practical approach and provide students with a clear and succinct overview of the subject.

These textbooks put the needs of students first, presenting the topics in a meaningful way that will help students to gain an understanding of the subject area. Covering the basics and providing springboards to further study, these books are ideal as accessible introductions or as revision guides.

Other books in the Business Briefings series:

Quantitative Methods, by Les Oakshott

Research Methods, by Peter Stokes

Marketing, by Jonathan Groucutt

Human Resource Management, by Michael Nieto

Financial Accounting, by Jill Collis

Management Accounting, by Jill Collis

ORGANISATIONAL BEHAVIOUR

MIKE MAUGHAN

BLOOMSBURY ACADEMIC
LONDON • NEW YORK • OXFORD • NEW DELHI • SYDNEY

BLOOMSBURY ACADEMIC
Bloomsbury Publishing Plc
50 Bedford Square, London, WC1B 3DP, UK
1385 Broadway, New York, NY 10018, USA
29 Earlsfort Terrace, Dublin 2, Ireland

BLOOMSBURY, BLOOMSBURY ACADEMIC and the Diana logo are trademarks of
Bloomsbury Publishing Plc

First published by Palgrave Macmillan 2014
Reprinted by Bloomsbury Academic 2024

A catalogue record for this book is available from the British Library.

A catalog record for this book is available from the Library of Congress.

ISBN-13: 978-1-137-31242-6 paperback

Series: Business Briefings

To find out more about our authors and books visit www.bloomsbury.com and sign up
for our newsletters.

This book is dedicated to my old friend, colleague and mentor, Clem Wilkinson, whose unflappable calm I always admired but have never been able to emulate.

CONTENTS

List of Figures   viii

List of Tables   ix

Preface   x

Acknowledgements   xii

  1 **What is Organisational Behaviour?**   1

  2 **Individual Differences**   41

  3 **Perception, Beliefs and Attitudes**   79

  4 **Motivation**   114

  5 **Working in Groups**   149

  6 **Leadership**   187

  7 **Structuring the Organisation**   220

  8 **Culture in Organisations**   250

  9 **Power and Politics in Organisations** 282

10 **Managing Change**   311

11 **The Future for Organisational Behaviour**   340

Index   365

LIST OF FIGURES

1.1	A simple linear system	7
1.2	The organisation as a simple system	20
1.3	Linear problem solving	22
2.1	Cattell's 16 Personal Factor constructs	46
3.1	A simplified diagram of the perceptual process	82
4.1	Maslow's hierarchy of needs	117
4.2	Expectancy theory as a cyclical process	124
6.1	Blake and Mouton Management grid. Reproduced by permission of Gulf Publishing Company	195
6.2	Fiedler's leadership styles	202
6.3	House's path–goal theory	206
6.4	Leader functions in action-centred leadership	209
7.1	Simplified hierarchical structure	224
7.2	A matrix of academic business programmes	233
7.3	The main features of core-periphery model	236
7.4	Comparison of a petroleum company's organisation chart with its real-world communication patterns. Adapted and reproduced with permission from Elsevier Publishing	240
8.1	Schein's model of organisational culture	253
10.1	Lewin's change process	320
10.2	The action research cycle	326
10.3	Haverton Advice Centre Organisation Chart 1	332
10.4	Haverton Advice Centre Organisation Chart 2	333

LIST OF TABLES

2.1	Erikson's eight stages of personality development	48
2.2	An outline of how different theories are used in workplace learning	62
2.3	A comparison of men's and women's career progression at the English Bar	67
4.1	How Alderfer's ERG theory relates to Maslow's hierarchy of needs	120
5.1	Main differences between formal and informal groups	153
5.2	A summary of the Belbin Team Role descriptors. Reproduced with permission of Belbin Associates	169
5.3	Factors influencing group vs. individual decision-making	171
6.1	A summary of Hersey and Blanchard's leadership styles	207
7.1	Organic vs. mechanistic structures	222
9.1	Summary of characteristics of differing perspectives across three key parameters	287

PREFACE

Organisational behaviour (OB) is a field of study that takes its intellectual legacy from a disparate set of academic disciplines: psychology and sociology are its main sources, though anthropology, economics, communication and cultural studies also make their contribution. OB itself has influenced the study of Management to the extent that the two areas of study are often seen as the same. I resist taking this view, which has ideological undertones. Management focuses on how to make the running of organisations more effective. It can sometimes be charged with being too managerialist and too compliant with the aims and values of twenty-first-century capitalism. OB, I hope, takes a more dispassionate and critical stance, challenging some of those assumptions and seeking to understand a range of alternative approaches, some of which go beyond a Western (and largely Anglo-American) understanding of organisations.

As with other disciplines, OB breaks its content down into discrete topics. This is for the greater convenience for learners. However, this in itself can pose problems. When we work in organisations, and especially when we have management responsibility, the problems we confront rarely present themselves as clear-cut problems obviously falling within the scope of one of the OB topics. So we can't be sure whether we are dealing with, say, a culture problem, or a leadership problem, or something which arises because of issues of power and organisational politics. Consequently, we have to avoid suggesting to learners that the challenges they face are soluble by the application of a limited theoretical perspective.

Moreover, because OB deals with human systems, the application of theory to practical issues is not one of theory, as it were, being 'done' to a passive set of others. Those others have ideas, values, personalities, emotions and susceptibilities which may be resistant to, or even uncomprehending of, what is taking place. The individuals attempting to apply a theoretical solution to a problem, of course, are not without their own set of beliefs, values and personal characteristics, which will influence their approach. This is the distinction made by Schön between academic learning taking place on the high ground, whilst everyday practice takes place in the swamp. In other words we teachers simplify the world to make learning easier and more convenient, but perhaps do too little to prepare our students for the complexities of a professional life where problems arise unformed, with uncertain causation and often without the possibility of a satisfactory outcome.

To make, however inadequately, an attempt to address this, you will find many points in the text where are asked to consider the complex versus the simple, the rational versus the non-rational, the planned versus the emergent and the rhetoric versus the reality. Moreover, you will find that the case studies after each chapter are often equally suited to the content of other chapters. The Ecintel case is a prime example. I wrote this case many years ago and I have used it, sometimes with small modifications, for work on structure, individual differences, motivation, leadership and change. I believe most of the cases will be similarly flexible. The questions that follow the cases usually ask the learner to use the chapter material to analyse a situation. Which parts of the material they use is up to the learner; this provides an interesting exercise in observing how different perspectives (and often different personalities) frame an issue differently.

Most of all, however, I hope you find the material clearly explained and useful as a learning resource.

ACKNOWLEDGEMENTS

I have to begin by thanking all those who have spent time and energy over the generations researching and writing about organisations. Many of them are indeed giants on whose shoulders the rest of us have to stand on the off-chance of seeing a little further, and learning a little more.

More specifically I want to thank the staff at Palgrave, especially Ursula Gavin for trusting and supporting me in this project and for her extreme patience.

Finally, this book would never have been completed without my wife Carol whose insights and comments were never less than inspiring and whose determination that the project would be completed often exceeded my own.

1

WHAT IS ORGANISATIONAL BEHAVIOUR?

LEARNING OBJECTIVES

- Introduce the discipline of organisational behaviour
- Trace its intellectual roots
- Discuss the value of studying OB
- Outline the main threads and interests of OB to date

THE ORIGINS AND PURPOSE OF ORGANISATIONAL BEHAVIOUR

As the name suggests, Organisational Behaviour (or OB as we shall usually refer to it) is the discipline we have developed to try to understand how the behaviour of people influences the effectiveness of the organisations they belong to. It focuses mainly on business and work organisations, though not exclusively, and concerns itself with four dimensions of the organisation:

1. **The individual dimension,** which examines the relationship of individuals to the organisations they work in. In this dimension we study things like how people can be motivated to produce their best work; how individuals differ so that management can select the best person for a job or role; the part played by our perceptual faculties in making decisions and understanding the context of the organisation.

2. **The group dimension,** where we look at how people can work most effectively together by studying group dynamics, roles and interactions. Most of the work in organisations is done by groups, both formal and informal, and OB tries to understand how groups contribute the effectiveness of the organisation in different contexts.

3. **The dimension of the whole organisation,** where we study how groups and individuals combine and interact to create and maintain organisational effectiveness. This dimension concerns itself with things like organisational structure and culture, power relationships and decision-making at the level of the whole organisation.

4. **The dimension of the organisational context,** by which is meant the variables, both internal and external, which affect the organisation's operations. These include the business sector the organisation is in, the technologies used, the legislative and social framework in which it has to operate, the means by which the organisation is financed, the beneficiaries of its activities, etc. OB specialists are also interested in how organisations respond to demands for change.

We often hear or read of things which organisations do or decisions they have made. This is a kind of shorthand which hides a great deal more complexity. The word organisation (spelt *organization* in American English) is an abstract noun. This means that it is an idea, a mental construct, not a physical thing. The physical aspects of an organisation exist in its buildings and machinery, and, most importantly for the study of OB, in the people who work in it and for it. When organisations *do* something, it is the people of the organisation who have caused that thing to be done. The fact of its being done may well have been the subject of a great deal of discussion, or even conflict, before the decision was made. What is often presented to the public as the necessary and obvious thing to do may well hide a long and difficult process between competing groups and individuals in the organisation to get their particular view of what should be done accepted. It is this complexity in all four dimensions which is the concern of OB.

In the financial services sector the trading of debt-based derivatives has exposed the western economies to the most serious crisis in modern times. The companies which traded these derivatives were doubtless very efficient and effective in what they did, but the end result was disastrous for their customers and many of their employees, while the knock-on effect on the banking systems, markets and governments of those economies has been nothing less than catastrophic.

VIGNETTE

Organisations supply goods or services to users (customers, clients, etc.) outside the organisation, so to study the organisation in isolation from its context is to miss the point of why an organisation exists. Moreover, if an organisation is to effectively fulfil its primary tasks, there needs to be a system in place to combine the efforts of the people in the organisation with other resources in order to achieve those tasks. We refer to this system as *management*. Consequently, there is a great deal of overlap between OB theory and management theory. However, it would be mistaken to see the study of OB as the same as the study of management. The study of management is the study of how to use the available resources to make the production of goods and services as effective and efficient as possible both in the present as well as in the future. It is not surprising that there is a temptation to see the two areas of study as interchangeable. Certainly, OB usually forms a small but key part of business and management courses where learners can critically examine some of the theories and practices which can help to understand and deal with the complexities of management. However, while OB (and this book) shares this aim, a wider interpretation of OB goes further. It is also an academic study, and as such it has the job of dispassionately and critically examining organisations and how they operate at internal, local and societal levels. Clearly the phenomenon described in the Vignette is the subject of the urgent scrutiny of economists, but there will certainly be those from the field of OB interested in the management of these organisations trying to understand, among other things, how strategic decisions came to prevail which allowed these trades to continue indefinitely.

HOW DO WE STUDY ORGANISATIONAL BEHAVIOUR?

The approaches to studying and researching organisations come from the social sciences: psychology, sociology and anthropology. Psychology helps us to understand aspects of individual behaviour in areas like perception, learning and motivation, while sociology assists us in studying how groups behave, giving us insights into understanding group development and effectiveness, interpersonal relationships, working with seniors, peers and subordinates as well as looking at organisations as part of wider societal phenomena. Study of organisational culture and interest in ritual in organisations owes a lot to the discipline of anthropology, which is the study of how societies develop coherence and deal with conflict and diversity.

Social science research processes

There are two broad approaches to carrying out research in the social sciences: quantitative and qualitative research. The former is based on statistical analysis of observations. First of all a hypothesis is developed – in other words an educated guess based on experience, received wisdom or insight. This is then tested by collecting data. This can be done by methodical observation, surveys, interviews and so on. often using specialised and sophisticated data collecting techniques. The data is then subjected to a variety of statistical analyses leading to a conclusion as to whether the original hypothesis is valid, partially valid or invalid.

However, not all social phenomena are easy to quantify, since we often want to understand about people's beliefs, perceptions, symbolic meanings, personal experiences, etc. To carry out this kind of research we use qualitative studies. These rely on interviews, diaries and other reflective processes and are evaluated by very sophisticated types of analysis in order to be able to produce reliable and credible findings.

When looking at social science research we tend to evaluate it at several levels: The hypothesis itself – is it a credible and plausible thing to investigate? The research method selected – are the data (data is a plural word when we use it in research, even though it is colloquially used as a singular noun) collected likely to give us the answer to our hypothetical question? Is the statistical method or other forms of analysis used appropriate and does the interpretation of the results give us a believable answer. Are the conclusions generalisable – i.e. to how wide a set of circumstances do they apply? Or what applicability do they have in practice?

These approaches to researching and developing theory come with a health warning, however. Theory developed in this way is very different from theory in the natural sciences. In the latter scientists are searching for 'laws' – theories that are applicable at all times in all cases. So we know according to Newtonian physics that if we let go of a pencil, it will fall to the floor. As will anything else, because of the law of gravity. And this will happen to any pencil at any time in the same circumstances.

Social science theory, however, because it is looking for trends and averages and often uses probability as a measure of outcome, cannot be relied on to predict the behaviour of all people all of the time. We must therefore take care to use these theories intelligently, as guidelines and as analytical tools, rather then as predictors of behaviour. For example, many theories are based on fundamental beliefs. If you don't share those beliefs, then you are unlikely to want to apply theories founded on them. You may, for instance, hold the belief that leaders are born, that they possess leadership qualities because of their genetic inheritance (after all monarchies and political or business dynasties are founded precisely on this belief). If so, you will accept a version of the 'trait' theory of leadership, where leaders are identified by recognising specific personal traits which they have inherited. If, in contrast, you believe that exposure to the right kind of experiences can help develop leadership skills, then you will most likely turn to other explanations about leadership.

Perhaps also worthy of mention, however, is the fact that OB, possibly uniquely among academic studies, from its earliest days has fostered interaction between academics and practitioners. Frederick Winslow Taylor, the founder of scientific management, whose ideas on how to organise and manage industrial production were more influential than anyone else's, was himself a manager. A look at the staff of the major business schools will

serve to show the reliance they put on having people who have been practitioners holding senior positions in their colleges. This has given research
into organisations and management greater credibility, since there is less of
the 'ivory tower', academic versus the down to earth practitioner type of
conflict which arises in other fields.

WHAT HAVE WE LEARNT FROM OB SO FAR?

Writers, philosophers and practitioners have always been interested in how
organisations work. The great walls, pyramids and palaces of the ancient
world needed just as much co-ordination of people, material, planning
and human effort as any modern major project. However, OB tends to be
interested in the development of ideas about organisation and productive
effectiveness over the last 100 or so years, that is, since the industrial revolution to the present day. The huge development of productive technologies
of the nineteenth century enabled production of goods on a mass scale that
had never been seen previously. This called for a greater attention on how
work was to be organised so that the new technologies could be exploited
to the full. The development of technologies and the supply of goods and
services based on those technologies continues to this day, giving many
organisations a global reach and all of us as individuals virtually instant
communication in almost any field.

OB research has identified four loosely connected approaches to organising and managing. However, it must be emphasised that the work that is
encompassed within these approaches and the groups and individuals who
developed these ideas had little sense of belonging to coherent schools of
thought. Rather our way of understanding the development of OB uses the
gift of hindsight to suggest links and complementary or contrasting ways of
approaching the subject. The four broad approaches are:

1. **The classical approach,** which emphasises organisational and productive efficiency. In this approach we see work which attempts to seek the
   optimum way of combining human effort with the technologies of production, along with the development of key principles of management
   and organisational structure.

2. **The human relations approach,** in which greater attention is placed on the social, emotional and psychological aspects of organising. The underlying assumption behind this approach is that work has important meaning to human beings, consequently an organisation which provides meaningful, satisfying work will be an effective organisation.

3. **The systems approach,** which looks at organisations in a more dynamic way than the previous approaches. The term 'system' here means an analysis of the organisation as having three interrelated processes (Figure 1.1).

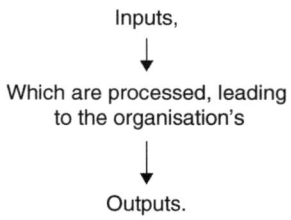

Figure 1.1 A simple linear system

Looking at organisations in this way enables us to observe and understand them in their environment. It is also a useful analytical tool since an examination of the three systemic processes will often give managers an indication of where changes need to be made.

4. **The contingency approach,** which suggests that there is no 'one best way' that suits all organisations at all times, but that managers need to be aware of the situational variables that impact on their organisation. Contingency theorists assume that every organisation is unique and has to solve its problems with regard to its own unique circumstances.

THE CLASSICAL APPROACH

Productive efficiency

Perhaps one of the greatest insights into the organisation of work comes from Adam Smith. In 1776 he published his 'An Inquiry into the Nature and

Causes of the Wealth of Nations', which introduced and developed the idea of *division of labour* where production is broken down into its sequential constituent processes, with each carried out by one person or small group before passing the work on to people carrying out the next process. Smith gave the example of the production of pins. This had traditionally been work which had been put out to people working in small workshops. Each individual carried out all parts of the pin-making process. Smith claimed that it would be difficult for someone new to the work to produce more than about one pin a day. Smith broke the process down into eighteen stages and trained each person in carrying out one, two or three of those stages. This meant that each individual became highly competent in those parts of the process which they carried out. When these principles of division of labour were applied to this task, it brought about a staggering increase in productivity.

Smith's breakthrough in the organisation of work heralded one of the important threads in OB: how to arrange work and technology so as to maximise productivity.

> **Adam Smith and division of labour.**
>
> I have seen a small manufactory of this kind where ten men only were employed, and where some of them consequently performed two or three distinct operations. But though they were very poor, and therefore but indifferently accommodated with the necessary machinery, they could, when they exerted themselves, make among them about twelve pounds of pins in a day. There are in a pound upwards of four thousand pins of a middling size. Those ten persons, therefore, could make among them upwards of forty-eight thousand pins in a day.

VIGNETTE

At the end of the nineteenth and beginning of the twentieth century, Frederick Winslow Taylor further developed this approach with what he termed 'scientific management'.[1] Taylor's approach to organising work was 'scientific' in that it analysed work, measured tasks, used specialised equipment and combined the results to identify a 'one best way' to carry out any task. He broke industrial processes down into a logical sequence of tasks, each of which would be easy for any worker to learn. Special tools were designed to make these tasks as productive as possible. For example in one of his first studies, a labourer, Schmidt, was given a specialised shovel to move pig iron from a pile into a vehicle. He was trained to use it appropriately and given a standard of performance to achieve and a pay rate dependent on the quantity moved. His productivity rose from 12.5 tons of pig iron moved in a day, to 48 tons using the 'science of pig iron moving' developed by Taylor. Later, other workers were trained to this job and, like him, received a much higher wage for their higher productivity.

Taylor maintained that all work could be scientifically designed to maximise productivity. There would be for each job a 'science' of that job. To achieve this, he developed a number of key principles:

- It was the job of managers to analyse work and organise the most efficient sequences of tasks.

- Each task should be simple enough to learn rapidly and carry out effectively using the 'one best way' designated by managers.

- Workers should be chosen according to their ability to carry out the task.

- They should be paid by results to encourage high productivity.

- There was to be a strict demarcation between the role of the managers and that of the worker.

Perhaps Scientific Management, or 'Taylorism' as it is also known, received its greatest recognition when it was taken up by Henry Ford at his new car plant in Detroit. His famous Model T car, produced between 1908 and 1927, was the first mass production automobile. He was able to produce the car at an affordable price largely because of his adoption of Taylorist principles on his production line.

From that time on the production line became the classic production method of the twentieth century. They are still to be seen in mass production factories today, though the balance of effort has shifted from manual labour to automation in the most modern factories.

Scientific management was further developed by Frank and Lilian Gilbreth. Recognising that human beings did not come in a standard size with identical abilities, they developed the 'motion study' of work. This identified the important movements required for specific tasks and trained people in those movements. The example Frank Gilbreth used was of the tasks involved in laying bricks. He identified all the key motions necessary to carry out this task efficiently and trained workers in these tasks so that they became proficient. Subsequently many jobs in many industries were subject to 'time and motion' studies (though rarely with the enthusiastic support of the workers who had to then follow the procedures developed by the studies!).

Until the advent of computer technology, scientific management reached its most sophisticated in the operations research carried out by the British government during the Second World War. Using very sophisticated mathematical and statistical modelling OR was applied to problems from rationing of the food supply to the wartime population to reducing the number of shells needed to shoot down enemy aircraft (from 20,000 per hit in 1940 to 4,000 per hit in 1944[2]). The arrival of computer technology has led to the ability to model and simulate larger and more complex scenarios so that jobs can be designed more 'scientifically' and better management decisions can be made.

Criticisms of scientific management

While scientific management undoubtedly leads to greater productivity, the main criticism comes from the workers who have to carry out the work. People doing this work unfailingly find it tedious and unsatisfying. It is, after all, designed precisely to be simple and repetitive. Right from its earliest applications scientific management approaches led to industrial unrest. Taylor's own implementation of his ideas met with resistance to the point where a Congressional committee was convened to discuss it. They concluded that, whilst Taylor's approach led to undoubted benefits, the separation of the worker and the management with the great decline in the former's involvement in the planning and sequencing of the work would only lead to greater resistance.

Taylor's view of people's behaviour at work was based on the concept of the 'rational-economic man'. This view held that the purpose of work was to maximise economic benefit to the individual and that people would act in a rational way to achieve this. Consequently, if greater reward were offered for adopting more productive work practices, the worker would accept them. Our modern understanding of human psychology finds such a view very simplistic, since it takes no account of the social and psychological factors of work. The reduction of the human worker to little more than an adjunct of the technology is repugnant to many people.

Theories on management

Hand in hand with the development of productive efficiency went work on understanding the function of management. The French practitioner Henri Fayol produced his classic work 'Administration Générale et Industrielle', though this was not published in English until 1949.[3] Although other writers have developed or modified Fayol's elements and principles, they remain very influential when the key tasks and roles of management are discussed.

In this work Fayol suggested that management consisted of five 'elements':

- **Planning** – Deciding what tasks have to be carried out, by when and to what standard

- **Organising** – Arranging human, material and financial resources to carry out the planned tasks

- **Command** – Giving direction to the workforce by applying and delegating power and authority

- **Co-ordination** – Ensuring that all activities contribute to the effective achievement of the planned task

- **Control** – Developing systems which monitor progress of activities to ensure successful completion of planned tasks.

In addition to these elements, which represented what a manager spent his time doing, Fayol also highlighted 14 'principles' of management which gave an organisational context and set of key values to a manager's work. These were:

1. **Division of Work** – Work should be broken down into its constituent parts so that workers can specialise in their own job and deliver greater productivity.

2. **Authority** – The leadership of the organisation delegates power and authority to managers at different levels in the organisation.

3. **Discipline** – Expectations of behaviour and performance should be clear and adhered to by everyone.

4. **Unity of Command** – Employees should have only one direct supervisor so that they clearly understand the lines of authority.

5. **Unity of Direction** – Management should be consistent and focused on achieving agreed plans.

6. **Subordination of Individual Interests to the General Interest** – The implied bargain between employees and employers is that the former are paid to carry out the requirements of the latter without seeking to promote personal agendas or interests.

7. **Remuneration** – Pay and any other benefits should be fair and reflect the effort and skill of the work.

8. **Centralisation** – This principle reflects the degree to which decisions are made by senior managers and staff at the centre of the organisation compared with localised decision-making.

9. **Scalar Chain** – The number of levels in the hierarchy of the organisation.

10. **Order** – Everyone in the organisation should understand how to get things done, where everything is and how to access resources.

11. **Equity** – Employees should be treated with consistency and fairness.

12. **Stability of Tenure of Personnel** – Staffing levels should be as stable as possible consistent with having competent staff at all times.

13. **Initiative** – Employees and managers should, as far as possible, have the freedom to make decisions which directly affect their work.

14 **Esprit de Corps** – Management should attempt to create a feeling of support and belonging in the organisation.

Fayol's attempts to classify key aspects of managers' work are still very influential. Other writers have followed his lead and argued for similar principles and elements,[4] with slight additions or modifications. Brech,[5] for example suggested management consisted of four elements: planning, control, coordination and motivation. The first three are identical to elements proposed by Fayol. The last, motivation, gives us a clue about how Brech developed Fayol's notions. Brech believed management was a social process. In other words, managers had to get the job done by working with and through other people. Brech does not share the Taylorist belief in the rational-economic man view of human motivation. Writing in 1963, he was able to draw on work on the social and psychological aspects of work published after Taylor.

Structuring organisations

The approach to organisational structure which we tend to include in the classical approach was developed by the German sociologist Max Weber. In contrast to Taylor and Fayol, Weber was an academic, not a practitioner. He was not seeking to find and recommend an ideal organisational structure, but his development of the idea of bureaucracy accompanied his work on what he saw as the increasing rationalisation and intellectualisation of both states and organisations in the western world. For him the bureaucratically organised company or government service represented a modern alternative to more primitive forms of exercising power in the service of production. Though we often have a negative view of bureaucratic organisations now, the idealised conception of them that Weber proposed offered many benefits and was in keeping with industrial and societal development of the late nineteenth and early twentieth centuries. The main characteristics of bureaucracy are:

- Clearly delineated roles and responsibilities (job specifications)
- Job specialisation
- Centralised decision-making
- Levels of authority from senior to operational level (the scalar chain)
- Rationalised and open pay and conditions according to level
- Open selection for recruitment and promotion
- Selection and promotion by ability

- Work and conduct prescribed by rules and regulations
- Clear line management responsibilities.

Weber's conception of the ideal bureaucracy was that it created openness and fairness because everyone knew how the system worked and everyone was subject to the same rules and regulations. Moreover, those rules and regulations governing work and professional relationships in the organisation led to more rational decision-making. Personal and sectional interests would be harder to promote in such a climate.

Most medium to large organisations, both in the public and private sectors of the western economies probably have some degree of bureaucracy in their structure. However, a number of criticisms can be levelled at it. First of all, the bureaucratic decision-making process is seen as slow, unresponsive to changing circumstances, and lacking in the dynamism and organisational flexibility needed in a changing world.

Not only that, but the reliance on written rules and records can come to seem an end in itself rather than a means to an end. Moreover, a thorough understanding of how rules and procedures can be manipulated enables those with that understanding to influence decisions in their own interests. Such control of the means of decision-making leaves the door open to patronage, nepotism and empire-building – some of the very things Weber's conception of bureaucracy wanted to eliminate,[6] Finally, bureaucracy discourages independent thought or action, let alone risk-taking. Many people believe that precisely these attributes are the ones required for success in market-led economies. The challenge, perhaps, is to maintain the benefits of equity, stability and accountability that bureaucracy can offer, whilst finding room and resources for the organisational entrepreneurs who can develop new products and services.

Conclusions

- On the face of it the three writers we put forward as representing the foundations of the classical approach have little in common. Weber was a political activist on the left (he co-founded the German Social-Democratic party) as well as a philosopher and pioneer in the new discipline of sociology. In contrast Taylor was a proponent of American market capitalism.

Fayol was a mining engineer turned management thinker. However, what they have in common is the period of history they lived in, which shaped the way they saw the world. They were what we call with hindsight 'modernists'. That is to say they had seen what the application of science and technology could deliver when rationally planned and resourced. Consequently they all had the modernist confidence in the human ability to solve problems using logic, reason and science, and they all saw these phenomena as superior to what had gone before. This confidence led them to attempt to seek the most rational ways to structure and manage organisations and, in Taylor's case, to create the most efficient way of harnessing human effort to the technologies of production.

- We know that these ideas and practices have some value because they are still with us in many forms. They represent the early paradigms of organisation and management which subsequent practitioners and thinkers have, with varying degrees of success, challenged, modified, criticised or championed.

THE HUMAN RELATIONS APPROACH

In 1924 a series of studies began at the Hawthorne plant of the General Electric Company in Chicago. The studies were intended as a scientific management experiment to find the optimum physical conditions to maximise worker output. They began with a study which changed various conditions in a controlled way and measured output following these changes. Changes included varying the lighting in the work area and, later, changes to break times and changes to the hours of the working day. Most of these changes were made in consultation with the workers in the study (all female). The results of these experiments were so surprising to the team carrying them out that a range of experiments continued until 1932, a period of eight years. The Hawthorne studies, as they became known, were to have a profound effect on thinking about the human aspects of work. The study results were surprising because the changes to work conditions led to changes to output that the study team did not predict. Generally speaking, the changes that the workers were involved in led to higher productivity, even those which the experimenters predicted would lead to lower output.

The final experiment of the Hawthorne Studies was in the 'Bank Wiring' room, where a group of men fitted electrical circuits. The interesting result of this study was that no matter what changes to conditions were made, production levels remained constant. This team was physically quite isolated from the rest of the plant and consequently was a very close-knit group. The study team concluded that the bank wiring workers were deliberately and informally controlling their output. This prompted researchers to try to understand the dynamics of the informal aspects of organisations

The studies continued with experiments where key variables, like piece-work rates (a payment system where the individual worker is paid according to a measured quantity of output), were held constant, while others were varied. The study team and management at the plant reached the conclusion that there were psychological and social factors at work which had a much greater impact on productivity than the mechanistic improvement or worsening of working conditions. To try to understand the meaning of the study results, the team undertook thousands of interviews over several years with staff at the plant. One of the major conclusions they arrived at was that the workers built up a relationship with the study team carrying out the studies and interviews, whose members seemed interested in them and their work. This led to them increasing their output even when some of the work conditions were worsened and the scientific management hypothesis would predict a lessening of output. This phenomenon has become known as the 'Hawthorne Effect'.

The consequences of the Hawthorne Studies

Taken together the results of the Hawthorne studies presented researchers with a set of unexpected questions about the meaning of work for employees, and presented managers with questions about the human complexities of optimising productivity. So the studies are perhaps best seen as raising questions about people's relationship to work rather than as a finished set of studies which provide us with definitive answers about how to make work more productive. What is clear from the studies is that work is much more than a negotiated economic deal between the employee and the employer. The studies raised questions which researchers have been trying to investigate ever since. Subsequent studies have focused on:

- The psychological and emotional needs of workers: that is the degree to which a job satisfies needs of recognition, achievement, security and a sense of belonging.
- Work organisations as formal and informal social systems, giving members opportunities for friendship, self-expression, status and personal development.
- The power of the informal organisation both to support or to inhibit the aims of the formal organisation.
- Organisations operate only on a limited (or 'bounded') rationality. Human beings have powerful social and psychological needs which work can satisfy. Work can also inhibit the fulfilment of these needs. Moreover, rationality is itself contested since supposedly rational decisions are themselves founded on a value-based set of assumptions which may conflict with the values of other constituents in the organisation.

Just as the classical approach to understanding organisations influenced research into technological efficiency and the search for the underlying principles of effective organisation, the Hawthorne studies were a central influence on studies into motivation, leadership, group dynamics, organisational culture, perception and individual differences,[7] Collectively, this interest in the relationship between people and the work they do has come to be known as the Human Relations approach. It has come to be seen as a contrast to the classical approach for two main reasons:

1. It is based on the assumption that people are more productive when their key social, psychological and emotional needs are met and consequently,
2. It places people, rather than technology, at the centre of organisational effectiveness.

Whilst these assumptions still have many supporters, they are far from proven. There has, from the outset, been a steady stream of criticism of both the methods used in the Hawthorne studies and the interpretation of the results,[8] In 1991 R. Gillespie[9] produced a comprehensive review of the studies, showing how there were competing interpretations of the results at the time, and of the role of the study leader, Elton Mayo, in ensuring that his own interpretation became the accepted one.[10] A very interesting and insightful article by E. A. M. Gale[11] contextualises the studies and cautions us to remember that the societal context in which the Hawthorne studies were carried out was very different from today. Moreover, he also looked at what subsequently happened to the plant itself and some of the key staff involved in the studies.

Since we cannot be sure of the validity of either the received results and assumptions that come out of the studies, what are we entitled to make of them?

Like scientific management, the Hawthorne studies and the work which followed have had a profound effect on subsequent research right up to the present day. Understanding the relationship of the individual and group to the effectiveness of organisations is as important now as it has ever been. Perhaps most importantly the Human Relations approach challenges the reductionist view of workers as rational-economic beings and that is its most valuable outcome. However, the essential political and ideological conflict remains: is work an essential human activity giving identity and satisfaction to the individual or is it no more than the harnessing of human effort in the service of capital and the elites who control it?

Conclusions on the Human Relations approach

- The Human Relations approach is largely based on the Hawthorne Studies which led to surprising results. Changes to output brought about by changes in working conditions were often the opposite to those predicted by the researchers.

- This became known as the 'Hawthorne Effect'.

- There is disagreement about interpretation of the Hawthorne Effect. Many believe that the workers' response was brought about because people (the researchers in this case) were taking an interest in them and their work. An alternative view is that close monitoring of performance will lead to workers feeling that they have to perform at a consistently higher level.

- Whatever the interpretation, a great deal of research has been carried out on issues which arose from the Hawthorne studies.
  - Job design
  - Work motivation
  - Group dynamics
  - Formal and informal structures
  - Leadership vs. management
  - Understanding the social and psychological needs of people at work. This contrasts with the 'rational-economic' perspective of scientific management.
- The main premise of the Human Relations approach is that workers who have their social and psychological needs met by work will be more productive and more fulfilled. The evidence on this is inconclusive.

THE SYSTEMS APPROACH

Scientific management and the Human Relations approaches developed principles and precepts which, if followed, would make organisations effective, at least according to the proponents of those principles. The focus of both approaches is on the organisation itself and the activities it is engaged in.

Organisations as open systems

In contrast, the systems approach is more a way of understanding the organisation in its context. It is an approach to understanding organisations that makes comparisons with the biological sciences.[12] To view an organisation as a system is to see it in relation to its environment, in a similar way to how biologists try to understand living organisms. The organisation takes people, material, knowledge and other resources from its external environment; and it organises and uses those resources in order to produce the goods and services it is set up to provide. Those goods and services are then put out into the environment to be used by customers, clients and others. However, it is not only goods and services which are the output of organisational systems. Organisations are often, for example, careful to manage their external reputation; moreover, they may pay dividends to shareholders, invest in other organisations or projects, or develop areas of expertise and knowledge. There are many varied outputs over and above the goods and services they are set up to deliver.

We refer to this three-part breakdown of the organisation as an 'open system' (Figure 1.2). It is open in the sense that it needs resources from its environment and returns the results of its activities to that environment. It is also open in the sense that changes in the environment will mean that there may need to be changes to elements of the organisation. Seeing an organisation as an open system recognises that the organisation is dynamic, not static. It also implies that inputs need to be monitored and evaluated to ensure that they are effective and that the organisation receives feedback about its outputs.

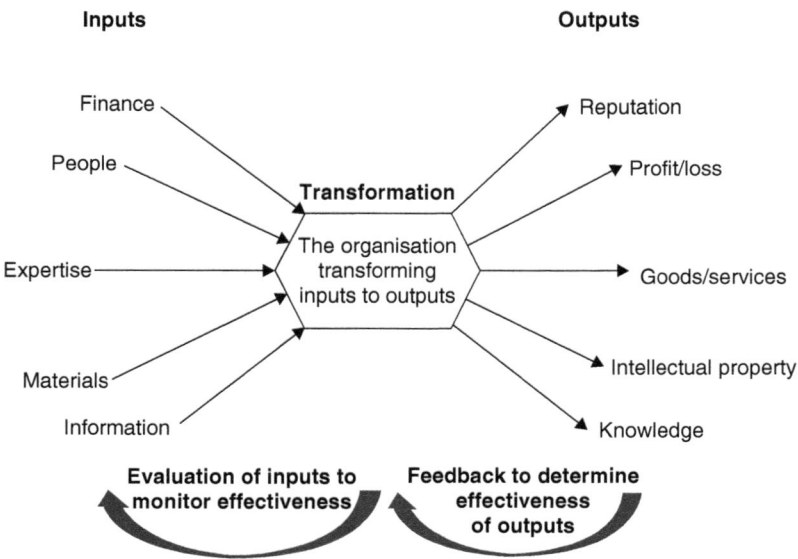

Figure 1.2 The organisation as an open system

The organisation itself can also be seen as a number of interacting sub-systems, each receiving inputs from other sub-systems, transforming those inputs and creating outputs which become in turn inputs to other parts of the overall system. Depending on the nature of its inputs, its transformational processes and the outputs it is creating, a system is more or less complex. The more component parts there are to any system, the greater the complexity and, consequently, the more challenging the management of the system, and the greater its unpredictability.

Socio-technical systems

This systems approach was recognised and researched by Trist and Bamforth from the Tavistock Institute in London in the late 1940s and early 1950s.

In the 1940s the British government nationalised the coal industry. Recognising that coal was a vital national resource, the government invested heavily in new technology for the mines. This raised the need for significant changes to the way coal was mined. Previously, each shift had carried out the whole process of tunneling, supporting the tunnels, mining the coal and removing it to be taken to the surface. Now each shift had its own task which was different from the work of other shifts. However, it quickly became apparent that the expected productivity benefits of the new technologies were not being achieved, creating inter-group friction and a loss of generic mining skills.

Eventually, in order to restore the productivity benefits of the new technologies and to improve industrial and inter-group relations, the Coal Board used Trist and Bamforth from the Tavistock Institute to investigate the problems. Based on their findings the Coal Board developed a system whereby the teams once more became multi-skilled with more autonomous decision-making in the groups, and the shifts much less specialised.

This approach to organising work was named 'socio-technical systems' because it attempted to optimise productivity by applying production technology to the prevailing social and working norms of the workers. While we might observe that coal mining, with its inherent dangers, is unique as an industry, and that in such an environment trust between workers is critical to safety and effective working, nevertheless the Trist and Bamforth findings have been seminal to modern thinking about how to effectively combine human and technical systems to optimise productivity.

Organisations as complex systems

The essence of systems thinking as it is outlined above is that if you can identify and understand the cause of a problem, you can manage a transition to a more desired state. So, for example, if an organisation is experiencing high levels of absence and high staff turnover, the management may well decide to investigate the causes. If they find that this is caused by, say, over-autocratic behaviour by managers, they may well replace or retrain their managers. Equally, depending on how they view the problem, they may look to a disciplinary procedure instead. The essential point is that this is a *linear* approach to dealing with the problem. It can be simply shown as in Figure 1.3:

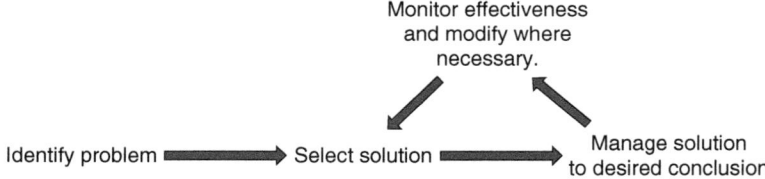

Figure 1.3 Linear problem solving

At a micro level, linear problem-solving may well be appropriate and effective. However, there are a number of problems which arise at each stage of this approach:

- **Identifying the problem**: It is surprisingly difficult to find agreement about what the problem actually is! In the example given above, one individual might see absence as more important than staff turnover, for example. Others may not see these issues as problems at all. This can often become even more difficult when you are trying to identify the cause of the problem. A manager whose department is experiencing these problems is unlikely to agree that poor management is the cause. In fact, there may be several other contributing causes: uncompetitive pay, poor physical working conditions, boring work and so on. Most probably, there are several causes acting in combination. Different people will have a different view about what is the main cause. Consequently, identifying the problem is often a consensus, rather than an indisputable, obvious feature of problem-solving.

- **Select the solution:** The solution may be obvious, or there may be many different solutions available, some of which maybe outside the scope of a manager's experience or competence or knowledge. So managers may go for solutions with which they are familiar. Moreover, the solution itself may be seen as a risk. What if it doesn't solve the problem? Or, just as problematic, what if it leads to other problems. For example, if you needed to invest a large amount of money to solve the problem, would it be worth it?

- **Manage the solution:** How this is done will depend on several factors, such as what has been done before, the confidence and competence of those whose job it is to implement the solution, the degree of acceptable risk in implementing a solution and numerous other possible factors. Are there the resources? Are those who are responsible for solving the problem given enough power to achieve the solution? Is the solution the one which is best for the organisation?

On the face of it the linear approach seems a clear, unambiguous way to proceed. However, in the brief illustration above, we can see that problem solving involves much more than can be captured in such a simplified algorithm. Issues of competence, reputation, experience, power, the way individuals see their world and many other things are involved.

Consequently there is a contemporary focus on non-linear management processes which try to understand this complexity. Much of the thinking behind this originates in the evolutionary and biological sciences, where researchers have been theorising about the adaptive features of organisms. The principles of this approach are also being applied to economies, markets and organisation theory.

We can classify these processes under the heading of *complex systems theory*.[13] This has most often been seen in the fields of organisational strategy, organisational change, decision-making and problem solving. The key features of a complex system are:

- **Complexity** – By complexity we mean that a system has many elements to it with many and variable relationships between elements. Put simply, this idea suggests that a complex system consists of many smaller, often simple relationships, which interact with one or more of the other elements of the system. The complexity comes with the number and variety of these relationships. They give the system its dynamism and its variability. In such a system the identification of causation is problematic whereas the linear approach assumes a relatively easy understanding of cause and effect. Complexity, in contrast, tells us that except in very low level interactions with very few agents, causation is far from clear. The weighting of causative factors is problematic, as is the predictability of the outcome.

- **Emergence** – This is a property of complex systems whereby features and defining characteristics of the system emerge over time. The example is often given of the game of chess, where there is a restricted, clear, unambiguous set of rules about what moves are allowed, by whom and in what order. In spite of this, it is not possible to predict the outcome of any chess game. How it unfolds at any given time is unique and emergent. Similarly, organisations can look for clarity in their design, in their standards of performance and behaviour and the clarity of their purpose, but the experienced features of that organisation will emerge over time and will be influenced but not constrained by those formal organisational processes.

- **Self-organisation** – This is the process in which some form of order or pattern arises from the many varied interactions among the elements of the system. Examples of self-organising complexity are: evolution by natural selection, human cultures, markets, large crowd actions. There are countless others. The important feature of self-organisation is that it arises spontaneously. In such a system management interventions are important but form only one of the many contributing influences. Self-organisation is observable at the macro level, though its causes originate at the micro level of the system.

- **Adaptability** – Complex systems adapt to changes in their environment. They are sensitive to changes at the micro level which change behaviour and consequently alter the nature of interactions between agents in the system. Over time adaptations will be observable at the level of the whole system.

- **Homeostasis** – Roughly, this means stability or equilibrium. The need for homeostasis is the driving force behind complexity. All systems can be destabilised by change. In this state they are unable to function effectively. Consequently they need to seek and find a form of stability which will allow them to continue to function.

What does this mean for the management of organisations?

In the traditional view of organisational management, managers decide on the purpose of the organisation, organise and co-ordinate resources and apply them to the achievement of the organisation's goals. Under the open systems approach, managers monitor the effectiveness of the sub-systems, note areas for improvement and organise resources to achieve this.

However, in a complex system, management action is only one of the interventions, albeit an influential one, in the system. Over time other features may well emerge that are unintended and even unwelcome. A good example of this is the 'Bank Wiring Room' study at the Hawthorne plant. The management's intention was to improve productivity – to improve the ratio of resources input to output produced. At a very local level, however, the workers, for cogent reasons of job protection and security, rationed output and set up very effective social controls to ensure that the output level was maintained.

Recognition of the power of informal groups has led some managements to try to harness this by creating a working environment where groups and their individual members are given greater autonomy and are consulted more on imminent changes than would be the case under a more traditional, autocratic system. Such an approach is more in tune with a complex systems approach and we can see this approach underlying several management processes. For example:

- **Autonomous work groups** – Where groups work within a general framework of what is to be achieved, but are given autonomy to determine how this is carried out.

- **Organisational development** – This is an approach to managing change which works by facilitating change at the operational level. It enables those involved in the change to own the process and, to some extent, the direction of change. It works on the basis of negotiation and consensus and attempts to tap into the emergent properties of a complex system.

- **Management styles** based on consensus and leadership rather than on the application of top down authority.
- **Emphasis on networking** – This creates patterns of relationships that go beyond the standard view of role and task and cross disciplines and boundaries.

Conclusions on the systems perspective

- In contrast to the classical and Human Relations approaches, a systems approach is not a set of precepts or principles for managing an organisation. It is much more a way of understanding and analysing the organisation as part of its environment.
- It is a dynamic approach which attempts to capture the key features of the organisation and their relationship to each other and to the world outside the organisation.
- At its simplest it analyses the organisation in term of its inputs taken from the environment, the application and transformation of those inputs to achieve the desired organisational outputs. Accurate feedback from each part of the system or its constituent sub-systems enables management to modify the system to make it more effective.
- Changes at any stage of the system can mean changes to other stages.
- The organisation can also be seen as a group of interacting sub-systems taking inputs from each other and creating outputs which are used as inputs in other sub-systems.
- The socio-technical system focuses on integrating the human and technical systems of the organisation to take advantage of the cohesiveness and adaptability of the former and optimising the efficiencies of the latter.
- Complex systems theory focuses on the emergent and self-organising properties of organisations.
- In complex systems management interventions are only one of the causative variables.
- Complex systems have many interactions at the micro levels which produce observable unities at the macro level.

- Complexity requires an acceptance of a variety of alternative, or even competing, intentions in organisations and of management processes which accept this and can work with it.
- The environment can be understood using analytical tools like PESTEL (see below). This analysis will provide information which will enable management to make changes to inputs, transformations or outputs to the system.

Contingency

When we use the term contingency in OB, we are referring to the features of the environment in which an organisation finds itself. Contingency theory sees each organisation as unique since no other organisation can have exactly the same environmental circumstances. From this perspective, we can understand contingency theory as part of an open system approach.

Contingency theory suggests that there is no generic best way to structure or manage an organisation. The optimum structure is contingent on both internal and external factors. Consequently, what is best for one organisation is necessarily different for another. Contingency theory is often seen in opposition to the search for the 'one best way' approach of the classical writers on organisation theory, since these approaches, it is claimed, ignore the unique set of circumstances in which each organisation finds itself.

In the late 1950s Joan Woodward[14] carried out important empirical research to establish the variables which had the greatest influence on an organisation's structure and operations. The principal interacting variables she identified were the technology and the production systems which made use of it. She developed classifications for production technologies:

- Unit based for small scale production
- Mass based for large scale production
- Continuous process for things like gas, water, electricity and so on.

These technologies determined the type of structure that an organisation would use.

Woodward further analysed structure according to:

- The number of management levels
- The supervisory span of control
- The ratio of managers to total workforce
- The skill levels required for the technology being used
- The overall structure of the organisation, from mechanistic to organic.

When she combined these characteristics, she was able to identify the kinds of overall structures in use in different types of organisation.

It is important to understand that Woodward's classifications are *descriptive,* not *prescriptive.* That is to say she is reporting on her observations and generalising from what she has observed. She also introduced some key concepts which are now common currency in the study of organisations.

- Her definition of technology goes beyond the usual understanding of the term. She uses the word to mean the sequence of physical techniques, knowledge, and equipment used to turn organisational inputs into outputs.
- The 'number of management levels' refers to the levels of seniority in the hierarchy of the organisation. This is also known as the 'scalar chain'.
- 'Span of control' refers to the number of subordinate staff who report to one manager. So, a manager with three staff would have a small span of control, while a manager with 30 staff would have a span of control ten times bigger.
- The 'ratio of managers to total workforce' refers to the number of managers in the organisation compared to the total number of workers. This is likely (though not certain) to correlate positively with the depth of the scalar chain.
- The 'skill level of workers' refers to the capacity of the workforce to effectively operate and contribute the technology underpinning the production system.

Woodward also introduces the terms the terms 'organic' and 'mechanistic'. These are metaphors taken from biology and mechanics respectively to help us understand organisation structures in different contexts. The terms were originally coined by Burns and Stalker[15] in the late 1950s. They suggest that an organic structure is likely to exist in periods and circumstances of uncertainty, where the organisation will have to react swiftly to threats from its environment to avoid instability or failure. Because of its flexible communication systems an organic structure reacts to its environment much more rapidly than a mechanistic one.

Burns and Stalker introduced the *PESTEL* process of environmental scanning, so that the organisation can identify threats and opportunities and react accordingly.

The PESTEL acronym stands for key factors an organisation needs to analyse:

Political

Economic

Societal (or social)

Environmental

Legal.

Understanding these factors, according to Burns and Stalker, will give an organisation important clues as to how they should react when confronted by change.

Lawrence and Lorsch,[16] following a similar research trajectory in the U.S., looked at the key concepts of *differentiation* and *integration*. Differentiation is necessary in any organisation. It refers to the need for different functions to be carried out. Organisations will vary as to how they divide up their required functions, but functions like production, marketing, personnel, finance and so on must be carried out. In smaller organisations it is relatively easy to control and mange these functions. Very few people are involved, communication is easier and the scope and range of activities is smaller. However, as an organisation gets bigger, the problem of management and control increases. This leads to the need for greater and probably more formal integration of functions. The balance any organisation achieves can be critical to its effectiveness. Lawrence and Lorsch suggested that different types of function or task in the organisation would be structured differently depending on the contingencies of that function. Some functions will have a long term perspective some short term; some will be directly concerned with the core operations of the organisation, others will support those operations.

Read the case below and try to answer the questions which follow.

The Ecintel Case

Ecintel is a small company founded to research and market economic intelligence to commercial organisations. Andy and Brian started the company four years ago after leaving their lecturing jobs in a university to start the business. They had identified this type of business as one in which they could exploit their subject and research expertise. Up until eight months ago the company consisted only of Andy, Brian and Carol. Andy researched the Far Eastern economies, while Brian took care of Eastern Europe and Russia. Carol was taken on at the beginning to carry out administrative and basic financial tasks. Andy and Brian discuss most of the important business issues before a decision is taken.

The company until eight months ago:

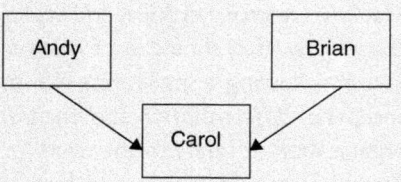

The quality of Andy and Brian's research brought them two lucrative contracts eight months ago. These represented a departure for the company because they were specific, focused contracts for a specific client. Previously their work had been produced and published as a series of occasional bulletins and was available to anyone who wanted it and could afford to buy it. Three months ago, as a result of the success of the bulletins, they had set up a subscription service for this part of the business, delivered quarterly either online or in print form and this was just beginning to build up. It clearly had potential to generate a relatively predictable cash flow, but obviously as it grew it would need resources applied to maintain the research impetus as well as to market and administer it.

As for the new projects, they were awarded on the basis that Andy and Brian would each head one of the projects according to their expertise.

In financial terms these contracts were too good to pass up, but they required an immediate expansion of staff in order to maintain the subscription service intact as well as to work on the new contracts. The following new staff were taken on seven months ago:

Doug, 27 years old - a recent PhD in economics who has an excellent track record in research, but this is his first job in a commercial environment. He has an A level in Russian. His research has been into the economic reforms and emergent markets of Russia and the other countries of the old Soviet bloc. Apart from one or two conferences a year, Doug's work has been largely solitary, which is really the way he likes it. Although he is a focused and capable researcher, he has been used to managing his own time and workload. Consequently he has found it difficult to slot into the disciplines of a small commercial organisation. He tends to see his own projects as sacrosanct and is difficult to pin down to carry out essential administrative work like logging time and expenses, reporting on progress of his work and so on. He can become touchy when he is obliged to deal with these things and tends to give off the sense that it is all a bit of a chore. With the new contracts taking up most of Andy's and Brian's time, he will be involved in supporting Andy on the Eastern Europe project. However, he will also be expected to continue his other ongoing research for the bulletins. This will mean a significantly greater workload for him and it will be important that he keeps the clients and Brian and Andy abreast of what he's doing.

Ellie, 22 years old - Ellie is a recent graduate in Chinese with Economics. She has been hired specifically to research the potential of various Chinese markets for the other corporate client under the supervision of Brian. Ellie has little research experience apart from her final year dissertation on the liberalisation of China's economy. She was principally hired for her linguistic and cultural understanding of China. Andy and Brian intended to train her in research skills on the job as well as giving her further opportunities as yet unspecified to develop her economic and commercial knowledge. Ellie herself has also expressed a long term goal to learn another oriental language, an ambition Andy and Brian are enthusiastic about. Ellie is energetic and keen, gets on well with people and is very methodical and organised.

Fran, 19 years old - Fran was taken on to assist Carol. She was to develop some simple financial control systems with a medium term plan to make her responsible for the billing and credit control of the business. Carol will eventually take on the role of administrative manager, with Fran reporting to her. Fran was taken on a few months ago straight from school with three good A levels in business studies, economics and English. She opted not to go to university because of the cost though she would have had no problem getting in. So far she has shown herself extremely capable and hard working and has devised some simple but effective systems to keep financial control. She has more than paid for herself by the effectiveness with which she gets the money in. She is clearly not stretched by this work, however, and Carol is worried she might go into further study or a more interesting job. Andy, Brian and Carol want to keep her.

The company at present (the lines on the chart are only a guide and do not necessarily reflect accurately line, staff and functional relationships):

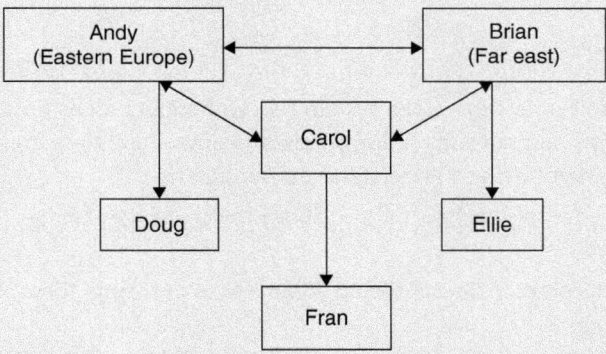

Andy and Brian had not given much thought to the future of the business while they were making a good income from their initial work. The expansion necessitated by the new business has forced them to take a hard look at the future of the company. If the two major contracts are successful the clients have indicated that other work would follow and a close partnership would be in the offing. Andy and Brian are unsure about what direction to take. Currently they are concerned about cash flow. Although there will be some interim payments from the new contracts, these could well be offset by falls in sales of the commercial intelligence the company was set up to provide, unless Andy and Brian, with Doug's and Ellie's assistance, can continue to satisfy subscribers to the bulletins and build that side of the business *as well as* putting in the time on the new contracts. Naturally the additional cost of the new staff has compounded the problem, so that the company has had to take on a significantly increased overdraft facility with the bank. Both Andy and Brian appreciate that their current human resource capability will not see them through anything more than the short term, but the company's finances will not permit the employment of any more permanent staff for the foreseeable future, though Andy and Brian do not rule out more flexible short-term arrangements.

Your Task

- Analyse Ecintel as an open system (i.e. with inputs, transforming processes and outputs). Can you identify any other OB features which might help us understand the situation?
- What does this analysis tell you about the challenges facing Ecintel?
- What recommendations would you make to overcome these challenges?

GLOSSARY OF TERMS

Bureaucracy A rational way of giving an organisation a structure and way of making decisions. It is characterised by rules and procedures.

Classical organisation theories An approach to organisation which seeks to find the optimum way of organising efficiently and productively.

Complex systems The view that organisations with many constituent parts and many low level interactions will eventually self-organise at the macro level. These systems will adapt to changes at the micro level which will over time bring about change at the macro level.

Contingency theories These look for the key identifying features of an organisation to determine the most effective way of organising its resources.

Decentralisation Where important decision making responsibilities are devolved to various parts of the organisation.

Differentiation The division of tasks in a process into identifiable discrete activities.

Formalisation Where the key activities in an organisation are controlled by rules and procedures

Hawthorne effect The apparent rise in productivity when workers feel someone is paying attention to their views. This interpretation has been challenged.

Hawthorne Studies A series of studies carried out at the Hawthorne plant of General Electric in the 1920s. The studies uncovered the importance of the social and psychological importance of work.

Homeostasis A state of equilibrium which a complex system will try to achieve.

Human relations theories This approach puts people at the heart of the productive process and suggests that satisfied workers are more productive.

Integration A system of controlling and communicating with all parts of an organisation.

Open system A way of looking at an organisation taking inputs from its environment, transforming them into goods and services and returning them to the environment as outputs.

Rationality The use of reason and logic to determine means and ends.

Scientific management A way of measuring work activity to determine the most efficient way of carrying out a task. Developed originally by F. W. Taylor.

Socio-technical systems The attempt to strike a balance between effective division of labour and the social needs of work groups.

Standardisation Procedures and task in an organisation are designed to be carried out in a standard way.

KEY POINTS

1. Organisational behaviour is a research-based academic subject, but it also tries to develop ways to help organisations become more effective.
2. It takes principles and methods mainly from sociology, psychology, anthropology and even biology.
3. It focuses its research on theories about individuals, groups and whole organisations
4. It has developed several 'schools of thought' or approaches over the last one hundred years.
5. These can be summarised as: classical theories, Human Relations theories, systems theories and contingency theories.
6. Organisational Behaviour continues to develop.

REVISION QUESTIONS

- What are the main differences between the study of management theory and the study of OB?
- What evidence is there in favour of a Human Relations approach to running organisations?
- How helpful is an Open Systems approach to understanding organisations?
- Do we still need the so-called Classical theories of organisation?

GOING FURTHER

An earlier part of this chapter suggested that OB has a rather split personality. On the one hand it is an academic study of how organisations work. On the other it has been used to develop principles and precepts about how to make organisations more effective. This is partly the result of OB being studied not only by academics, but also by practitioners. Naturally, the latter are keen to distil their experience and try to find principles which can be used in the day to day running of organisations. How then are we to decide what is sound academic research and what is perhaps written to influence a particular point of view or set of interests?

Below is a series of questions which are useful in deciding on the credibility of what you read:

- Who wrote the article, book or web publication? Who are the intended readers?
- What are their affiliations? In other words, are they connected with any organisation such as a university, research centre, consultancy, company etc. including one which they own, run or work for?
- What topic(s) are dealt with?
- What approach to writing this piece has the author, or authors, taken? Is it clear what is being discussed and how it has been investigated? Is there a methodology and is it discussed and justified?
- What are the themes or arguments put forward? Do they accept, challenge or modify currently held views on the topic?
- What are the conclusions of the piece? Do they arise logically from the investigation? And do any recommendations arise logically from the conclusions? Is there recognition of other perspectives even if they are challenged or dismissed?
- What have you, the reader, learnt from the piece? Has it reinforced or challenged your understanding of the topic? Has it pointed to any gaps in your knowledge?

Not everything you read will be produced by rigorous research. That does not mean it is of no use. However, it does mean that you need to evaluate its accuracy and usefulness carefully. Quite often practitioners will write articles or books from their own experience. Although they may have no training in academic research, nevertheless, what they have to say may often be very useful to another practitioner.

There is a lot of material available on all aspects of OB and management. An important source of material comes from articles in academic journals. These are valuable because before any article is published it is peer reviewed. That is, the draft article is sent to other academics in the field who will review it and possibly suggest changes before publication. Consequently, you can be confident that where this has happened the article will have been evaluated first. There are hundreds of journals in the field, many of which specialise in a particular area of OB or management. One example is the *Journal of Organizational Behavior* (in the USA it is spelt 'behavior' in UK and most other English speaking countries we spell it 'behaviour').

More popular, though equally respectable publications are also invaluable, and more accessible. Examples of these are *The Harvard Business Review* and *Management Today*.

Useful material to widen your knowledge of the various sections of this chapter are listed below:

Research methods:
- Lewis, P., Saunders, M. N. K. and Thornhill, A. (2009) *Research Methods for Business Students*, Harlow, England, Pearson Education.

Useful academic journals:
- *Journal of Business Research* published by Elsevier.
- *Organization Studies*
- *International Journal of Industrial Organization*
- *Journal of Organizational Behavior Management*

Management:
- *Academy of Management Journal*
- *Journal of Management Studies*

Books (many of which are available as ebooks):
- Handy, C. (1993) *Understanding Organization 4th edition, New York, Oxford University Press.*
- Morgan, G. (2006) *Images of Organization 4th Revised Edition,* Thousand Oaks, Ca, Sage Publications.
- Clegg, S. (1990) *Modern Organizations: Organization Studies in the Postmodern World by Stewart Clegg,* London, Sage.
- Reed, M. and Hughes, M. (1992) *Rethinking Organization: New Directions in Organization Theory and Analysis,* London, Sage.
- Linstead, S. (2004) *Organization Theory and Postmodern Thought,* London, Sage.

- Arnold, J., Randall, R., Patterson, F., Silvester, J., Robertson, I., Cooper, C., Burnes, B., Harris, D., Axtell, C. and Hartog, D. D. (2010) *Work Psychology: Understanding Human Behaviour in the Workplace*, Harlow, England, Financial Times Prentice Hall.

There are tens of thousands of books on organisations and management, so inevitably the list above is highly subjective and very short. Nevertheless, these books will give you a starting point into further exploration of OB. As you progress through the book, there will also be a selected number of references and suggestions for further study which relate to the chapter you are working on.

NOTES

1. Taylor, F. W., 1911, *The Principles of Scientific Management*, Harper and Brothers, New York. Accessible online at http://www.gutenberg.org/catalog/world/readfile?fk_files=2268784&pageno=1.

2. Operational Research Society (Great Britain). Kirby, M. W., 2003, *Operational Research in War and Peace: The British Experience from the 1930s to 1970*, Imperial College Press.

3. Fayol, H., 1949, *General and Industrial Management*, Pitman, London.

4. See amongst others: Urwick, L., 1943, *The Elements of Business Administration*, Harper and Brothers, London; Drucker, P., 1954, *The Practice of Management*, Harper Collins, London. Each of these writers, as well as many others, has their own perspective on management. What they have in common is a search for universal, or at least contemporaneously generalisable principles.

5. Brech, E. F. L., 1963, *Principles and Practice of Management*, Third Edition, Longman, London.

6. Weber himself was aware of these potential shortcomings. He always stated that his conception of bureaucracy was an idealised one. It presented a view of power and authority which was 'rational-legal', which was to be preferred to the alternatives – charismatic and traditional power structures. He believed that western society as a whole was

adopting a rational-legal ideology in its government and structures and bureaucracy was an organisational reflection of this.

7. These topics now form a large part of the OB curriculum and are often classified as 'neo-human relations'. The changing nature of work from the 1950s on meant that workers increasingly did jobs requiring more skill and judgement rather than simple production line tasks. The management of an increasingly skilled and educated workforce meant that managers needed to modify their 'command and control' paradigm to take into account the needs and expectations of such workers.

8. Franke, R. H. & Kaul, J., 1978, 'The Hawthorne Experiments: First Statistical Interpretation', American Sociological Review, vol.43, pp. 623–643.

9. Gillespie, R., 1991, Manufacturing Knowledge. A History of the Hawthorne Experiments, Cambridge University Press, Cambridge.

10. See Mayo, E., 1933, The Human Problems of an Industrial Civilization, Harvard University Press, Cambridge, MA.

11. Gale, E. A. M., 'The Hawthorne Studies – A Fable for our Times?', QJM: An International Journal of Medicine, vol. 97, no. 7, pp 439–449. Accessible online at http://qjmed.oxfordjournals.org/content/97/7/439.full.

12. von Bertalanffy, L., 'Problems of General Systems Theory: A New Approach to the Unity of Science', Human Biology, vol. 23, no. 4, Dec. 1951, pp. 302–312.

13. For a fuller picture, see: McMillan, E., 2004, Complexity, Organizations and Change, Routledge, London and New York.

14. Woodward, J., 1981, Industrial Organization: Theory and Practice, 2nd edition, Oxford University Press, London.

15. Burns, T. & Stalker, G. M., 1994, The Management of Innovation, New Edition, Oxford University Press.

16. Lawrence, P. R. & Lorsch, J., 1967, Organization and Environment: Managing Differentiation and Integration, Harvard Business School Division of Research, Boston.

2

INDIVIDUAL DIFFERENCES

LEARNING OBJECTIVES

- Show the importance to organisations of an understanding of individual differences
- Describe the key theories of personality
- Describe and discuss theories on intelligence
- Describe the key learning theories
- Discuss issues of unfair discrimination in relation to gender and ethnicity
- Discuss the contexts in which these theories are applied

WHY STUDY INDIVIDUAL DIFFERENCES?

Individuals differ in many ways: they have different social and cultural backgrounds, different levels of educational attainment, different personal qualities, different expectations and ambitions about work and careers, as well as different experiences of life. This is without the differences which arise directly from our genetic inheritance such as gender, height, left- or right-handedness, hair and skin colour, and so on.

Patterns of migration and globalisation of business have meant that it is increasingly rare to find culturally and ethnically homogeneous workforces in many parts of the world. Consequently, we can no longer be confident that our assumptions about attitudes, motivations and expectations in the workplace are shared between management and staff.

Organisational behaviour focuses on these differences for several reasons:

- Understanding individual differences is important when you are recruiting staff and allocating work so that you get the best fit between person and job since making sure that the right person is in the right job is a major contributor to organisational effectiveness.

- Our understanding of how people differ influences job design. Physical differences and differences in ability are at the core of designing work which is productive, challenging and rewarding.

- It enables us to treat people fairly and ethically. In many countries it is not only unethical but illegal to discriminate against people because of certain differences. In the UK for example, you may not discriminate against an individual on the grounds of their nationality, ethnicity, gender and, increasingly, age. The problem is that when you select someone for a role or for promotion or for further development what you are doing is discriminating. You are trying to pick the best person for the task at the expense of someone who you believe will be less capable. So the question is not whether you are discriminating or not, because you are. The question is whether you are discriminating *fairly*. An understanding of how individuals differ may well provide you with the tools for examining your decision impartially.

- As an employee you are much more likely to get satisfaction and fulfilment from work which suits your personality, ability and physical capacity.

- As a manager or employee you bring your own individual qualities, characteristics and beliefs to the work you do. This will have an impact on the behaviour of those you come into contact with and their responses to you are as important as your responses to them.

The body of theory behind our understanding of difference comes mainly from those areas of study which examine the relationship of human beings to their environment. These theories attempt to capture and make sense of the complexities of difference. We can often find this challenging since any given theory may not match our own experiences. Moreover, there may be several theories which attempt to explain the same phenomena, but which look very different from each other. This simply highlights the complexity researchers are trying to get to grips with. Individual difference is multi-faceted and the theories about difference reflect this. This means that we have to take a sophisticated approach to making use of the theory. This kind of theory often looks at trends in specially identified groups of people (referred to by researchers as 'samples'). Researchers use sophisticated statistical calculations to make their findings as credible as possible.

The issue for people in organisations is that we have to deal with real individuals, not with trends or statistically selected samples, and those individuals may not fall neatly into the categories the theorists have identified.

However, the theory can be very helpful in turning a complex, often confusing set of characteristics and occurrences into a coherent, organised model. And we can often use these models to help us sort out a better understanding of the complexity which confronts us. The theory won't often give us a recipe for solving the problem (though sometimes it claims to), but it will help us to put a structure on the problem which may help us understand it. We then have to use our imagination, sensitivity and experience to provide a solution.

A chapter which attempted to deal with all the conceivable ways in which people differ would be impossibly long and detailed. Consequently this chapter will concentrate on some of the key differences which affect the work effectiveness of the individual: personality, learning and those areas where, knowingly or unknowingly, we can discriminate unfairly, ethnicity, gender and disability.

THEORIES ON PERSONALITY

There are several approaches to theorising about personality. Organisational behaviour has tended to highlight two broad approaches, the nomothetic and idiographic approaches, though there are others. Each, as you will see, is founded on a different view of what personality is.

Nomothetic research assumes that our personality is largely resistant to change and is consistent over time. It is thought to be mainly inherited, with influences from our environment playing a relatively insignificant part, though theorists disagree about the exact influence our environment can have.

The underlying assumption is that there are a number of important personality types and traits which can be identified and measured. The measurement of the strength of each of these traits in a given individual will give us his or her personality profile. Nomothetic approaches have led to the development of tests and questionnaires to profile personality in order to predict work performance.

VIGNETTE

At some point in your career, you are likely to undertake a personality questionnaire (for selection for a job, for example). When you have completed the questionnaire, you will be awarded a score. These scores, known as 'raw scores' are of little value in themselves. They only become useful when they are 'normed'. That is, when they are compared to the scores that are achieved by people carrying out roles for which the test is being used. For example, you would expect the personality scores for a librarian to be significantly different from those of salesperson or an airline pilot. It is only by collecting scores for these occupations, and then comparing the raw score with these averages (or norms) that we can see whether the test result puts the individual in the expected score range for the occupations being tested for.

The work of Eysenck

One of the most influential psychologists working in this field was Hans Eysenck.[1] Eysenck comes from the positivist school of research. This involves the testing of a hypothesis by collecting data from large, carefully selected samples of the general population, in this case hundreds of members of the armed forces. His statistical analysis of his sample led him to conclude that there were two measurable differences: extroversion and emotional stability. So he examined extroversion on a continuum from *introversion* to *extraversion* and emotional stability on a continuum from *emotionally stable* to *emotionally unstable.* By intersecting these continua this produced four quadrants:

- Introverted and unstable
- Introverted and stable
- Extroverted and stable, and
- Extroverted and unstable.

Within each of the quadrants formed by these continua are a range of secondary traits formed by combinations of these major dimensions. Eysenck developed tests which measured the strength of these primary and secondary traits in order to attempt to predict how an individual will respond in a variety of situations.

The work of Cattell

In the 1960s Cattell undertook a substantial project to identify the major traits of personality. He surveyed thousands of people and obtained data about them from friends and colleagues. Using a range of statistical techniques he identified two principal types of personality trait:

- Surface traits – behaviours which seem to cluster consistently over a range of people and
- Source traits – characteristics which appear to be influencing our behavioural responses.

Cattell identified 16 source traits, which he referred to as 'personal factors' (Figure 2.1). The '16PF' personality questionnaire is today one of the best known and most trusted of the personality tests used by organisations. Like Eysenck's types, each of the personal factors is placed at one end of a continuum with its opposite at the other. People taking the test are given a number of statements about their likely behaviour and are scored on the strength of their response to each statement. This score is then mapped onto the 16PF chart and a profile of the individual's personal factors is drawn up. The profile is then 'normed', or statistically compared with the optimum profile for a given role or occupation.

Cool	- - - - - - - - - -	Warm
Concrete thinking	- - - - - - - - - -	Abstract thinking
Affected by feelings	- - - - - - - - - -	Emotionally stable
Submissive	- - - - - - - - - -	Dominant
Sober	- - - - - - - - - -	Enthusiastic
Expedient	- - - - - - - - - -	Conscientious
Shy	- - - - - - - - - -	Bold
Tough-minded	- - - - - - - - - -	Tender-minded
Trusting	- - - - - - - - - -	Suspicious
Practical	- - - - - - - - - -	Imaginative
Forthright	- - - - - - - - - -	Shrewd
Self-assured	- - - - - - - - - -	Apprehensive
Conservative	- - - - - - - - - -	Experimenting
Group-oriented	- - - - - - - - - -	Self-sufficient
Undisciplined	- - - - - - - - - -	Controlled
Relaxed	- - - - - - - - - -	Tense

Figure 2.1 Cattell's 16 Personal Factor constructs

The five factor model

Research to further refine the trait model of personality has continued since this early and influential work. A consensus has developed around the 'big five' model.[2] This suggests that there are five core dimensions of personality: Openness, Conscientiousness, Extroversion, Agreeableness and Neuroticism (often remembered by the mnemonic OCEAN).

Data from testing and observation of performance over a long period has tended to show the consistency and reliability of this model. Indeed, there is some evidence to show that these traits may well be applicable across cultures, though this whole approach to modelling personality has its critics. The main criticisms are:

- The descriptors used are imprecise. Bentall[3] suggests that they are 'tainted by the investigators' values'.
- Test subjects who are competing for a job have a good idea of where they need to be on the personality profile, so may not respond honestly to the questionnaire.
- Some traits are more stable than others
- The reliability (consistency of scoring between individuals and over time) and validity (confidence that the test measures what it claims to measure) of the tests can be compromised if they are not properly administered and interpreted.
- There are other ways of understanding personality than trait theories.

The idiographic approach to understanding personality

In contrast to nomothetic approaches, which see a relatively fixed set of traits distributed across all human beings, with individuals differentiated by the strength of each trait, idiographic approaches see personality as the development of the concept of self in each individual. Researchers who take this approach argue that we cannot understand an individual's personality without seeing it in its social and cultural context, since it is input from our social environment which influences our perceptions of the world around us and our interactions with others. They take the view that personality is dynamic – that it changes over time and that it is too complex to capture in a set of universal traits. Some of the key champions of this alternative approach are Carl Rogers, G. H. Mead and Erik Erikson. Within this broad group we can also include the Myers Briggs Type Indicator and Kelly's Personal Construct Theory.

Carl Rogers stressed the need for psychological growth of the individual over a lifetime. He believed that we all seek self-actualisation; the capacity to be fulfilled in all aspects of our existence. This can only take place in the context of people's relationships which are the main source of fulfilment and growth and on which we develop our sense of self.[4]

G. H. Mead[5] saw the development of personality as a dynamic inter-relationship with an individual's community. Personality developed as an individual learned and internalised the norms of personal conduct. Mead differentiated the *I* from the *Me*. *I* represents the unique, spontaneous aspects of the self, whilst *Me* is the self that develops from interaction with the community.

Erik Erikson,[6] like Rogers and Mead, saw personality as dynamic, developing and changing throughout our lives. He identified eight differentiated life stages (see Table 2.1), each of which present the individual with challenges and conflicts at the various stages. Successful resolution of these challenges and conflicts leads to psychological health and stability. However, an inability to deal effectively with such problems early on may later cause difficulties.

Myers-Briggs Type Indicator. Basing their research on work by the early psychologist Carl Jung which suggested deep-rooted internal causes for introversion and extroversion, Isabel Briggs-Myers and Katharine Briggs suggested that individuals differed according to a number of cognitive factors: thinking, feeling, sensation and intuition. Using these dimensions and later including a further dimension, style of living, they developed their Type Indicator. This and subsequent research is important for understanding the relationship between personality types and the kinds of job they are attracted to.

Table 2.1 Erikson's eight stages of personality development

Stage 1	Trust	V	Mistrust	1st year
Stage 2	Autonomy	V	Doubt	2–3 years
Stage 3	Initiative	V	Guilt	4–5 years
Stage 4	Industry	V	Inferiority	6–11 years
Stage 5	Identity	V	Role confusion	12–18 years
Stage 6	Intimacy	V	Isolation	Young adult
Stage 7	Generativity	V	Self-absorption	Middle age
Stage 8	Integrity	V	Despair	Old age

Kelly's personal construct theory. Central to Kelly's ideas is that personality is an individual's way of interacting with his or her world and should not be separated out from understanding all other aspects of the individual.

Kelly developed the 'repertory grid' as a way of dealing with the large amounts of subjective personal information he needed to collect for his research. The repertory grid enables the subjective view of people and events to be discussed until a set of 'constructs' emerges. These are taken to represent how the individual constructed (or perceived) the world and was consequently influenced to respond to situations. The repertory grid is used in organisations to support organisational development, employee training and development, job analysis, job description and evaluation.

Conclusion: There are key differences between nomothetic and idiographic conceptions of personality:

- Nomothetic approaches assume that there is a pool of characteristics which make up personality.
- This pool of characteristics is relatively stable over our lifetime.
- Each individual possesses these characteristics to differing degrees.
- These characteristics can be reliably measured producing an individualised personality profile.
- Creating personality profiles in this way will enable us to predict behaviour and the right fit for a job or role.
- Idiographic approaches see personality as dynamic and changeable over time.
- Personality cannot be separated from the social context of the individual.
- To understand the complexity of personality you need to understand the individual's need for psychological growth.

Application of the theories to organisations

Nomothetic theories of personality are the more widely used of the two competing approaches. This is largely because tests have been developed to measure personality traits for each of the models within this theory. This is a very attractive notion for human resource professionals. You can produce test results to differentiate between individuals for recruitment and selection in many contexts. You can rely on the fact that these tests have been rigorously developed and statistically validated.

These tests, along with ability and aptitude tests (that is, test which respectively assess your ability to carry out certain skills, or they test your aptitude – potential – for specific abilities) and other tests such as interest inventories, creativity, etc. are collectively known as psychometric tests. These often form part of a range of activities which candidates for new posts are asked to complete. Other activities may include group activities, presentations and interviews. The purpose of these events is to gain as much information about the candidates as possible to help in making a decision. Although the companies which produce these personality and other psychometric tests do all they can to make sure that they are valid (that they test the things they claim to test) and are reliable (the results are consistent between the individuals tested, between different people administering the test and produce consistent results over time) no-one would claim that they are foolproof. There are always a few capable candidates who do badly and some less capable who perform well. Consequently, any results from personality or other tests need to be supported and reinforced by information from other sources.

While nomothetic theories are mainly used for assessment purposes, idiographic influences can be seen in several activities that modern organisations engage in to improve performance or support personal and professional development. Counselling, for example, relies on the skill of the counsellor to support the client in identifying and framing problems which are an obstacle to effective work performance and personal development. However, it is not an activity which can be carried out without training, since you may be engaging with highly emotionally charged events or behaviours. If you are unskilled in dealing with these, then you can end up doing more harm than good.

Similarly, the mentoring process is often used to support the development of personnel, particularly in professional jobs. It shares many of the core principles of the idiographic approach. It is based on the idea that a mentor can help an individual identify their personal and professional goals and provide opportunities to develop abilities to achieve those goals. It does not seek to discover how an individual is similar to or different from other individuals. It seeks to bring out the individual's strengths and to help them improve areas where they are not strong in the context of the role they have in the organisation.

In contrast to nomothetic approaches, which tend to be a rapid, pragmatic way of differentiating personal differences between individuals at a single event, counselling and mentoring require a longer term commitment and investment, and a focus on the specific needs of the individual.

INTELLIGENCE

The notion of intelligence, rather like that of personality, is rather slippery. There is the everyday usage, which can be rather vague and there are the attempts to define the concept more precisely by researchers. The problem with the latter is that it is very difficult to agree on what is meant by the term.

Moreover, intelligence, perhaps more than any other of the topics in which psychologists are interested, has fallen foul of the nature versus nurture debate. In other words, do we inherit our intellectual abilities from our parents (nature) or are they the consequence of our interactions with our environment (nurture)? Or are they some kind of combination of the two – and if so, how do they work together to give each of us our individual intelligence?

Clearly different kinds of work demand different kinds of intellectual ability. A doctor needs to be able to listen to a patient and from the details presented, be able to apply a huge volume of medical knowledge to correctly diagnose the problem; then he or she has to consider what treatment would be most effective.

In contrast a footballer, say, has to assess the changing game situation with incredible rapidity and be able to react with the right decision. All this has to be done almost instinctively, with no time for the slower deliberation which the doctor uses. A sales person has to listen very carefully to what a prospective customer is saying in order to spot the openings for a sales pitch. So all we can say for certain about intelligence is that it is a term which covers a very wide range of human cognitive abilities. That being so, how have researchers tried to capture and understand that diversity?

Perhaps one of the best known (and most controversial) approaches is that of the *intelligence quotient* or IQ test. This was developed by Terman[7] in the USA developing work done in France with children with learning difficulties by Binet. Terman used the following formula to calculate IQ:

$$\frac{\text{Mental age}}{\text{Chronological age}} \times 100 = \text{Intelligence quotient}$$

Thus a twelve year old child, assessed as having a mental age of twelve, will have an IQ of 100.

Of course, the validity of this formula depends entirely on being able to accurately assess a person's mental age and it is precisely the nature of these tests (though by no means exclusively the tests) which has fuelled much of the controversy over IQ tests. The idea that intelligence can be reduced to a single score has also been widely challenged.

Spearman dealt with this challenge by suggesting a two-factor model of intelligence[8]. He argued that for any kind of specific intellectual ability to be used there had to be some kind of general intellectual ability underpinning it, which he referred to as **g**. *g* consequently enabled more specific abilities, referred to as **s**.

Later Vernon placed the specific abilities in a hierarchy, all depending ultimately on *g*. He claimed that, deriving from *g* there were several 'major factors' such as verbal ability, spatial ability and so on and, from those, more minor factors like verbal reasoning, spatial awareness and so on, and finally each of the minor abilities lead to specific operational skills such as the ability to précis text without losing the central meaning or to carry out actions requiring high levels of manual dexterity.

Some have argued that because some people have an ability in one of the major factors whilst having a much lower ability in another, the concept of *g* is not particularly useful. Thurstone considered that it is much more useful to have a profile of scores[9] across a range of abilities than a single score and it is certainly the case that an employer is more concerned with the range of abilities needed to carry out a particular role. Consequently a profile of the sort that Thurstone suggests is of more practical value than a broad IQ score.

More recently, Howard Gardner has used research on how the human brain works to go beyond the notion of multiple abilities and to refer to them as multiple intelligences. Recognising that modern methods of brain scanning show different parts of the brain in use for different cognitive activities, he has claimed that the notion of an overarching general intellectual ability is redundant.

Gardner[10] has so far suggested six 'intelligences': linguistic/verbal ability, logic/mathematical ability, spatial awareness, bodily/kinaesthetic ability, musical ability and personal intelligences. All of these can be further broken down into more specific skills and activities. Musical ability, for example, can be broken down into the abilities required for playing music, composing music or simply listening to music. All of these activities call upon varied combinations of different parts of the brain.

Gardner's category of personal intelligences is the starting point of Daniel Goleman's development of the idea of emotional intelligence.[11] Goleman suggests that high performing professionals possess high levels of emotional intelligence (EI). He has identified four components of EI: self-awareness, social awareness, self-management and relationship management. Those four can be further broken down into about 18 specific competences. Tests have been developed to assess these individual competences and provide a profile of an individual's EI.

What this means for organisations

Most employees in an organisation will only be superficially aware of the debates about intelligence, so situations where intelligence or aspects of intelligence are needed must be handled with extreme care. In practice it will be rare for an organisation to make use of an IQ score. IQ has been shown to be a good predictor of academic achievement, but a poor one for effectiveness in employment. The intellectual abilities required to carry out any given role can be analysed and tested for specifically in several ways. First of all, an organisation can use ability or aptitude tests. There are many around which have been rigorously produced to give the best possible levels of reliability and validity. But, as with personality questionnaires, they should not be used in isolation. Competent interviewing can also play a part. For example, talking to people about specific situations in which they had to make use of the skills you are interested in can be very revealing, as can detailed references. In other words, focus on the specific intellectual abilities you are interested in and get as much information about them from as many sources as possible.

LEARNING AND THE INDIVIDUAL

Individuals arrive in organisations with different levels of educational attainment, varying abilities, different capacities for learning and different motivations for learning. This matters to management for several reasons:

- Managers want their staff to be able to work productively to as high a standard as possible, so staff will need to be able to learn the tasks required for the job they are being paid to do.

- Modern organisations exist in a climate of constant change. In order to confront and successfully deal with the challenges raised by change, managers have to be confident that their staff can adapt to new situations.

- Organisational effectiveness depends on the knowledge held within the organisation. That knowledge needs to be developed, shared and applied to the goals of the organisation. Knowledge and its application require an ability to learn. The 'intellectual capital' of the organisation, as this management of knowledge is called, is increasingly being recognised as a key competitive asset.

- Most people are interested in developing their careers and work offers many opportunities for personal and professional development. However, management need to be aware of how they can support their staff's development and individual staff members have to be able to identify opportunities and have the capacity to exploit such opportunities.

Knowledge is rapidly becoming one of the most important economic assets for both individual organisations and whole economies. The ability to acquire, transmit and exploit knowledge is a key competitive element of twenty-first-century business. Organisations which can identify and make use of the knowledge and creativity of their staff will be able to innovate more effectively and gain competitive advantages. This idea has seen the emergence of a field of study and research in OB known as 'knowledge management'

VIGNETTE

THEORIES ABOUT LEARNING

Learning is an important and fundamental human activity. All of you reading this book will have undertaken several years of formal education, otherwise how would you be able to read it? Because it is so important, researchers for many years have been trying to understand exactly how people learn. As with nomothetic and idiographic approaches to understanding personality, approaches to understanding learning have also differed in similar ways. Some theories have tried to understand in general terms what happens when we learn, attempting to develop an overarching theory which applies to all learning in all situations. Others, paralleling the idiographic approach, have emphasised the uniqueness of the individual and have championed approaches to learning which have seen learning as a transformative process rather than as the mastery of knowledge and skill. These approaches are not necessarily mutually exclusive and many organisations embrace both ways of looking at learning. Obviously, any organisation is going to insist that its staff have the knowledge and skill needed to perform effectively. All staff carrying out similar tasks will need similar knowledge and skill. At the same time, most organisations offer opportunities, both formal and informal, for personal and professional development tailored to the abilities and needs of individuals and the organisation's future requirements.

Main groups of learning theory

Behaviourism

The behaviourist approach was an early attempt to understand how people learn. As the name suggests, this approach emphasised the learning of behaviour appropriate to the situation.

Behaviourist theorists examined the interaction between the learner and his or her immediate environment. They limited themselves to observing the input from the environment and the learned response from the learner. They did not concern themselves with the psychological and cognitive mechanisms by which the individual processed information and made decisions about how to respond to it. They considered the mind to be a 'black box' to which they had no access and which, consequently, they could not examine.

Early work on developing behaviourist theories of learning was done by I. P. Pavlov in Russia and B. F. Skinner in the USA.

Pavlov, using dogs as his experimental subjects, famously used their salivation response to the presence of food to develop his theory of classical conditioning. By signalling with a bell, or some other stimulus, the presence of food, he found that after a short time his dogs would salivate at the stimulus whether food was present or not. Through repetition and habituation, the animals were producing an unlearned response (salivating) to a stimulus (the bell) even though the reward (food) was not always present. This is known as classical conditioning.

Skinner[12] developed the notion of operant or instrumental conditioning. Again working with animals, he used the prospect of a reward, usually food, to encourage them to learn to carry out some activity to obtain the reward. This entailed the animal finding the correct lever to press so that the reward was delivered. Again with repetition and habituation, the animal learned what had to be done to obtain the food. Skinner believed that the key to embedding learning was reinforcement, that is, some form of reward for engaging in appropriate behaviour.

The notion of reward as reinforcement is central to the behaviourist approach. The opposite of reward – punishment or deprivation, we know as negative reinforcement. The difference between the two as effective prompts to learning (apart from the obvious – one is pleasant, the other not) is that positive reinforcement gives a clear message about what the appropriate behaviour is, whilst the other only tells you what should not be done, leaving you to make possible wrong inferences about what is right.

Behaviourism has received much criticism. For example, can we say that there is no learning unless we can observe behaviour based on that learning? If in some way you have increased your knowledge or understanding of something, can that always be demonstrated by some change in your behaviour? For instance, if you learn that there are 319 bones in a dog's body, will it change your behaviour as a dog owner? And conversely, can we always accurately infer learning from observation of behaviour?

This is a problem that behaviourism has always had, since it doesn't concern itself with the internal processing of information, only with the stimulus provided by the input and behavioural output of conditioned learning.

However, behaviourism is pervasive in workplace learning. Every time someone has a performance review and a pay rise results from that review, management have applied a behaviourist process to that member of staff even if they don't realise it. Certain behaviours are being rewarded. Moreover, a lot of workplace learning, especially the learning of manual skills, is carried out through the process of demonstration, practice and feedback – a behaviourist reinforcement process.

Cognitive theories

In contrast, theories on cognitive learning concern themselves mainly with psychological processes – the very processes with which behaviourism has traditionally refused to engage. They are attempting to uncover what actually happens in the 'black box' of the mind when we learn.

Cognition focuses on how we perceive, process and store information from our environment. And on how we use what we have stored to make decisions about how best to act or react to a situation. It poses questions about knowledge and memory to which modern research is only beginning to find answers.

If behaviourism assumes that all learning is a response to an external stimulus, cognitive theories suggest a higher order set of processes where we look for patterns in the world around us and develop and modify theories of action in order to function in the world. A useful example is language learning. Where behaviourism will (quite rightly) encourage the practice and repetition of language forms, a cognitive approach will stress learning the grammar or rules of language. The difference is that once you have learned and internalised the grammar, you are free to say things which you have never before said.

We should perhaps not see one theory as being in opposition to the other, but rather understand that cognition attempts to understand what behaviourism ignores. If a pigeon learns that pressing the right hand lever produces food, whilst pressing the left hand lever produces nothing, then the bird must have a 'rule' which enables it to select the lever which will give it the most benefit. Behaviourists are not really interested in how the rule was formed, cognitivists are. The latter are also concerned to understand how we can generalise from the rules we make – the 'grammar' of situations.

The psychologist Kohler,[13] who worked with chimpanzees, developed the notion of 'insightful learning'. He noticed that a chimp would often repeat an action which had been successful previously even if the situation was slightly different. Kohler concluded that the animal did not simply respond to the immediate environment, but understood the problem more abstractly. In other words it had made a generalised rule for solving that particular problem. Kohler was one of the proponents of *Gestalt* psychology. Gestalt is a German word meaning pattern or form and the Gestalt psychologists saw the process of learning not as a gradual incremental building of solutions from mastering discrete parts of a problem, but as the development of insight into the problem as a whole.

Social learning

Social learning is the interaction between the individual and his or her environment. It involves the identification of those people who are seen by the individual as appropriate models for emulating.

The key features of social learning are:

- Finding an appropriate model to observe
- Motivation to learn
- Application of what has been observed.

Many professions and occupations build in a social learning element to their training. Typically apprentices had a 'master' who showed them how to do the work and supervised their progress. Many organisations now have systems of mentoring to provide guidance from more experienced and senior personnel for novices.

Learners have to see the need to learn, and have to feel that they have the capacity to learn.[14] Both of these are indispensable conditions for any kind of learning to take place. In situations where mentoring takes place, learners are often put into challenging and unfamiliar situations and will struggle to learn if they do not have the confidence and motivation to succeed, as well as the help of the mentor to overcome barriers to learning.

Experiential learning

Kolb[15] developed a very influential model for workplace learning. He suggested that learning was cyclical; that learners went through four stages as they learned from the experiences they had and repeated those stages when they met similar situations in order to refine and improve their performance:

1. **Concrete experience** – This may be planned or unplanned. It is something where the learner is expected to act or respond in some way.

2. **Reflective observation** – the learner should honestly reflect on what happened and their part in it. That reflection should consider what led up to the event; how he or she responded; whether that response was successful; what they might have done differently.

3. **Abstract conceptualisation** – this stage poses the question, 'What have I learned?' This is the stage at which the learner develops an understanding of the event and looks for ways to formulate rules and principles for successfully dealing with similar events in the future.

4. **Active experimentation** – at this stage the learner will put his or her rule or theory (often referred to as 'theories of action') into practice. The theory of action will become embedded if it is successful. If it is not, the cycle enables the learner to once more reflect, theorise and practice until a theory of action is developed which will enable him or her to respond to situations effectively.

Because most situations and events don't repeat themselves in exactly the same way, the experiential cycle enables the learner to develop more and more sophisticated theories of action over time as they modify their responses and build competence.

Although the experiential learning stages themselves, as well as the cyclical nature of learning, have been challenged, this approach to workplace learning remains highly influential. If you have been on a training course where the trainer has asked you to carry out an activity, then asked you how well it went, followed by asking what you have learned and what you would do differently, then you will have had a taste of the experiential learning cycle.

Imagine you are driving a car. Because of the speed at which events can unfold, you often don't have to time to consciously consider all the available options, but act almost instinctively. It is not really instinct causing you to behave like this, but knowledge you have learned and which has been embedded in your brain to be used when required. This important knowledge and behaviour has become tacit.

VIGNETTE

Reflective practice – Focusing more profoundly on the reflective aspects of experiential learning, Donald Schön[16] developed the theory of reflective practice. Drawing on work with trainees in the professions, Schön effectively combined experiential with social learning. He saw professional development as being led by an expert practitioner helping a novice to reflect on what they were doing. The learner was to do this not only after the event, as in the learning cycle (reflection *on* action), but also during the process of carrying out a task (reflection *in* action).

The purpose of this was to develop a learner's 'tacit knowledge'. That is, to embed the knowledge which produces effective action, at almost subconscious level. This kind of knowledge enables an expert to act effectively without having to consciously think things through every time. Developing and relying on tacit knowledge is one of the most extraordinary and fascinating phenomena of the human brain. Information is processed incredibly quickly and promotes immediate response. Compared to our tacit processes, our explicit, or conscious, processes are very slow and ponderous. Imagine having a conversation in your mother tongue. You may occasionally have to stop and think of the right word or phrase, but most of the time the words just flow. Your tacit knowledge is enabling you to make appropriate selections of grammar, vocabulary, tone and emphasis without your being consciously aware of these selections. Moreover, you will also be taking in the responses you are getting from the person you are conversing with and rapidly modifying your own utterances.

Modern research[17] into how the brain works supports the importance of tacit knowledge in enabling us to perform effectively. But it also poses questions about reflection. Reflective practice theory is premised on a number of key assumptions:

- Both the learner and the tutor-expert can bring their tacit knowledge to the surface and articulate it.

- Once surfaced, the tacit knowledge of one individual can be communicated to another.

- Someone else's tacit knowledge is useful to another person's learning.

Like experiential learning, reflective practice has become very influential, especially for professional learning.

Action Learning

This approach to learning is mainly focused on managers. It is an extreme form of social learning where individuals decide that they need to learn to improve their performance. They seek out other, like-minded individuals and collaborate to explore and find solutions for day-to-day problems they are experiencing. They learn collaboratively in autonomous, self-organising groups, or learning sets. This approach was developed by Reg Revans[18] in the 1950s and 60s. It assumes that there is no need for attendance at formal courses, since members of a learning set are capable of identifying their own learning needs and can collaborate to satisfy them.

Conclusion

The variety of different theories and approaches to learning may appear confusing. However, they tend to deal with a particular aspect of the learning process, or examine it from differing perspectives. Some theories seem to be linked to specific learning contexts. Table 2.2 below gives an outline of how different theories are used in workplace learning.

This list of theories on learning is not exhaustive. However, it represents the main theoretical approaches found in organisational learning.

Individuals within an organisation will have varied capabilities for learning. They will have had different learning experiences before coming to

Table 2.2 An outline of how different theories are used in workplace learning

Type of theory	Learning context
Behaviourism	Tasks (especially motor skills) which can be broken down into a series of routine procedures.
Cognition	Less routine tasks and procedures. Situations where planning and problem-solving are important.
Social learning	Learning how to function effectively in a particular organisational, professional or social context
Experiential learning	Experiential learning can cover many learning contexts.
Reflective practice	This approach is principally used for the development of professional learning. It is highly personalised.
Action learning	Managers/professionals who take responsibility for their own learning and collaborate to share knowledge and solve problems.

the organisation, some successful, some less so. Many will display blocks to learning which may well be an obstacle to their effective performance. Identifying what these are and finding approaches to learning which are user-friendly may well help overcome these obstacles.

Learning in the workplace

All organisations have to rely to some extent on public and private education systems in their country. This will give managers a good idea what to expect at different levels of educational attainment. However, to expect people to carry out the roles required by the organisation, there will certainly have to be some training carried out in the organisation. This can be expensive and time-consuming, especially for small organisations. Consequently, a wide range of techniques and approaches have evolved to try to ensure an effective and capable workforce.

Learning is seen as an important competitive feature of modern organisations. The ability to confront change and adapt to changing circumstances may well be critical to an organisation's continued health. Individuals differ in what they are good at learning, how quickly they learn and how confident and motivated they are to learn. Organisations which take change and innovation seriously also take learning seriously.

ETHNICITY

The globalisation of business, and consequently of work, means that managers of organisations can no longer assume that their workforce will share the same national or ethnic culture. In modern organisations we will usually find ourselves working with others from different ethnic cultures than our own. Since our culture largely determines our expectations of, and our approach to, work, we have to be more prepared to examine and challenge our own assumptions, which themselves arise from our culture as well as to explain our own expectations to others.

Moreover, relations between ethnic groups, both historically and in the present, can be a source of tension. If issues like this are not confronted and dealt with, it will be difficult to operate effectively.

Most of us are familiar with some of the stereotypes about cultural differences: Asian people work for the good of the group, whilst in the West we are more individually orientated. Westerners value punctuality and directness in inter-personal relations; in other cultures the slow building of rapport and trust is needed before deals can be struck. Japanese managers typically work in similar conditions to their staff whilst in the West the size and quality of your work surroundings is an indicator of status in the organisation.

How then are we to try to understand these complexities? Is it possible to make generalisations which are of any use to us in the work organisation?

There have been some notable attempts to clarify the important differences that emerge from the varieties of culture and ethnicity.

One of the most important is the study carried out by Geerd Hofstede.[19] Hofstede is important because of the sheer number of people in his study. He surveyed more than a hundred thousand members of staff of one multi-national company with branches in 40 countries.. The value of having all his sample from one corporation is that none of the variations he found could be attributable to company policies or practices. Consequently the variations he found could, he argued, be reliably attributed to cultural differences. Moreover, these variations were more attributable to culture than to sex, age, status or role.

Hofstede identified four key dimensions of cultural variability and later added a fifth:

1. **Individualism versus collectivism**: By individualism is meant that people are largely responsible for their own acts and omissions and those of immediate family. In an individualistic culture, the individual is given, and expected to exercise, a large range of choice on his or her own behalf. Hofstede correlated individualism with high levels of affluence in the society. Collectivism, by contrast, is mostly to be found in less affluent societies, and demands a strict loyalty to the group, whilst in return, the group will give support and protection.

2. **Power distance:** This concept highlights the differences in respect for and acceptance of differences in power. Hofstede found that in countries like India and the Philippines there was greater respect paid to those with greatest power. Titles, ranks and other symbols of status were regarded as very important. In countries with low power distance, such as Israel, Denmark and Austria, differences in power between individuals were rarely referred to.

3. **Uncertainty avoidance:** This characteristic describes the extent to which members of a particular culture confront risk. It is impossible to predict with certainty what is going to happen. Societies with low scores on uncertainty avoidance tend to be relaxed about this, showing a high degree of confidence that they will be able to cope with unpredictability. Cultures which score high on uncertainty avoidance tend to manifest high anxiety and nervousness. There is a tendency to have little tolerance for difference or individuality of thought.

4. **Masculinity versus femininity:** This is perhaps the construct which has provoked most criticism, largely because it is easy to perceive the descriptors of these characteristics as gender stereotypes. These terms are often replaced these days by *achievement* versus *nurturing orientation*. Masculinity, according to Hofstede, is signalled by assertiveness, competitiveness, material acquisition, a 'sink or swim' attitude to others. In contrast, femininity is characterised by an emphasis on good relationships, a society where there is concern for others and on good quality

of life for all. He identified Japan as having high masculinity, whilst femininity is found in some of the Scandinavian countries.

5. **Long-term versus short-term orientation:** This construct addresses the way a culture behaves in relation to time. A long-term orientation suggests the individuals prefer to forego immediate results for a future, longer-term benefit. Consequently, you will often find that people in these cultures will have high levels of savings, will undertake longer-term enterprises and will show greater persistence in striving for longer-term goals. People with a short-term orientation tend to plan less and put less of their income into saving.

Hofstede's work, unsurprisingly, has attracted criticism. First, like much social science research, it deals in averages and trends, and in the workplace we have to deal with real individuals who may differ significantly from their cultural norm. Consequently, we have to be very careful that we don't simply use Hofstede's work as an evidential basis for ethnic and national stereotyping. Secondly, there has been criticism that by only surveying employees of one multi-national – in this case IBM – we may not be using a representative sample of the population of a country. We would expect IBM employees to be fairly well educated and perhaps have a better understanding of global business than many members of some populations.

Lastly, is national culture dynamic or static? How is it influenced by such things as economic development, political upheaval and societal changes? Will the growing gap between rich and poor in the UK over the last 15–20 years have any influence on, say, the power distance score of the British in the future? A useful link for looking at the Hofstede scores across the world is http://www.clearlycultural.com/geert-hofstede-cultural-dimensions/.

In spite of such criticism, the work of Hofstede, as well as that of Trompenaars[20] and others, has shown a consistency in national and ethnic differences, across different measures and constructs. The question then arises as to what we are to make of these differences in work organisations.

In many countries, including the UK and across the European Union, there is legislation explicitly forbidding unfair discrimination on the grounds of someone's ethnicity or nationality. However, in spite of the development of the legislation in the UK since the first Race Relations Act in 1965, the evidence suggests that many people of ethnic minorities do less well at school, find getting a job more difficult, are paid less than their white counterparts and are disproportionately found carrying out unskilled work.[21]

It shouldn't surprise us that the tendency to discriminate exists. We are all more comfortable with people who are like us. It is easier to work with those who share similar attitudes and expectations to ours. The more different someone seems to be, the more opportunity there is for misunderstanding. However, increasingly fewer parts of the world are ethnically homogeneous, with greater permanent and temporary migration probable. Many of us will find ourselves working in other countries, as well as needing to work in our own countries with people of different ethnic origins. This would appear to be one of the growing accompaniments to globalisation. The message is clear: organisations must find ways of operating effectively with very diverse workforces.

GENDER

In the UK there has been legislation outlawing discrimination on grounds of gender for more than 40 years. Nevertheless, a report in the Guardian newspaper in August 2010 discussing a report by the Chartered Institute of Management, stated that women's pay was, on average, only 79% of men's pay. This was only slightly bettered by the average for the European Union as a whole, where the rate was 82%.[22] There are a number of reasons suggested for this disparity.

• Discrimination in pay has been widespread since the early industrial revolution. Andrew Ure, discussing the mechanisation of cotton spinning stated:

> It is, in fact, the constant aim and tendency of every improvement in machinery to supersede human labour altogether, or to diminish its cost, by substituting the industry of women and children for that of men; or that of ordinary labourers for trained artisans. In most of the water-twist, or throstle cotton-mills, the spinning is entirely managed by females of sixteen years and upwards. The effect of substituting the self-acting mule for the common mule (types of spinning

machines), is to discharge the greater part of the men spinners, and to retain adolescents and children. The proprietor of a factory near Stockport states, in evidence to the commissioners, that, by such substitution, he would save £50 a week in wages in consequence of dispensing with nearly 40 male spinners, at about 25s.[23]

- A 'gendering' of work has continued to take place. More women, for example, work in the caring professions and in catering, where the wages are usually very low.

- Whilst women have increasingly entered prestigious professions like law and medicine, fewer of them seem to reach very senior positions.[24]

A report on women in law presented figures for women's progression in perhaps the most elite profession – the English Bar – as well as for solicitors. We can see from Table 2.3, the wide discrepancy between women and men at the self-employed Bar and even more so in the elite status of those who become QCs. The situation for solicitors is more evenly balanced, although there is still a 20% differential.

- The 'glass ceiling' is said to exist in many professions, occupations and organisations where men want to make it difficult for women to get through the ceiling into more senior positions

Table 2.3 A comparison of men's and women's career progression at the English Bar

Bar	Men	Women
Barristers in self-employed Bar	71%	29%
QCs	92%	8%
Employed Bar	56%	44%
Called to the Bar in 2003/04	51%	49%
Law Society		
Solicitors on the Roll (with and without practising certificates)	59.4%	40.6%

Source: Increasing Diversity in the Legal Profession: A Report on Government Proposals, Department for Constitutional Affairs. 2006

- Women may want, or feel obliged, to take on most of the child-rearing activities for the family. In spite of statutory maternity pay and leave now being in some countries extended to male partners too, this task falls overwhelmingly to women. This can often mean several years out of the labour market. When women want to return to work they find they have lost seniority, so have to start from a relatively junior position, or their skills need updating to equip them for modern work.

- Controversially, Catherine Hakim has suggested that women make deliberate choices about how far they want to progress in their jobs. She believes that about 20% of women see their role as and get their personal fulfilment from being home makers. About the same percentage want to progress as far as they can in their careers. The remaining 60% want employment and want to be treated equally with their male colleagues, but do not aspire to the top jobs. Hakim challenges the idea that most women are unhappy with their employment lot.[25]

CONCLUSIONS

There are clearly many more ways in which one individual differs from all others than those discussed above. There are those differences which arise from our genetic inheritance such as height and complexion. We differ in terms of age, health and so on. In fact each of us differs from others in every aspect of our being. This chapter has looked at the differences that the study of organisational behaviour tends to regard as being important for good performance in the workplace. For example, when we write a job specification or advert we try to match the job to the ideal characteristics of a person who would do the job competently. When we get to the selection process, we use a range of techniques to try as far as possible to make sure we get someone who is a good 'fit' for the job. Many of you will have been through an 'assessment centre' when applying for a job. This will often include ability tests to make sure you have the skills needed, as well as personality questionnaires, which are based on one of the models of personality highlighted earlier in the chapter, and are intended to ensure that your package of personal qualities matches those needed for the job. After all, it is quite rare to find an introverted sales person!

Learning is critical to the health of modern organisations. In a climate of challenge and rapid change, the organisation whose members can adapt and learn to handle new situations is the one that will thrive. People often have negative experiences of learning, particularly from their school days. Unless an individual's ability to learn in the workplace can be stimulated and developed, then they are likely to be little use to the organisation. Their career progress will be thwarted and the organisation will fail to get the best from that member of staff. An organisation which identifies and supports the learning of its staff is one which is more likely to have a motivated, confident and adaptable workforce.

Many countries outlaw discrimination on grounds of ethnicity, gender, sexual orientation, age or disability. The legislatures of those countries clearly see that such discrimination is not in the national interest let alone in the interests of individuals who find themselves discriminated against. From an organisational perspective, what case can you make for failing to employ, select or promote someone for any reason other than their inability to do the job? All you are doing is reducing the available pool of talent which the organisation can draw on. This is the stark business case, without even considering the ethical and moral aspects of unfair discrimination.

At the very least members of organisations need to understand the law on discrimination and ensure that they comply. However, many organisations take their social responsibilities much further by introducing systems of work and training to ensure that all members are treated fairly and openly. It is common in the UK for organisations to declare in their job adverts that they are 'an equal opportunities employer'.

Finally, we have to remember that each of us is an individual who differs from every other individual. We too have our personal characteristics, experiences and upbringing which lead us to see the world in our own way and which influence our behaviour towards other people. Understanding individual differences isn't just something we do to others, it helps if we try to understand ourselves as well.

Read the information given below and carry out the tasks indicated.

Below are the organisation charts of two companies. One is a small veterinary practice, the other a manufacturing company which has recently been taken over by a German company.

Both companies want to take on a new member of staff. You are provided with information on the key features of each job.

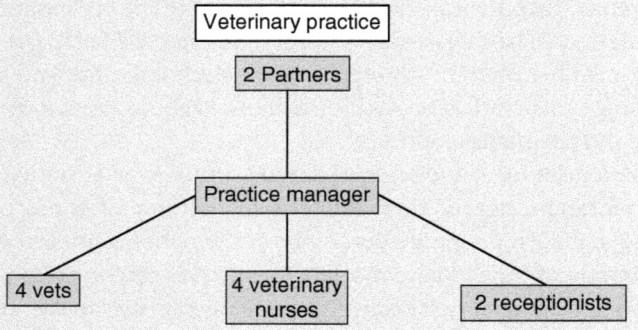

The veterinary practice wants to employ a receptionist. The main duties of the job are:

- To answer the telephone and greet people coming to the surgery.
- To arrange and keep a record of appointments.
- To deal with queries from customers.
- To set up and operate a reminder system for appointments.
- To take and record payment for medication and treatment.
- To operate and maintain the records of customers' animals and their treatments.
- To assist the veterinary nurses in routine matters such as weighing animals.

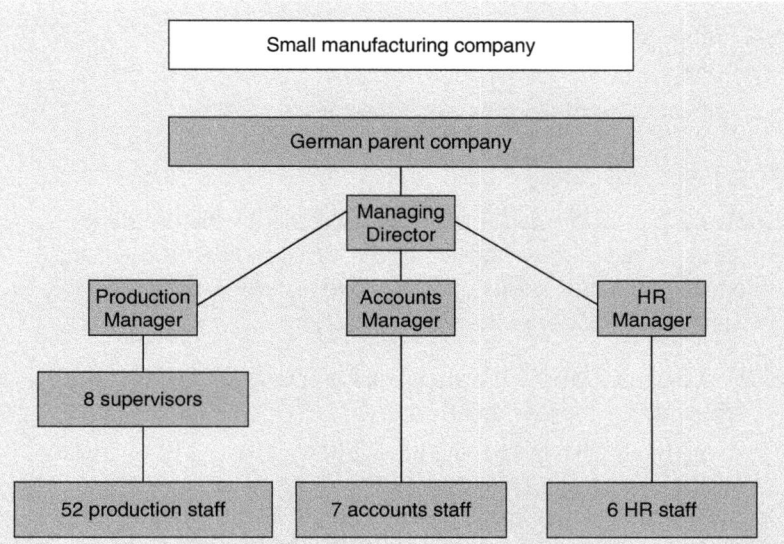

The manufacturing company wants to employ an accounts administrator. The key duties of the role are:

- To pay maintenance suppliers and contracted maintenance companies by due date.

- To verify plant maintenance work has been carried out and goods and services supplied according to contract.

- To follow up non-payment quickly and expeditiously.

- To liaise with plant and warehouse managers to verify goods and services delivered are as specified.

- To liaise with suppliers in the event of non-payment or late payment.

- To keep up to date, complete and accurate records of payments to suppliers.

- To inform suppliers if payment is to be withheld because of faulty supplies.
- To prepare a monthly summary of payments.

Your Task

Below is a part of the person spec (the document which employers use to describe the characteristics of the ideal candidate). There are other categories, but we are only using the 'Intellectual ability' and 'Personal qualities' categories on this occasion.

- Try to describe what you would look for in terms of intellect and personality for the jobs on offer.
- You might also like to consider how you would assess these qualities at the selection process.

The person spec has columns for 'Essential' and 'Desirable' characteristics. How would you decide on what is essential and what is desirable?

Part of person specification

Characteristic	Essential	Desirable
Intellectual ability		
Personal qualities		

GLOSSARY OF TERMS

Action learning A learning process where a group of learners take responsibility for their own learning. They support, encourage and challenge each other.

Behaviourism A theory about learning which is based on shaping behaviour by rewarding the correct responses to external stimuli.

Classical conditioning Part of behaviourism. This entails inducing a non-learned behaviour, such as salivating, in response to a stimulus.

Cognition The way we perceive, process and make decisions about our world. This includes important processes like decision making, remembering and planning.

Emotional intelligence A concept developed by Goleman which is comprises self-awareness, social awareness, self-management and relationship management.

Experiential learning A learning process which focuses on learning from things that we have experienced, observed or otherwise taken note of.

Extroversion Where the man focus of the individual's attention is directed externally, to other people and events.

Idiographic theories of personality This approach to understanding personality assumes that the personality varies over time with ongoing exposure to new events and situations.

Intelligence quotient A score arrived at by testing individuals, which purports to represent their intelligence compared to the average for the population. The mean average for the population is 10.

Introversion Where the focus of the individual's attention is directed internally to the individual.

Nature versus nurture debate This is an ongoing difference of view between those who believe that our intelligence is the result of our genetic inheritance and those who believe that the environment in which we find ourselves is the main determinant of our intellectual ability.

Nomothetic theories of personality These theories assume that our personality varies very little over time. Therefore we can develop classifications of personality types which we can assess through psychometric instruments.

OCEAN An acronym representing the 'big five' personality traits: openness, conscientiousness, extroversion, agreeableness and neuroticism.

Operant conditioning Part of behaviourism. This entails inducing a learned response, such as choosing to press a lever, in response to a stimulus and reward.

Reflective practice A process of professional development where the learner is encouraged by a more experienced professional to develop key skills and knowledge. The mentor is there to facilitate and challenge the learner.

Social learning This is a learning process where we interact with and try to emulate key individuals in our environment.

Source traits Personal characteristics which influence our behaviour.

Stereotyping This is a tendency to attribute a given characteristic to a group of people and to assume that every member of that group will have that characteristic.

KEY POINTS

- Individuals differ in countless ways. It is important to understand important differences so that work may be allocated to suit the capacities and competences of the individual. Selection for things like promotion, training and other special tasks should also take account of individual talents and preferences.

- Personality can be understood using either nomothetic or ideographic theories. The former use a range of personal characteristics which we are all supposed to share to a greater or lesser degree. Personality question- naires test for the exact profile of the individual along the constructs of any given theory. The latter proposes a theory based on the possibility of change of personal characteristics over time. So application of these theories usually centres around working with the individual, rather than comparing them with a group.

- Intelligence is a very contested concept. The first attempt to under- stand intelligence, the IQ test, is still in use today. However, modern understanding of genetics and brain function is beginning to present us with a much more complex view of what intelligence might be.

- Individuals exhibit different abilities in their capacity to learn and their preferences for different learning approaches.

- Behaviourism is an early attempt to understand how people learn. It relies on stimulus and response to model behaviour. However, it pays no attention to the workings of the mind, focussing exclusively on targeting appropriate behaviour.

- Cognitive theories, in contrast, try to understand what is going on in the mind of the individual when learning takes place. This approach focuses on problem solving in particular.

- A great deal of workplace learning is experiential; that is, people learn by carrying out activities, and by incrementally improving their performance.

- Reflective practice is used mainly for the development of professional expertise. It involves a form of mentoring and enabling by the mentor.

- Ethnicity is an important factor because it shapes culture, which in turn influences behaviour in such things as ambition, work relationships expectations and many other aspects of the work environment.

- Gender has traditionally been a source of discrimination in the workplace. Such discrimination is deemed to be illegal in many countries.

REVISION QUESTIONS

- You supervise a small team. Two of your staff members have recently been guilty of producing work that is below standard. One of them is struggling to manage the workload and some work is not properly completed, while the other, who is normally on top of the job, seems careless and distracted. How would you approach these problems? Would your approach be the same in both cases?

- How far do you agree that many jobs are better done by men, whilst others are better done by women?

- How good are you at assessing someone's intelligence? What criteria do you use?

GOING FURTHER

This chapter has tried to give an overview of some of the key issues in understanding the importance of individual differences. If you have to write about any of these topics, or if you are interested in finding out more, then the resources listed in the endnotes of the chapter are a good starting point. Additional resources below may also be useful. Materials on these topics are plentiful and easy to access.

- A very useful work is Chapter 3 of *Work Psychology*, 4th edition, by John Arnold with Joanne Silvester, Fiona Patterson, Ivan Robertson, Cary Cooper and Bernard Burnes, published by Pearson Education, 2005. This book, as its title suggests, is heavily based in psychology research with lots of tables, examples and questions.

- ACAS, the Advice, Conciliation and Arbitration Service of the United Kingdom produces many leaflets on gender, race and other forms of unfair discrimination. These outline the legislative responsibilities of employers and indicate sources of help in training to eliminate unfair discrimination.

- The Management Charter Initiative have developed a set of performance standards for managers. These standards form part of the NCVQ approach to workplace learning and are now the responsibility of the Management Standards Centre. The standards are arrived at by breaking the manager's work down into clusters of discrete behaviours against which the learner is assessed. You can easily navigate to the standards at http://www. management-standards.org/standards/standards.

NOTES

1. Eysenck, H.J., 1960, *The Structure of Human Personality*, London, Methuen.

2. Mcrae, R. R. and Costa, P. T., 1989, 'More Reasons to Adopt the Five Factor Model', *American Psychologist*, vol.44, no. 2, pp. 451–452.

3. Rogers, C. A., 1980, *Way of Being*, New York, Houghton Mifflin.

4. Mead, G. H., 1934, *Mind, Self and Society*, Chicago, University of Chicago Press.

5. Erikson, E. H., 1980, *Identity and Life Cycle,* New York, Norton.

6. Terman, L. M., 1916 *The Measurement of Intelligence,* New York, Houghton Mifflin.

7. Spearman, C., 1927, *The Abilities of Man,* New York, Macmillan.

8. Thurstone, L. L., 1938, 'Primary Mental Abilities', Chicago, University of Chicago Press.

9. Gardner, H., 1993, *Frames of Mind: The Theory of Multiple Intelligences,* Second edition, London, Fontana.

10. Goleman, D., 1996, *Emotional Intelligence,* London, Bloomsbury.

11. Skinner, 1953, B. F. *Science and Human Behavior,* New York, Macmillan.

12. Kohler, W., 1925, *The Mentality of Apes,* New York, Harcourt Brace.

13. Dweck, C. S., 1999, *Self Theories: Their role in Motivation, Personality and Development,* Ann Arbor MI, Edwards Bros.

14. Kolb, David A., 1984, *Experiential Learning: Experience as the Source of Learning and Development,* New Jersey, Prentice Hall.

15. Schön, D., 1987, *Educating the Reflective Practitioner: Towards a New Design for Teaching and Learning in the Professions,* San Francisco, Jossey-Bass.

16. For a useful and informed overview see Blakemore, S.-J. And Frith, U., 2005, *The Learning Brain: Lessons for Education,* London, Blackwell Publishing.

17. Revans, R., 2011, *ABC of Action Learning,* London, Gower.

18. Hofstede, G., 1980, *Culture's Consequences: International Differences in Work-related Values,* Beverley Hills, Sage.

19. Trompenaars, F., 1998, *Riding the Waves of Culture,* London, McGraw-Hill.

20. For a useful summary of this, see: Arnold, J., Silvester, J., Patterson, F., Robertson, I., Cooper, C. and Burnes, B., 2005, *Work psychology: Understanding Human Behaviour in the Workplace, Fourth edition,* London, FT Prentice Hall.

21. *Equal pay for women not likely till 2067, says research,* Katie Allen, The Guardian, 19 August 2010.

22. Accessible online at http://www.fordham.edu/halsall/mod/1835ure. html

23. McManus, I.C., Sproston, K.A., 2000, 'Women in Hospital Medicine in the United Kingdom: Glass Ceiling, Preference, Prejudice or Cohort Effect?', *Journal of Epidemiology and Community Health,* vol.54, pp. 10–16.

24. Hakim, C., 2005, 'Lifestyle Preferences as Determinants of Women's Differentiated Labour Market Careers', *Work and Occupations,* vol.29, pp.428–459. Cited in: Arnold, J., Silvester, J., Patterson, F., Robertson, I., Cooper, C. and Burnes, B., 2005, *Work psychology: Understanding Human Behaviour in the Workplace, Fourth edition,* London, FT Prentice Hall.

3

PERCEPTION, BELIEFS AND ATTITUDES

LEARNING OBJECTIVES

- State the importance our perceptions have in the decisions and judgements we make every day in the workplace
- Describe a simple model of the perceptual process and how it enables us to construct our individual view of the world
- Describe the biases that this can lead to and the problems which arise from these biases
- Show how our perceptions beliefs and attitudes are in a dynamic relationship and influence attitude and behaviour change over time.

INTRODUCTION

We all see, hear and feel the world through our five senses. Our world is populated by other people, animals, cities, deserts, jungles, oceans and so on. We take in this world through the senses of sight, smell, touch, hearing and taste. It is almost as if the world is projected on to a small screen in our minds, with the extra advantage of being able to reach out and touch it, smell it or taste it. But there is no screen in our heads. Instead we have billions of brain cells forming hundreds of billions of connections and pathways which are constantly growing or shrinking and receiving and sending signals to other parts of our bodies. Our brain is also storing information in our conscious and unconscious memory. After all, we could not function if we had to continually reinvent our understanding of the world every time we received information through our senses. Our memory helps us to sort out the important from the unimportant, the relevant from the irrelevant.

The wonderful and mysterious property which emerges out of all this activity is our individual consciousness. This phenomenon, though at present poorly understood, is immensely powerful. Through our consciousness we are able to create our own view of the world and this enables us to act in ways which are consistent with our intentions and interests.

This means that although we might agree with others about the objective realities of the world, we will differ in greater or lesser degrees in the meanings we place on those realities. Each of us will put a personal and different interpretation on to the same event. The basis of this difference is what we refer to as our *perception*. Through our perceptual processes we construct our understanding of the world and we interpret what we perceive in accordance with our own construction of the world. We only have to listen to people discussing, say, a football match or a movie to see that even though they watched the same event, each person has their own interpretation of what happened and why it happened.

This chapter is concerned not only with how we perceive the world, but also with how those perceptions influence our attitudes which in turn influence how we act. Moreover, perception is not a one-way process. Our own actions are part of the perceptual process of people around us. How they see us also influences how effective we can be. Consequently, we need to be aware of how we are perceived.

The organisational world, as well as the world at large presents us with a variety of different contexts in which we have to act. These contexts often prescribe the relationships we have with those around us. At work we are subordinates to our managers, colleagues to those we work with and senior to those who work for us. In addition to these formal relationships, there are many other, less formal relationships we have to deal with – staff from other departments we need to work with, specialists both from within and outside of the organisation, clients, suppliers, etc. Each of these different contexts requires us to take a different role and how we carry out the role is a consequence of how we perceive it. How we carry out each of these roles can often determine the effectiveness of our work performance.

At the root of all of our decision-making about work and about relationships within the organisation is our view of the world – our perception.

THE PERCEPTUAL PROCESS

Imagine the company you work for has decided to relocate to a different part of the country as part of a rationalisation process. There are generous relocation expenses for those who decide to make the move or generous severance payments for those who opt not to go, depending on length of service. What will influence your decision to go or stay? The factors you take into account will be very different for each individual: Career prospects, family ties, age, your attitude to new challenges and many other factors will all play a part in influencing your decision. How you *perceive* the situation as it presents itself to you will be different from how everyone else perceives it.

VIGNETTE

Taking in stimuli

How we turn information (stimuli) from the world around us into an understanding of that world can be shown in Figure 3.1 (bear in mind that this is a very simplified version of an extremely complex process).

We are constantly bombarded by stimuli from our surroundings: noise, visual events, smells, tastes and touch. So much so that it would be impossible to take in everything and make any kind of sense of it. Without some means of sorting out what is useful and what is not, we would exist in a state of complete chaos. So, we need to limit the amount of data we take in from these stimuli or we would be overwhelmed. Moreover, we need to be able to pay attention to those things which are important for us to be able to function effectively. Consequently, we need to filter out those stimuli we don't want or need.

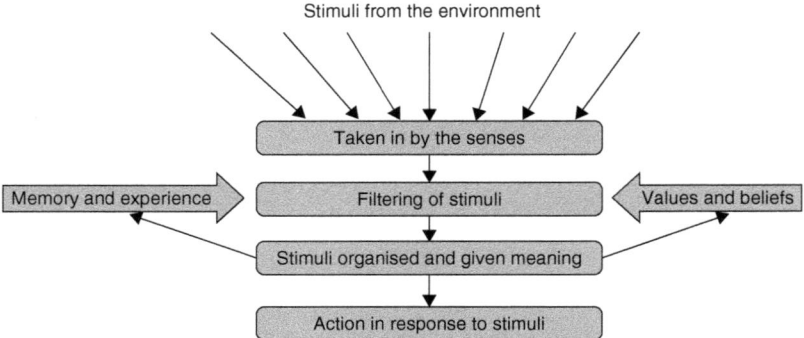

Figure 3.1 A simplified diagram of the perceptual process

FILTERING STIMULI

Broadly speaking, these filters come from two sources: our remembered experience and our value and belief system. What we have learned and experienced in the past is a valuable guide to what will be useful to us now. When we drive a car, for example, we pay attention to information about other road users and traffic signals. We know that if we see a red traffic light ahead we will have to stop until it turns green. Other lights mean different things. Some are important to what we are doing, others not.

If, however, you are a passenger being driven to the shops, you may well want to pay attention to other stimuli which the driver will want to filter out.

The second kind of filter, our beliefs and values, is important when we have to decide between alternatives: whether one course of action will be more effective than another; whether a course of action may have ethical or moral consequences; where your decision to act may promote one set of interests at the expense of another; whether your actions will hurt the feelings of others. We are making these decisions constantly. However, they are rarely decisions which are subject to a solely rational analysis. Our own feelings, our beliefs about what is right or wrong, our strategic sense (opting to do something which delivers benefits in the long term, even though there may be short term disadvantages) all come into play.

ORGANISING AND GIVING MEANING TO FILTERED STIMULI

There is a very famous picture, published in the magazine *Puck* in November 1915. When you look at the image, you either see an old woman, or an attractive young woman. Some people find it hard to see either, while some can easily see both. What you see depends on how you filter and organise the stimuli provided by the form of the image.[1]

Of course, at its most basic, the stimulus is really is no more than a set of black marks on a white background. Turn the picture upside down and you will see what I mean. It is impossible to make any sense of it. However, if (when you have turned it the right way round again) you can discern the image of a young, beautiful woman or a sad looking old woman it is because you have organised the information from the stimulus so that it makes sense to you. How you have organised the stimulus information will determine whether you see the old or the young woman. What this image shows is the need we have to make sense of the information our senses present us with. If you can see an old woman you will see her with a large nose and a loose headscarf. If you can see a young woman, the same lines that makes up the old woman's nose make up the cheek and jawline of the young woman. What is the old woman's left eye is the young woman's left ear. The old woman's lips form the young woman's necklace.

Although this image is a relatively simple way of illustrating the point that we need to make sense of what we perceive, it nevertheless requires the application of several internal processes to arrive at a perception of an understandable picture.

First of all, the observer needs to expect and accept that marks, colours and shapes made on a two-dimensional medium can be perceived as a representation of three-dimensional reality. Most human cultures seem to do this. It happens not only with images on paper, but we carry out this process when we watch a movie or video. So what are the main internal factors which support or inhibit our ability to make sense of our world?

- **Our sensory thresholds:**

    The levels of sensory perception that human beings have evolved are limited. Our sense of hearing or smell is not as acute as a dog's. We can't see as well as a hawk during the day or a cat at night time. Nevertheless, our senses are fine for our purposes. However, that does not mean to say that we are all the same. People differ in the sensitivity of their sensory tolerance. Some people are quite happy to go to loud music gigs while others can find those levels of noise literally painful. Some people are very sensitive to smells, others much less so. Many people need to have their eyesight corrected with spectacles or contact lenses, while others have very acute vision. As we age, we suffer a decline in most of our sensory capability. For example research into driving found that older drivers processed information more slowly and responded less quickly than younger drivers.[2]

- **Schemata:**

  From early childhood we have a need to understand what is going on around us in order to be able to function in the world effectively. For this we engage our innate learning process to create and develop a system of 'schemata' (this is the plural of the word 'schema'; some writers use the more conventional plural 'schemas'). This concept was used by Piaget in his work on child development.[3] It suggests that as we are exposed to more and more of the world, so we have to revise our schemata, or even abandon them altogether. For instance, when you begin a new job, you will already have a schema in place for how an organisation works, which you will have developed from other organisations you will have experienced. You will, perhaps have a schema which tells you that there is an authority system which creates levels of management and subordinates. You may also have a schema that tells you that senior/subordinate relations are formal, and that subordinates are careful what they say when more senior staff are around. If relations between seniors and subordinates in the new job are much more informal, with open communication, you will need to revise your organisation schema. Whilst a schema needs to present us with a comprehensible explanation of what we perceive, it often needs to have a predictive purpose. We need to know that in a given context in order to achieve result r we must carry out action a. Argyris and Schön[4] refer to schemata like these as 'theories of action'. Consequently, the filtering process is not only about gaining an understanding of the world, but also about getting information which enables us to act effectively. Moreover, the development and modification of schemata enable us to learn.

PERSONAL FACTORS

We all have different personalities, intellectual capabilities, goals, needs and interests. These all interact to determine what we pay attention to, what we ignore and, consequently, how we form our schemata. It is why we can confidently make the claim that we all see the world ('construct' the world, in the words of psychologists) in our own individual way. This complex interaction between the individual and the environment is referred to as our *perceptual set*. Working on the way we process information (our 'cognitive styles' Witkin et al.),[5] by focusing on one cognitive style – field-dependency vs. field-independence – showed that field-dependent individuals took their action cues from the environment and adjusted their behaviour according to their reading of the context. Field-independent individuals, on the other hand, tended to be more reliant on and confident in their internal constructs for reading the situation. Of course, field-dependency is a continuum, so it is rare to find an individual who is wholly field-dependent or wholly field-independent. It is more likely that most of us can move along the continuum depending on circumstances.

VIGNETTE

Two people happen to go into a small organisation on the same day. One is a job applicant arriving for an interview for a job. The applicant has just successfully completed a long programme of professional training and is keen to get her first job now that she is qualified. The other is a potential investor coming to discuss the possibility of investing in the company. The investor has to decide between putting his money into this company or into a rival organisation. The company CEO will carry out the job interview and will later go into discussions with the investor.

In both of these situations, one of the parties has something the other wants – in the former, the company has a job to offer, in the latter, the investor has something the company wants.

In the case of both the job applicant and the investor, they are going to want to know as much as possible about the company. The former so that she can present herself as a good job candidate, the latter so that he can make a considered choice about his investment. But assuming that the CEO is not at either extreme of the dependency continuum, what would you predict about his field-dependency in each of these scenarios?

CULTURE

Through the development of our schemata, we ready ourselves to filter out those stimuli that we don't need, or want, to pay attention to. So how can we influence others to pay attention to something we want to convey? Most of the time we interact with others through the use of spoken or written language.

When we speak we use a combination of communicative processes to get our message over:

- **Words** – we use words to convey meaning on their own, or, more usually, in combination with other words to construct more complex meanings.

- **Body language** – this is a combination of posture, gesture and facial expression. These features help convey to the listener our feelings about what is being said, or to give the speaker some feedback on how what is said is being received by listeners. Our clothing and how close we stand to our listeners also transmit subtle messages.

- **Prosody** – stress, intonation and pauses all add important information to the message we want to convey when we speak. In English in particular, stress (the amount of emphasis you place on a particular word or syllable) and intonation (the amount your voice rises and falls) can be very important in subtly changing your meaning.[6]

When we use the written language we are communicating with people who are not present. Consequently, we can't tailor our message by reading or using body language. Prosody can, to some extent, be represented by punctuation, but it is a comparatively crude substitute. Therefore, to write powerfully so that your message is perceived and understood in the way you want it to be understood demands much more planning and consideration of the needs of your readers.

Language is perhaps one of the most powerful indicators of our culture and can convey infinitely subtle information. All cultures use the power of language to achieve this in their own ways. In addition, cultures are also rich in symbols and rituals,[7] which carry important meanings to members of those cultures which are difficult for non-members to completely understand. These symbols and rituals reinforce the values, beliefs and ideologies of individuals within their cultural context, which generally alter slowly.

EXTERNAL FACTORS

The perception process begins with our senses, so we need to make sure that our message at least gets noticed. The media, public relations and advertising industries are founded on their ability to do this. What then are the techniques we can use to grab people's attention? We know that we tend to notice things that are:

- loud
- bright
- in motion
- amusing
- emotionally intense
- surprising
- repeated.

Once through the initial filtering process, the person who you want to communicate with or influence must still somehow be persuaded to attribute meaning to the sensory stimuli.

LIMITATIONS OF THE PERCEPTUAL PROCESS

It has already been mentioned that our senses are limited. Humans don't have the eyesight of an eagle or the smell sensitivity of a dog. Many animals have better hearing than us and are more sensitive to touch. We also know that among people there are differences in our ability to use our senses. Some people have an 'ear' for music that others don't have. Some have better eyesight than others. Some are more sensitive to smell than others. Moreover most of our senses decline as we age.

When you get an opportunity, watch this advertisement from 2007 from a British chocolate maker: http://www.youtube.com/watch?v=TnzFRV1Lwlo

How do the advertisers use stimuli to get your attention and how do they create meaning for the audience, especially as you can't tell from the main activity in the ad what it is selling? Why do you think this advertisement was such a success both commercially and with the public?

Fortunately we can usually cope with our sensory shortcomings, largely because there is usually some redundancy in the sensory environment. That is to say that we don't only take information from one sense alone. Most of the information comes to several of our senses at the same time. You can see a fire. You might also be able to hear it, feel the heat from it and smell the smoke. Taking these stimuli together we build up a holistic impression of a situation – in this case a fire. Consequently, we become very confident of the completeness and accuracy of what we perceive. However, this confidence is often misplaced. Common beliefs about our perceptions, such as it being safer to talk on a hands-free phone than a hand-held phone when driving,[8] that we tend to make better decisions when we use our gut instinct,[9] or that we are often conscious of being stared at even if we can't see the person doing the staring, are incorrect.[10]

Work by Chabris and Simons[11] challenges these misconceptions and, in particular, highlights the phenomenon of 'inattentional blindness'. This is a phenomenon where an individual focusing on one aspect of their environment will fail to notice even very unusual occurrences which take place right in front of them. Chabris and Simons carried out a now famous experiment where two groups of people, one wearing white tops, the other wearing black tops were throwing balls to each other; observers were asked to watch and count how many passes of the ball were made by the 'white' team. During the course of this activity, a person dressed as a gorilla walked into the group and stayed for about five seconds before exiting. Approximately 50% of observers failed to see the gorilla. You can see this experiment if you click the web link at footnote 11. For a more detailed discussion of inattentional blindness see the 2003 article by Arien Mack.[12]

PERCEPTUAL BIASES

In our organisational life, we often find ourselves making formal or informal judgements about people and situations. Formal judgements may involve decisions about:

- job or role performance
- recruitment
- selection for roles, special tasks, promotion, etc.
- competence
- staff who deal with people outside the organisation such as sales staff, buyers, etc., who have to work with their perceptions about those people (conversely, people outside the organisation are making perceptions about those staff members).

Our informal perception may involve decisions about:

- How co-operative to be
- How helpful or informative to be

- Whether to include someone in your social circle
- How trustworthy or reliable people are as colleagues, seniors or subordinates.

It is important both for the sake of effectiveness and fairness that we try to make these decisions honestly. However, we know that we cannot perceive or even have access to all the information we need to make an accurate judgement. Even if we had such access, we would be overwhelmed by the sheer quantity of information. So human beings have evolved a repertoire of *heuristics* (rules of thumb or cognitive shortcuts based on our sense of the *probability* of being right) to enable us to make these judgement calls. The problem with a heuristic approach is that it is rather like betting. However good the odds of getting it right, sometimes we will get it wrong. And getting it wrong can cause problems for the organisation and for any individuals concerned. None of us would like to feel that we were being misjudged because of a predisposition against us that a decision-maker held.

Nevertheless we know that there are several perceptual biases that can come into our decision-making, because of the heuristic basis of our perceptions.

Stereotyping is where we attribute characteristics to a group of people – for example, all accountants are dull – then assume that those characteristics apply to all individuals in that group. This bias presents us with a number of problems. First, even if it is true that a majority of members of a group actually do possess a particular characteristic which typifies that group, there is still no basis for assuming that *every member of the group* will possess that characteristic. The only characteristic we should be concerned with, and which they all possess, is their ability to do accountancy. Second, stereotyping based on ethnicity, gender, age, class or religion may lead to decisions which deny opportunities to large parts of the population who are perfectly capable of filling roles and carrying out tasks effectively. Third, we have a tendency to prefer people who are like us: who share our values and beliefs and who behave like we do. The potential bias from stereotypes is similar to the attribution biases discussed below. The main difference is that stereotyping applies to whole groups, whilst attribution biases tend to apply to biases against specific individuals. However, it is possible to see how the two are connected.

1. **Halo/horns effect**: this is a biased response caused by forming a positive (halo) or negative (horns) impression about a person on first encountering them or based on what you already know or believe about them. It was first noted by Edward Thorndike in a study with the military in 1920.[13] So someone arriving at an interview late or inappropriately dressed may well have failed the interview before it has even begun because you may well try to evaluate their performance in the light of an initial negative impression. Evaluating someone from a positive perspective may be equally damaging if you are sufficiently swayed to offer someone a role or task they are not fitted for.

2. **Primacy and recency effects**: the tendency for information acquired early or late in an interaction to dominate our memory and consequently our judgement is well known. This applies both to a single interaction, where information presented at the beginning and at the end tends to be more memorable, and to a series of interactions, where interactions early or later in the series are more memorable. So if you are conducting, say, a series of interviews, then interviewees coming earlier or later may be at a greater advantage than those in the middle.[14]

3. **Attribution biases** – these arise when we believe we can explain the reasons or motivations for someone's behaviour. This can give rise to two kinds of bias:

   a. **The fundamental attributional error** says that we tend to attribute the causes of our own behaviour more to the context in which it occurs than to our personal qualities (positive or negative), whilst we attribute the behaviour of others more to their personal qualities than to its context. The issue with this is that when we make judgments about other people, we tend to pay more attention to their personal qualities than to context, while when we are judging ourselves, context plays a bigger part in our self-evaluation. A staff member having a performance review may well give the reason for poor performance as, say, the lack of completeness of information received. The appraiser, on the other hand, may consider that the staff member has not been sufficiently diligent in chasing up the information.

b. **The ultimate attributional bias** explains the tendency we have to favour people who belong in the same social groupings as we do and who share our values. We tend to explain good performance by these people from the perspective of their conscientiousness, capability and other positive characteristics that we believe members of this group possesses. To do otherwise may be a challenge to our own self-concept and judgement.

WORKING TO AVOID BIAS

Read the scenario below.

Summer jobs

You are a senior manager at a medium sized music software company. You want to take on temporary staff in your department over the summer, to cover holidays of permanent staff. You have two positions: one for a receptionist/general assistant, the other for a market research survey of current customers to obtain feedback on your products and to inform your product development.

The receptionist/general assistant job will entail meeting and greeting people who come into the building, finding their contact, issuing security badges, keeping a visitor log and helping in the administration department when not on front desk duties. You will need someone who is organised and professional in appearance, who will make a good impression on visitors.

The market research job will require someone to call customers by telephone or, occasionally, in person. Although they will have a list of questions already prepared you would also like someone who is able to follow up some of the issues that arise. They also need to be able

VIGNETTE

to record their findings accurately and in an agreed format. They will be working with one other member of the permanent staff.

You have seen two applicants from local schools who want to get a summer job to save some money before going to university.

Applicant one: Male, aged 18. Has just completed A levels in Maths, Physics and Computer Studies at a local comprehensive school. If he gets the required grades he will go to university to study science. He didn't have any idea how he'd done in his exams, but thought he'd done 'OK.' You know from your conversation that he plays in a local band and is very knowledgeable about the modern music scene.

He came over to you as rather diffident and lacking in self-assurance. He wasn't exactly scruffy in dress, but looked uncomfortable and a bit ungainly in a suit. However, he seemed to understand what the jobs required and wasn't fussed which one he got. His main motivation seemed to be to earn some money.

Applicant two: Female, aged 18 has just completed A levels in History, English, French and Music at an independent girls school. She plays the clarinet. If she gets her grades, which she seemed confident of doing, she was going to one of the top universities to study law. She wasn't very knowledgeable about the modern music business, although she was very well-versed in classical music.

She came over as very confident and professional. She did, however, make it clear in a tactful way that she wasn't as enthusiastic about the reception job as she was about the market research work. She was very keen to begin adding to her CV.

Your Task

What would influence your decision?

It is probably impossible to avoid bias altogether. However, this does not excuse us from confronting the problem. In an organisational context, we are constantly making assessments of other people – our seniors, subordinates, colleagues, customers, suppliers, etc. Many of these assessments are formal, that is to say, they are assessments on which decisions are made which commit the organisation to a course of action, so it is important for the effective functioning of the organisation that they are made as fairly as possible. However, most of our assessments are informal, and perhaps many are unconscious. We inevitably build up a perception over time of an individual's capabilities and personality. We tend to deal with them on the basis of this perception. How, then, might we do this in as unbiased a way as possible?

1. Recognise the probability of bias. We have already seen that our minds cannot process all the data we are surrounded by. Consequently, we take a heuristic approach and only pay attention to those stimuli we think matter. Over time we build our schemata, which allow us to refine what we perceive so that we tend constantly to strengthen those schemata. Once we understand this process, we are perhaps more open to seeing beyond our personal frameworks of understanding.

2. Ensure everyone involved in the process has been trained and understands the importance of making the process fair and unbiased.

3. Create structured processes for formal assessments such as recruitment, promotion, job review, selection for special tasks and so on. We should try to make these processes as reliable and transparent as possible. This means that there should be consistency between how those being assessed are treated, as well as consistency between how different assessors carry out the role.

4. Any assessment needs to focus tightly on the characteristics needed to carry out the function or role for which the assessment is designed. This can sound like a circular argument in which there is a danger of building bias into the design of the assessment process. To avoid this, we need to:

a. Identify as precisely as possible the purpose of the assessment.

b. Be specific about what performance indicators we should be applying to the assessment, and design criteria against which individuals can be assessed.

5. Gather evidence against the criteria and make judgements based on this evidence. It is important that you are clear about why and how you came to a decision. People often want feedback on their performance at an assessment, so it is crucial that you can give it based on how they measured up against the criteria. Moreover, in many countries it is unlawful to make decisions based on ethnicity or gender, so you need to be able make clear on what grounds you made your decision.

Of course making assessments about other people is never really so straight-forward. First of all it may be difficult to articulate the criteria. You may find it hard to agree with others whether all the criteria have equal importance. Or you may end up with individuals who fulfill different criteria at different levels of competence. What this means is that there is always a high level of subjectivity about even the most formal and well-designed assessment processes. Look again at the 'Summer Jobs' scenario above. What criteria would you use to help you decide which applicant to appoint to which job? How sure are you that these criteria will deliver an effective staff member? What difficulties do you face in making your decision?

BELIEFS AND ATTITUDES

While an understanding of the perceptual process may help us to challenge our immediate, habitual responses to people and situations and to maintain a focus on effective performance, we need to bear in mind that our construction of meaning through the perceptual process is dynamic. That is to say that it is constantly being strengthened or challenged. If our construction of meaning is supported by what we perceive, we become more sure of our understanding of the world. Where our construction of meaning is challenged, we have either to ignore it or to somehow fit any inconsistencies into a modified schema. So our constructions of meaning can become more subtle over time and we may become more confident of them. This leads to a system of beliefs about the way the world works, the nature of human beings and so on.

It may be appropriate at this stage to issue a word of warning. One of the problems of researching this area has been the problem of definition and categorisation of the terms used. The way the word *belief* is used in this chapter may also include what others call *values*. This may be further confused by how we use these words in our everyday language. The best way to deal with this confusion is to understand what the terms mean in this chapter and to bear that meaning in mind when other people use other terms.

Beliefs that we develop for ourselves are essentially probability-based. We observe or experience a range of phenomena and develop a belief that similar sets of circumstances will bring about similar outcomes. Obviously, we as individuals only sample a limited experience of the world. Nevertheless, we have to make judgements based on that sampling. The more our predictions appear to be right, the more confident we can be that our beliefs are valid. However, where we hold a belief very strongly, even when there is evidence that it is wrong, we often persist in holding to it. For example, certain sections of the British public (mainly women over the age of 45 and older people of both genders) believe that neighbourhood police foot patrols ('bobbies on the beat') are an important tactic in the fight against crime.[15] This is in spite of plenty of evidence to the contrary.[16]

However, perhaps more importantly than our own experiences and observations is the filter of our culture and society. A good example of this is religious belief, for which there is no objective evidence. However, people born into any of the world's religious traditions tend to identify with that tradition throughout their life. The same is true of political systems, moral codes and many other human constructs. The traditions we are born into represent a powerful agent for our construction of meaning and consequently of our sense of self. They are a crucial source for our beliefs and can make them resistant to change.

Attitudes. Attitudes are generally thought to be predispositions to respond and act positively or negatively towards things, people, situations, ideas and events. They have three components: the *affective* component, the *cognitive* component and the *behavioural* component.

The affective component is that part of our make-up which is centred around our emotions, values and beliefs. The cognitive component refers to our ability to evaluate situations and make decisions using our reasoning capacity. The behavioural component refers to the action we decide to take.

The influence each of these components will have in determining our responses will vary. For example, a strongly held belief may override a more reasoned approach – think of suicide bombers! In a more ordinary context, it is quite possible to have a positive attitude towards your employer and to identify closely with the aims of your organisation while at the same time having a negative attitude towards your actual job.

In such contexts, it is quite possible to have conflicting motivations as to how to act. You want to do well for the organisation with which you identify, but don't feel very motivated to carry out your particular role with any enthusiasm. This conflict is known as *cognitive dissonance*, a theory originally developed by Festinger.[17] Because attitudes are personal and individual, different people will handle this cognitive dissonance in different ways. One person may do his or her best for the good of the organisation, another will not be able to operate effectively because of the strength of a negative attitude to the actual job. Our personal goals will also come into play. We may, for instance, be prepared to carry out a role we are not enthusiastic about because such a course of action suits our longer term goal. So, if you have a longer term goal to advance your career, and believe from your own observation and from what you have been told, that management favour those who 'show willing', you may well be persuaded to make the best of things in the present to gain a later advantage.

RELEVANCE OF BELIEFS AND ATTITUDES

None of us comes into an organisation as a blank slate. We bring with us ready formed beliefs and attitudes about how the world works. These beliefs and attitudes will influence our perceptual process and will have an impact on how we perform, and how we relate to the organisation as a whole and to groups and individuals within it. They may well have an influence on our productivity, job satisfaction, career progress and important social aspects of the workplace.[18] They will also have an impact on things like our management style, our ability to work effectively with others and even our personal physical and emotional health.[19]

CHANGING ATTITUDES

Because our attitudes are dynamic, they change over time as we constantly modify them. Generally, this change happens slowly. However, our attitudes influence our behaviour, so it is important in organisations that behaviour is consistent and focused on the organisation's purposes. This means that organisations may want to engage in attitude change from time to time. There are a number of approaches that we can take to encourage attitude change:

- **Use of reasoned argument.** We all probably want to believe that we are creatures of reason and that we hold our beliefs as rational beings. Consequently, if we are given evidence or reasoned argument as to the rightness of a course of action, or the wrongness of the alternatives, we should accept the reasoned argument and act accordingly, even if this means changing our attitude or beliefs. However, this is rarely sufficient because:

  - Our beliefs and attitudes may be so deep-rooted that we think the reasoning or the evidence must be wrong. They go against 'common sense'.

  - Whoever presents the argument is good with words and ideas, but is not to be trusted (often *because* they are good with words).

  - You may be confident enough to have your own counter-arguments.

  - It is more often than not impossible to produce argument and evidence which is so conclusive that it cannot be challenged.

- **Use of fear or threats.** Such an approach may well produce the required action, but is unlikely to change attitudes or beliefs. At best it brings about a climate of *compliance*; in other words, people do what you want without believing in it or being committed to it. This approach has the added disadvantage of creating resentment and distrust.

- **Social pressures.** There is a tendency to align our beliefs and attitudes with those of groups with which we identify. Often, this does not require a major shift in attitude or belief, since we tend to seek out groups with members who are like us. In the organisational workplace, however, we have little choice over those we work with, so the challenges to our attitudes and beliefs may be stronger. However, the nature of group membership means that as a group becomes more cohesive, attitudes and beliefs tend to become more aligned.

- **Behaviour-led attitude change.** We know that attitude influences behaviour – it is one of the defining properties of attitude. However, can our behaviour lead to a change in attitude? There are several indications that it can. In 1974 the UK government brought in the Health and Safety at Work Act. The Act was brought in because of the very high number of days of work lost to work-related accidents and illness. Although the Act is a part of criminal law, meaning that if you break it you can be fined or even imprisoned, its main purpose is to create a safety-conscious workforce by imposing safe working practices and procedures.[20] Health and safety committees and officers were set up in organisations from among employees and management, whose task it was to implement and maintain these practices and procedures. The idea behind this approach is to create ways of working which become embedded and routine for everyone. When that happens attitudes can develop which lead to much greater awareness of safety issues. At the level of legislation, this approach has also been taken with legislation on unfair discrimination and on road safety.

- However, such an approach is not guaranteed to succeed. For example, legislation on equal pay for men and women has been in force in the UK for more than 30 years, but there is still a difference in average pay between the genders.

CONCLUSION

We saw in Chapter 2 that there are many ways in which one individual differs from another. The perceptual process is one way in which we become different and express that difference. The way each one of us sees the world is different from the way others see it. The importance we attach to what we perceive also differs. Consequently, an important part of management is influencing us to see situations in the same way so that priorities can be agreed, and action taken in a concerted and effective way.

Understanding the perceptual process is a good beginning.

Perception, among other things, highlights the complexity of human systems and the sensitivity and subtlety required to manage them.

Lisa's Dilemma

Read the case study and answer the questions at the end.

This case takes place at 'Gallagher's, a regional retail chain selling electrical and audio/video goods. The situation concerns the customer service department; the organisation chart for the department can be seen below:

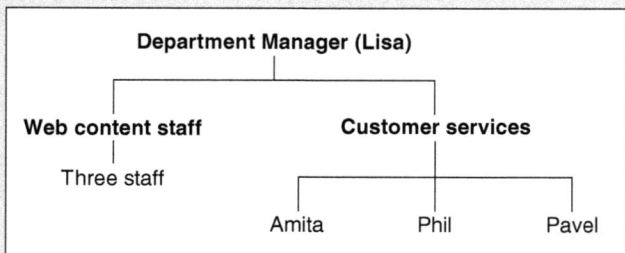

Lisa has just taken over as Customer Service Manager, having been recruited only six months ago. She has six staff in two sections: Customer Services and Web Content (see org chart).

The Web Content section:

- Maintains the product information on the company website.
- Deals with queries and complaints submitted through the site by customers.
- Liaises with Sales and Warehousing departments for online orders.

The section has three staff, all men. One of them has just handed in his notice as he has got a new job in another company.

The Customer Services section:

- Oversees customer service training for staff in the stores. This involves buying in and supervising training in customer care and problem-solving and managing a programme of seminars on product knowledge and development.
- Liaises with the Web Content section to update product information and deal with online customer problems and complaints The latter involves monitoring complaints, providing solutions to the Web Content team to communicate to customers, and dealing with problematic 'one-off' complaints either in person or by contacting technical staff in the supplying companies.
- Liaises with the call centre that handles telephone customer services, making sure that they receive and understand repair and replacement protocols. The department also monitors call centre satisfaction responses and handles difficult problems passed on from the call centre.

Lisa went to a meeting of department heads yesterday and was told that because of poor sales results in the last three quarters, there were going to be redundancies. This is the first time in the history of the company that this had happened and there were no procedures in place.

Lisa was told that she needed to cut two staff from her department and that she had to make recommendations as to who should go.

Because the Web Content section was losing one staff member already, that reduced Lisa's task to selecting just one staff member to go from the Customer Services section.

She was finding it difficult to make her decision, so she decided to make a review of her staff based on what she knew about them from her brief acquaintance and from a brief staff overview left for her by the manager she replaced, Max. These are the notes relevant to the Customer Service team she received from Max:

Dear Lisa,
Sorry we didn't have time to meet up for me to show you the ropes. I hope you enjoy the new job. I thought you might appreciate some information on your staff. A good bunch overall, they know their jobs but, like everyone, they have their foibles. I hope this information helps. Good luck.
Max.

1. Amita – age 26, has been with the company for four years.

She came straight from university where she studied marketing. She is working towards a professional qualification in marketing which the company is supporting through help with fees and time off to study.

Her job is to arrange customer service training for store staff. She doesn't carry out the training herself, but is responsible for contracting outside trainers. She has built up a lot of contacts in the training business and knows precisely who to go to when training is needed. She monitors the training by going through the feedback sheets and conducting training needs analyses. She also manages the performance review process in stores, often carrying out reviews of store management staff herself.

Without being spectacular, Amita is capable and conscientious. She generally gets on well with staff and management of the stores as well as with her outside training consultants. She can, however, be forceful when required and in the past has ruffled the feathers of some store managers who have been less than co-operative in allowing staff time to attend customer care courses or who have not taken the performance review process seriously. She has also been quick to terminate training contracts of consultants who have not delivered a high enough standard of training.

She gets on well with her colleagues in the department and will help them out in an emergency, though she makes it clear that her own job must come first.

You probably know that she applied for the job of department manager when I left. She was interviewed but the job went to you. Although she is professional in her attitude, maybe there's a sense of lurking resentment. I know that she thought the promotion was in the bag for her. She has been a little critical of management decisions sometimes without directly challenging them.

The formal feedback she received from the HR staff member present at the interview indicated that she did not have a wide enough grasp of the business. This is true. In my opinion she doesn't think like a manager – too focused on the detail and no sense of the 'big picture'. Could change with experience.

Lisa's note: All sounds quite accurate. Have noticed that A always the first to query decisions. Sometimes makes me feel that I miss the obvious!

2. Phil, with the company for nine years – almost from its beginning. Phil is the go-to person for product information. He is technically very capable and makes it a point of principle to keep himself up to date on new products and product development. He is often on courses put on by suppliers to update their customers about new developments. Consequently, he has a strong network of expertise outside of the company. His role is to liaise with the Web Content team, keeping them informed on new products and updates to existing ones. This is a crucial job as the company sells a wide range of electrical and audio-visual goods. He has to monitor online customer satisfaction with how their queries and complaints are handled. Any that are non-routine or unusual he will deal with himself, and any of those that he can't deal with he passes on to suppliers.

Phil is happier dealing with technical issues rather than the interpersonal relations which his job inevitably entails. He will try very hard, and usually successfully, to find an answer to a query, but doesn't cope well with customers who are angry or rude. Fortunately, most of his interactions with customers are online rather than by telephone or face to face.

I always felt that Phil often saw technical problems as a personal challenge, which he needed to solve for himself rather than passing them on to more knowledgeable people at the supplying companies to get a solution as quickly as possible. Phil is no team player – you'll find that out quickly. Phil is a fair bit older than the other members of the team and the other two regard him as a bit of a techie nerd, at the same time as relying on his expertise very often.

Phil doesn't seem to be very ambitious, and I don't see him as promotion material anytime soon, even if opportunities were to arise.

Lisa's note: Seems ok to me so far. A bit shy – seems more to be tolerated by the others than liked. <u>Very</u> good at his job. Everybody relies on him – what he doesn't know about product isn't worth knowing.

3. Pavel – with the company for three years. Pavel was born in the Czech Republic and came to the UK to study business. He has a degree in business and is about to enroll on a part-time MBA programme at a good local university.

Pavel is responsible for managing the company's link with the call centre they use. He has to make sure that they understand the repair and replacement protocols, and customer satisfaction levels. He is also responsible for producing help sheets and fixes for routine problems so that they can be dealt with immediately by call centre staff. He deals with non-routine problems and queries himself and has become very knowledgeable about the goods. He has also begun making useful contacts with suppliers so that he can get help from that source when he needs it. Phil is starting to get a bit twitchy about someone else muscling in on his territory. Phil likes to help out as the departmental technical 'expert', it seems he feels that Pavel is trying to usurp that role. Just something for you to watch out for!

Pavel is very ambitious, though he has yet to develop a real focus on where his career path should be, so he is quite happy to stay at Gallagher's for the foreseeable future, perhaps indefinitely if the right opportunities come up.

Additional information: Lisa knows much more about the details of Pavel's life than about the others because Pavel is her partner. They have been together for four years. In fact it was Pavel who told her about the vacancy at Gallagher's in the first place and encouraged her to apply. Naturally, she has kept quiet about the closeness of this relationship with other members of the department. Now, however, it is really difficult. Not only does she have to make a decision on the redundancy, but she has recently discovered that she is pregnant, expecting the birth in about seven months. Lisa and Pavel are planning to marry before the arrival of the baby. Obviously, from a personal point of view, she is very happy, but she really needs them both to continue working as they are going to need the money. She hasn't told her managers yet, but expects to take maternity leave about a month before the birth.

Your Task

Lisa is in a quandary. She wants to be fair in her decision, but doesn't know how to begin. She decides to confide in a close friend who has nothing to do with the company.

- If Lisa confided in you what advice would you give her about making a fair decision?
- From what you know of the case, and there will certainly be many details of which you are unaware, what biases may affect Lisa's thinking?
- From the information you have, what would you do if you were Lisa?

GLOSSARY OF TERMS

Affective To do with our feelings and emotions

Attitude A tendency, consistent over time, to act in a particular way in a given set of circumstances.

Attribution Particular characteristics or motivations that we believe are possessed by specific individuals.

Attribution biases A perceptual bias in which we think we know the reasons why someone behaves in the way they do.

Behavioural To do with the way we act.

Belief system A relatively stable set of beliefs about how the world *should* work.

Blank slate An idea of the mind which sees it as lacking any content until content is received from the external world.

Body language Combinations of gesture, posture and facial expression which communicate meaning to the observer.

Cognitive To do with our logic and reasoning processes.

Cognitive dissonance A mismatch between what our reason tells us *should* happen, compared with what *actually* happens.

Cognitive styles The approaches you take when you have to work think through a problem. The styles are dispersed over a continuum ranging from highly intuitive to highly rational.

Construction of meaning The stimuli we receive from the environment carry little meaning until we interpret them. We give them meaning by filtering them through our experience, beliefs and attitudes.

Criteria The standards we use to make decisions and judgements. They can be both explicit and implicit.

Dynamic Situations which change are dynamic. Opposite of static.

Filter A process by which some information is treated as useful or important, and consequently taken in, while other information is ignored or discarded because it has no importance.

Halo effect Where someone who makes a positive impression is thereafter seen in a positive light.

Heuristics Cognitive shortcuts to decision-making. Often used where the person making the decision feels he or she can rely on experience of similar situations dealt with in the past.

Horns effect The opposite of the halo effect. A negative impression influences further negative impressions.

Inattentional blindness Where you are focusing your concentration on a specific situation, you may often overlook other things of equal importance or interest which happen outside of your focus of attention.

Internal constructs Your internal, mental model of the world and how it ought to work. Similar to *schemata* defined below.

Perception Taking information from your external environment and giving it meaning.

Perceptual biases Tending to see a situation in only one way with a reluctance to change your view.

Perceptual process The process by which stimuli are filtered to construct meaning.

Performance indicators Metrics and other criteria from which we can deduce good or poor performance.

Primacy effect The tendency for events early in a series to be remembered more easily than other events, especially in the middle part of the series.

Recency effect The tendency for events late in a series to be remembered more easily than other events, especially in the middle part of the series.

Rituals Formalised occasions and actions which are repeated when specific events occur. Rituals are important ways to confirm cultural identity.

Schemata Your internal models of the world which influence attitudes, beliefs and behaviour. Similar to *internal constructs* defined above.

Sensory thresholds The physical limits to our senses

Stereotyping Holding a view about the attributes of a whole category of people or things and assuming that every member of that group will possess the same attributes.

Stimulus (pl. stimuli) Any external event or observation which triggers the perceptual process.

Symbols Artefacts or actions which contain meaning.

Theories of action Heuristic principles which are often internalised and which we rely on to manage many day to day situations.

Values Deep-seated convictions about what is good or bad, right or wrong, for example.

KEY POINTS

- We take in information about our world from our senses.

- We filter this information through our experience, belief system and cultural influences.

- We use this filtering process to create meaning – our 'construction' of the world. Consequently, each individual understands the world in his or her own individual way, which means that no-one will see the same event in the same way.

- The meaning we give to events in our world influence how we think we should act – our attitudes.

- The way we create meaning leads to important biases in our judgements of other people and situations which can lead to poor decision-making.

- When we are aware of the potential for bias in ourselves and in others we can take steps to reduce them through the creation of formal and informal processes

- Attitudes can be changed, but this needs time and constant reinforcement. There is no guarantee of success.

REVISION QUESTIONS

1. Two work colleagues are talking. One of them has studied the perception process and found it helpful in understanding aspects of the organisation they work for; the other hasn't studied it and feels that it would be a waste of time. Summarise what you think their respective arguments might be. What is your opinion?

2. From all the information available to us in our environment, how do we know what we should pay attention to? How do we make sense of these stimuli?

3. How serious a problem is perceptual bias? What can you do to minimise your own biases?

4. From your own observation and experience, how likely is it that you can change a deeply embedded attitude? How might you go about it?

GOING FURTHER

Modern research into brain function is revealing more and more about our ability to perceive the world, as well as the way individuals differ in how they construct their world. The number of books which explain these developments has grown proportionately. Fortunately, so much that is written about this complex process is written for a general readership, so we don't all need doctorates in neuroscience to understand the main thrust of the work. Below is a short, selective list of books on the topic.

- Sacks, O. (1998) *The Man Who Mistook His Wife for a Hat and Other Clinical Tales*, New York, Touchstone.
- Abbott, E. A. (1992) *Flatland: A Romance of Many Dimensions: A fictional foray into the mathematics of perception!*
  (Introduction by Banesh Hoffmann), London, Dover Publications.

- Tavris, C. and Aronson, E. (2007) *Mistakes Were Made (But Not by Me): Why We Justify Foolish Beliefs, Bad Decisions, and Hurtful Acts*, Orlando, Florida, Houghton Mifflin Harcourt.
- Peale, N. V. (1952) *The Power Of Positive Thinking,* New York, Fireside Books. *This is one of the best known 'self-improvement' books.*

NOTES

1. See the image in its various versions at http://mathworld.wolfram.com/YoungGirl-OldWomanIllusion.html. What do you make of it?

2. Joanne, M. Wood, 2002, 'Age and Visual Impairment Decrease Driving Performance as Measured on a Closed-Road Circuit', *Human Factors: The Journal of the Human Factors and Ergonomics Society Fall,* vol. 44, no. 3, pp. 482–494.

3. Piaget, J., 1928, *The Child's Conception of the World.* London: Routledge and Kegan Paul.

4. Argyris, M. and Schön, D., 1974, *Theory in Practice. Increasing professional effectiveness.* San Francisco: Jossey-Bass.

5. Witkin, H. A., Moore, C. A., Goodenough, D. R. & Cox, P. W., Winter 1977, 'Field-Dependent and Field-Independent Cognitive Styles and Their Educational Implications', *Review of Educational Research,* vol. 47, no. 1, pp. 1–64.

6. We can illustrate this by taking a simple sentence: *The cat sat on the mat.* If you stress the word *cat* more strongly than *sat* or *mat* - *The cat sat on the mat* – the sentence answers the question: Which animal sat on the mat? If, however you stress the word *sat* – *The cat sat on the mat* – you answer the question: What did the cat do on the mat? Similarly, if you were to read out loud the following one word sentences: *OK.* and *OK?* You would need to use different intonation to show which was the statement and which was the question.

7. Think, for example, what symbols and rituals are normal in your culture for, say, a marriage. How do they differ from those of another culture?

8. The British Royal Society for the Prevention of Accidents (RoSPA) strongly disagrees, see http://www.rospa.com/roadsafety/adviceand information/driving/mobilephoneswhiledriving/factsheet.aspx, accessed 13 November 2012.

9. Some interesting survey data on the extent of corporate decision-making based on intuition can be found at http://www.businessinsider .com/graphic-most-company-decisions-are-based-on-intuition-and-not-research-2012-6, accessed 13 November 2012.

10. Some psychologists agree with this and have an explanation for it. See: http://www.psychologytoday.com/blog/the-narcissus-in-all-us/ 201102/how-you-know-eyes-are-watching-you, accessed 13 November 2012.

11. Simons, D.J. and Chabris, C.F., 1999, 'Gorillas in our midst: Sustained inattentional blindness for dynamic events', *Perception*, vol. 28. There is also a website with downloadable video of several of Simons' and Chabris' experiments – www.theinvisiblegorilla.com

12. Mack, Arien., 2003, 'Inattentional Blindness: Looking Without Seeing', *Current Directions in Psychological Science,* vol. 12, no. 5, pp. 179–184.

13. Thorndike, E.L., 1920, 'A Constant Error in Psychological Ratings', *Journal of Applied Psychology,* vol. 4, pp. 25–29.

14. For a brief overview of this, see http://www.ere.net/2010/02/25/ the-recency-and-primacy-effects-in-the-talent-acquisition-process/.

15. According to a UK Home Office survey, Russell Bradley, *Public Expectations and Perceptions of Policing,* Police Research Series Paper 96, 1998, pp. 10–12, accessible online at http://library.npia.police.uk/ docs/hopolicers/fprs96.pdf.

16. See, for example the article http://www.bbc.co.uk/news/uk-17704354.

17. Festinger, L., 1957, *A Theory of Cognitive Dissonance,* Stanford, CA: Stanford University Press.

18. These aspects of organisational behaviour will be discussed in greater detail in the chapter on motivation at work.

19. See chapters on groups and leadership later in the book.

20. Health and Safety at Work Act 1974 creates duties on both employer and employee to maintain safe working practices. From time to time the Health and safety executive issue regulations for specific safety issues such as the reporting of accidents or the storage and handling of hazardous materials. For more information see www.hasawa.co.uk/.

4

MOTIVATION

LEARNING OBJECTIVES

- Discuss the meaning of the term motivation
- Evaluate content and process theories of motivation and their applicability in the workplace
- Develop a view about the role of financial and other rewards as motivating factors
- Discuss the motivational aspects of job design.

INTRODUCTION

The study of motivation goes to the heart of why human beings work. Nineteenth-century and early twentieth-century theorists believed in the notion of the 'rational-economic man'.[1] Harking back to times when the difference for many people between surviving and starving depended on whether you could find paid work, it is no real surprise that if anyone thought about motivation at all, it was in the context of individuals maximising their potential to earn. And it was rational since people needed to understand what their options were and make choices about how to behave in order to achieve maximum economic return.

Consequently, the motivation to work was above all an economic one. The underlying economic impulse to work is still at the heart the motivation question today. It is, of course, possible that you may have a powerful vocation to work in, say, education, medicine or in some form of artistic endeavour, where financial reward is not a major consideration. Literature has many examples of artists struggling in poverty but unable to do anything other than work at their art. In the UK the lure of music is so strong for some young people that they are prepared to accept a hand-to-mouth existence to try to make a living in a very tough industry. Many of them fail. In such cases pay may not feature as the most important motivation. However, most people's aspirations are much less demanding. For most of us the main reason we work is to earn a living in order to feed, clothe and shelter our dependants and ourselves. In all the discussion of motivation, we have to remember why people work. In spite of this, however, the degree to which financial rewards are in themselves a motivating factor is difficult to ascertain. Certainly, if you want to be paid, you have to get up and go to work, so that seems like some kind of motivation. However, is financial reward enough to make you enthusiastic about your job, or sufficient to make you want to do your best?

What is meant by the term motivation is itself a little uncertain. The term originates from the discipline of psychology. Psychology defines motivation as:

> the process that initiates, guides and maintains goal-oriented behaviors. Motivation is what causes us to act, whether it is getting a glass of water to reduce thirst or reading a book to gain knowledge.
>
> It involves the biological, emotional, social and cognitive forces that activate behavior. In everyday usage, the term motivation is frequently used to describe why a person does something. For example, you might say that a student is so motivated to get into a clinical psychology program that she spends every night studying.[2]

In a nutshell, this definition of motivation is a *descriptive* account of the reasons why we do things.

However, if we look at a definition from a business perspective, we get a slightly different understanding of the term:

> Internal and external factors that stimulate desire and energy in people to be **continually interested and committed to a job, role or subject**, or to make an effort to attain a goal.

Motivation results from the interaction of both conscious and unconscious factors such as the (1) intensity of desire or need, (2) incentive or reward value of the goal, and (3) expectations of the individual and of his or her peers. These factors are the reasons one has for behaving a certain way. An example is a student that spends extra time studying for a test because he or she wants a better grade in the class.[3]

Although the definitions of motivation are similar in both cases, the second quote has added a key feature to the definition (highlighted in bold). Workplace motivation studies have focused on the need to have workers who are interested, committed and enthusiastic about the job, the product or the organisation.

What began in academic studies of psychology as a *description* of motivation has become a search for a *prescription* of how to motivate workers.

Wanting people to be interested in, enthusiastic about and committed to their work is a clear legacy from the Human Relations movement which started in the 1920s.[4] The proponents of this movement, as we have seen, believed that people were more than rational-economic units of production and had emotional, psychological and social needs that work could fulfil. From a humanitarian perspective it is hard to argue that it is better that workers are satisfied and fulfilled in their work than not. The question still remains, however, of the relationship between motivation and productivity.

Even if we accept that this is the case, we still have to ask how applicable these theories are in practice: what can be done if someone is not motivated, for which there presently seems plenty of evidence.[5] Consequently, motivation studies in work organisations have tended to go beyond a descriptive analysis of motivation in order to concentrate on finding *what* motivates people (content theories) and *how* they become motivated (process theories).

CONTENT THEORIES OF MOTIVATION

Content theories of motivation have tended to emphasise the meeting of people's needs as the driving feature of motivation. They begin with the reasonable assumption that people have needs which they will take action to satisfy. Content theories attempt to understand what those needs are and to classify them in useful ways.

MASLOW'S HIERARCHY OF NEEDS

Probably the most widely known of the needs theories is that developed by Abraham Maslow in the 1940s and 1950s.[6] In it, Maslow identified five levels of human need, each of which has to be satisfied before an individual will attempt to satisfy needs at the next level – hence a hierarchy (see Figure 4.1).

Many people will be familiar with the five-stage hierarchy shown in Figure 4.1. What is less well known, though, is that Maslow later identified three other needs – aesthetic, cognitive and transcendent needs. He did not place these in the hierarchy, though others have subsequently done this. He did, however consider that the need for transcendence was a higher need even than self-actualisation.

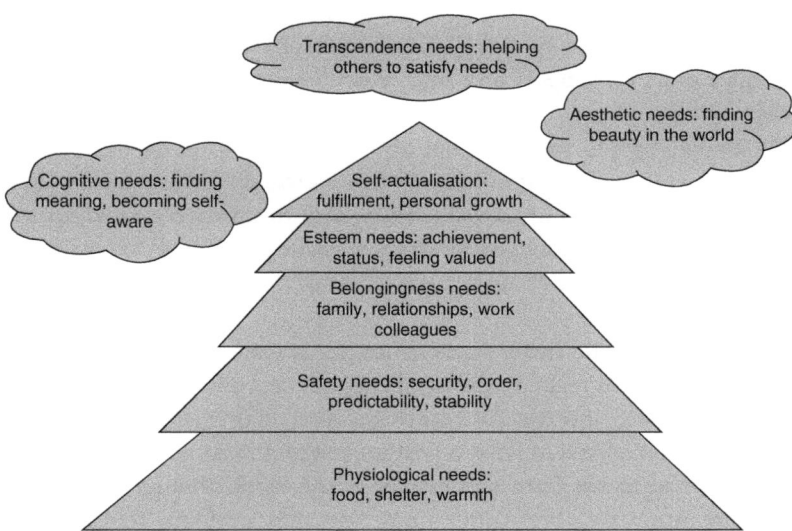

Figure 4.1 Maslow's hierarchy of needs

Maslow differentiated his original five needs into deficit needs (physiological, safety and belonging) and growth needs (esteem and self-actualisation) Deficit needs (sometimes referred to as 'lower order' needs), represent needs whose absence poses a threat to our well being, or even to our survival in the case of physiological needs. Growth needs, on the other hand, enable us to develop and become more rounded and satisfied human beings. Maslow's hierarchy is usually represented as a pyramid because he believed that fewer and fewer people managed to get to the upper levels.

The hierarchy of needs has high face validity. It seems very credible, for example, that if you are lost and thirsty in the desert, then you are not very concerned about the progress of your mortgage application. However, once you have been rescued and have satisfied your needs for food and water, then you might regain interest in how your application is proceeding because this represents a move to the safety and security level of needs.

Obviously, we are unlikely to focus on any other needs when we are threatened with death or other serious danger, so our physiological needs will take precedence in that situation. We can look upon safety needs, the second level, as giving us confidence that our basic needs will continue to be met for the foreseeable future. Once we are satisfied that that is the case, then we may well start to seek a place in our community or group in order to receive practical support and help when needed and to begin to find a social identity.

When we begin to feel confident of our social identity, we are then able to develop a sense of being valued, in other words, our esteem needs can be met. Finally, a minority of us will even be able to satisfy our need for self-actualisation. This need suggests that we are acting at a level that makes use of all our talents and positive personal qualities to achieve the optimum we can achieve.

Cognitive, aesthetic and transcendence needs were added later in 1970.[7] Our cognitive needs relate to the need to know and understand how things in our world work: how decisions are made, how things get changed, how to 'read between the lines' of what is written and said. Aesthetic needs suggest a strong desire to see form and beauty in the world through art, design, music, literature and other cultural processes and artefacts. Transcendence needs lead us to support and help others in their attempts to self-actualise.

Because Maslow found it difficult to fit these needs into a hierarchical framework, they shed light on to a major criticism of his theory: that needs do not fit into a hierarchy at all. Certainly, we can see the imperative of satisfying physiological needs before paying attention to any others, but it is not difficult to see that we can seek to satisfy needs at other levels without necessarily having to satisfy all needs at the previous levels. People who lead very insecure lives can often look for the satisfaction of social, esteem, cognitive or aesthetic needs to be met. Indeed, we may consider that making strong social bonds is one way of satisfying important security needs. In fact in many countries where people live in poverty, their social structures are their principal means of meeting safety needs.

Maslow has also been criticised for his methodology. As part of the humanist psychology tradition, he set great store by having people tell him their perspective on phenomena. For his research into needs, he interviewed 21 people he regarded as being self-actualising. This formed the basis of his data collection. However, such an approach is bound to be highly subjective. How far is Maslow's definition of self-actualising agreed? Can it be measured in any way? Can we establish reliable causation (that satisfying needs lower down the hierarchy has led them to this higher level of need) from the self-reporting of interviewees? The dangers of bias and lack of clarity are enormous.

Finally, Maslow has been criticised for producing a highly culture-specific model of motivation.[8] According to this model, the highest form of need is self-actualisation. This may be fine for a Western individualistic society, but how true would it be of collectivist cultures, where the role of the individual is less important than the cohesion of the family, community or ethnic group?

In spite of these criticisms, Maslow's needs theory continues to be a powerful model, especially in the field of management studies. Clearly the fulfilment of needs is a powerful force in motivation and the needs that Maslow identified have stood the test of time even if we struggle to agree with the model of the hierarchy.

As an analytical tool, however, it has its uses. It comes into play when organisations plan and mange their human resources. Such things as pay rates, job security, management styles and many other factors influence it.

It helps managers make sense of often complex and worrying events in the workplace, even if it provides no blueprint for solving those problems.

ALDERFER'S ERG THEORY

Alderfer's work can be seen as a modification of Maslow.[9] Instead of the five, later eight, needs identified by Maslow, Alderfer created three broader categories: **Existence** needs, **Relatedness** needs and **Growth** needs. Table 4.1 below shows how ERG theory relates to Maslow's. What is usually referred to as ERG is an acronym of these categories.

As well as simplifying the needs Maslow developed into three broader categories, Alderfer also differed in that he did not see his needs model as a hierarchy. He accepted that any individual could be trying to satisfy several needs at once. Clearly, if basic needs are not being met, then it is likely that a person would tend to focus on them, but not necessarily to the exclusion of other, so-called higher, needs. Alderfer recognised a greater degree of complexity in human motivation than can be encapsulated in Maslow's hierarchy.

Table 4.1 How Alderfer's ERG theory relates to Maslow's hierarchy of needs

Alderfer	Maslow
Existence Food, water, shelter, safety, physical well-being, confidence that these needs will continue to be met.	**Physiological needs** **Safety needs**
Relatedness Good relations with others, feeling part of a group or community, sense of identity, concern to be seen as valued member of group.	**Belonging needs** **Esteem needs**
Growth Need for sense of achievement, emotional and psychological growth, positive sense of self.	**Self-actualisation needs**

Like Maslow's model, however, ERG is perhaps more useful as a way of analysing the motivations of individuals than as a recipe for developing motivation. First, it may not be as simple as we think to identify the specific needs of a given individual. Second, even if we are able to do that, as managers, we may only have very limited strategies available to provide resources and opportunities to satisfy those needs.

HERZBERG'S TWO-FACTOR THEORY OR MOTIVATION-HYGIENE THEORY

In the 1950s and 60s Frederick Herzberg developed his 'Two-factor' theory of motivation. Other theories, like those of Maslow and Alderfer, believed that motivation, defined as the drive to do something, lay in the satisfaction of important needs.

Herzberg's research, however, found that if certain needs were not met, then the result was dissatisfaction. Moreover, if those needs were later met, the result was not greater satisfaction or motivation but absence of dissatisfaction. These factors he called *Dissatisfiers* or *Hygiene Factors*.

If other needs, on the other hand, were met, the result was motivation. These needs Herzberg classified as *Motivators*.

Broadly speaking, Hygiene Factors are those aspects of working conditions which are extrinsic to the individual worker. They are part of the working environment set up by management. They include:

- organisation's policies
- relationship with supervisor
- working conditions
- salary
- status
- security
- relationship with subordinates
- personal life

Motivators, in contrast, provide opportunities for individuals to meet important intrinsic needs such as:

- achievement
- recognition
- work itself
- responsibility
- advancement

Herzberg's apparent implication that hygiene factors and motivators are independent of each other poses some interesting questions: for example if the hygiene factors are all present to an acceptable degree (so that workers are not dissatisfied) but no motivators are present to any great extent (so that workers are not satisfied) what is the motivational status of workers? Is there a kind of 'neutral' state, where they are neither motivated nor demotivated, satisfied nor dissatisfied? Or what if some key motivators are present which provide motivation, but co-exist with significant negative hygiene factors? Which has the greater salience, the dissatisfaction because of poor hygiene factors, or the motivational power of the motivating factors?

It would appear that the theory is more complicated than it first appears. However, its great advantage is that it gives managers ideas about what to look for and what to do about it. If dissatisfaction can be prevented by paying attention to hygiene factors, then management can make some headway by doing so. Similarly, finding the intrinsic motivating factors of individual staff can lead to greater job satisfaction.

Interestingly, Herzberg found that interviewees reported that salary was not a great motivator, but an important potential source of dissatisfaction. If this is true, what are the implications for performance related pay schemes?

PROCESS THEORIES OF MOTIVATION

Whilst content theories of motivation looked at aspects of organisational life to discover how well they met workers' needs, process theories are concerned with *how* people become motivated. Content theories of motivation are difficult to implement since they require the manager to have an intimate knowledge of the needs of any individual. They then need to have access to the resources which can satisfy those needs. Process theories, on the other hand, are of interest to managers since they appear to be theories managers can use to direct workers to fulfil the needs of the organisation.

Expectancy theories

The underlying concept of expectancy is that an individual will strive to achieve a goal that they value. This basic concept was further developed by Victor Vroom.[10] It is often set out as:

Motivational Force (MF) = Expectancy × Instrumentality × Valency

Valency – how valuable the outcome is to the person carrying out the task;

Instrumentality – the likelihood that the valued rewards will be forthcoming when the task is successfully completed;

Expectancy – the belief that the effort input will lead to successful completion of a task.

There are consequently three key relationships in expectancy theory (Figure 4.2):

- Value to the individual of the reward for achieving the task, which determines how much effort someone will put in to achieve it (valency).
- The confidence that making the effort will result in successful completion of the task (expectancy).
- The belief that successful completion of the task will deliver the reward (instrumentality).

These relationships can be seen as cyclical:

First of all, the reward for successful completion of a task needs to be important to you. This will motivate you to put in the effort needed to succeed.

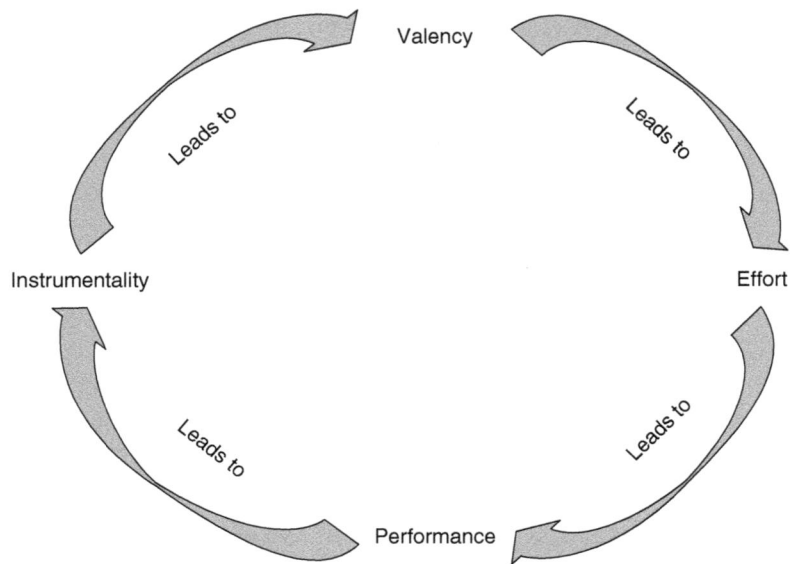

Figure 4.2 Expectancy theory as a cyclical process

Second, putting in the extra effort is not of itself sufficient; you need to be confident that the effort you expend will enable you to successfully complete the task. This is probably the most complex of the expectancy relationships, since some of the factors that lead to success will not be in your hands. Clearly you need the internal strengths of self-efficacy,[11] capability and confidence in the role you carry out. But the support you receive, the locus of control you operate under as well as the adequacy of resources made available all contribute to your success.

The final relationship, performance leading to a successful outcome, relates to two potentially separate outcomes: the first is that the task is successfully completed, the second is that the reward or outcome that initially motivated you to put in the effort will be available on completion.

Jo has called Robert into her office. She tells him that the department is under pressure to roll out new credit control software ready for the quarterly sales review in six weeks' time. The software has been available for several weeks, but the department has been too busy to put the time in to implement it. Jo tells Robert that he would be doing her and the company an important service by taking this on. She says she knows Robert is ambitious and the successful completion of this project would make him the strongest candidate for the post of International Accounts manager which would become available in the next few months as the present incumbent was retiring.

This looked attractive to Robert, who was indeed ambitious, so he agreed to take the project on.

However, he didn't find the task easy. He still had to carry out his normal work tasks, so he had to find time outside the working day to make sure the project worked out. He was given no extra resources and, realising his lack of knowledge of the software and the credit control process, he had to pester other people to get the required information. This made him a little unpopular, and some individuals avoided him or made excuses why they couldn't help.

Nevertheless, Robert's tireless efforts brought the software on stream in good time and he was quietly satisfied.

The International Accounts manager did in fact retire a couple of months later and Robert applied for the job. He was, however, mortified to find that he was not even interviewed for the post, which was given to a candidate from outside the organisation. He asked Jo what was going on but she was rather evasive, so he asked the HR department to give him some feedback on his application. They told him that he was not considered for two reasons: first, he was too inexperienced in the company's international business dealings and second he was seen as too abrasive a personality by some staff. He had realised that he was a nuisance to some staff when he was carrying out the software project, but assumed the urgency and importance of the task made his badgering of them acceptable.

What does expectancy theory tell us about this scenario? What is Robert's perception of the company likely to be? What lessons could a manager learn from this?

The final part of the cycle suggests that your experience of having your expectations fulfilled (or not fulfilled) will influence how motivated you may be in future tasks. If the desired reward was not forthcoming, or if you could not successfully complete a task because of unnecessary obstacles, not of your making, you may well reduce the effort you are willing to put into a task even if it is one you value.

The kind of reward that we see in this scenario is what is referred to as an *extrinsic* reward. By extrinsic we mean something that comes from outside of the individual – in this case it is the promise of promotion. However, Porter and Lawler[12] point out the power of *intrinsic* rewards – that is, something that we find within ourselves, things like satisfaction in doing a good job, a sense of achievement or wanting to feel valued.

Intrinsic reward is arguably important for managers. Since we tend to think of reward in terms of money or status or career progression, we also tend to think of it as having a cost, which needs to be outweighed by the benefits provided to the person being rewarded. However, if we accept that intrinsic rewards are powerful motivators (after all, Herzberg's interviewees stressed the importance of intrinsic satisfactions among the main motivators in his model), they tend to have more to do with interpersonal engagement with the employee, rather than a quantifiable cost to the organisation. However, it does presume that managers are aware that expectancy theories are about the expectancy of an individual. What motivates one person will not have the same valency for another.

To sum up, expectancy theory is calculative. It assumes that we make decisions about how to act depending on what we think is in it for us. It is about the motivation process of the individual; it has a number of key relationships which influence the decision to put in the effort to achieve a goal: how much the individual desires the goal, what extrinsic or intrinsic reward it brings and whether they believe the reward is actually available on completion of the task.

EQUITY THEORY

Like expectancy theory, equity theory is calculative. According to Adams[13] we weigh up the effort we put into a task and the reward we receive on its completion, similarly to expectancy theory. Where equity theory develops this idea, however, is in proposing that we not only calculate reward/effort relationship, but also make a comparison about how well or badly we do after completing the task compared to other people. We do not see the performance of the task as carried out in isolation from other people carrying out similar tasks, and we almost try to establish a kind of a 'going rate' which we calculate by comparison with what rewards others receive.

Adams saw the comparison as a relationship of *inputs*, or the effort that an individual puts into a task, with *outcomes*, the reward available on successful completion. Both inputs and outputs may be intrinsic or extrinsic.

Examples of inputs: Time, effort, skill, imagination, experience, conscientiousness, personal qualities.

Examples of outcomes: Money, status, position, satisfaction, praise, challenge, reputation, enhancement of your CV.

Extrinsic factors are much easier to make comparisons about than intrinsic ones. After all, an intrinsic factor is unique to the individual and it is arguably difficult to make comparisons about them.

There is implicitly a two-tier comparison at work:

First tier: the outcome reward has to be worth the effort, as in expectancy. This is a kind of internal equity.

Second tier (the focus of Adams' work): The outcome needs to be equitable in relation to the rewards others are receiving for similar tasks. This suggests that there is a 'market rate' for a given task or role, and it needs to be honoured.

The consequence of not honouring it will be a feeling of inequity, leading to discouragement and demotivation. Anyone feeling a sense of inequity will make efforts to restore an equitable balance, using a number of possible strategies:

Change inputs: You can do this by increasing or decreasing personal effort, or other inputs to the task.

Change expectations of outcomes: You can do this by raising or lowering what you expect to receive as a reward.

Change comparison: You may conclude that the person you are comparing your efforts with is not the right person for a comparison. In this case you need to change who you are comparing yourself to.

Influencing the inputs and outcomes of your comparator: If, for example, you find that someone else is carrying out the same task for a lesser reward, you may try to influence them to demand an increase in their reward. You may do this from a sense of fairness, or you may do it so that your own reward does not appear to be excessive – you are trying to change the 'marketplace'.

Of course, we are all different, so our responses to perceived inequity will be different. Huseman et al.[14] developed broad categories of responses:

Sensitives: These are people who are very concerned that there should be an equilibrium between inputs and outcomes.

Benevolents: These individuals tend to be tolerant of perceived under-reward, for example because they find intrinsic reward in other aspects of work rather than in the task they are engaged in.

Entitleds: These people tend to prefer situations in which they are over-rewarded, in other words, the outcomes for their inputs are better than those of their comparators.

Criticisms of Equity Theory: Even a very brief experience of a work organisation will serve to show how important the concept of fairness is in the workplace. Equity theory therefore seems to be tapping into a rich source of influence over people's behaviour. We can imagine (or may well have experienced) the demotivating power of inequity. In such a case, equity can be seen as one of Herzberg's hygiene factors. It has the power to demotivate, but if equity is restored, it does not have the power to improve motivation. If, on the other hand, equity is a motivator, then managers would do well to ensure that it is an important presence in the workplace.

However, the work done on equity is very inconclusive as to its influence on work behaviour. Criticisms address three areas:

1. Equity is a perception and consequently highly subjective. What I may consider equitable may be thought of as inequitable by others. It is not unusual for subordinates to differ in what they perceive as equitable from what their managers think is equitable. Moreover, perceptions of equity differ in different sociological and demographic circumstances. In the UK at the time of writing, 2013, there is a lot of political discussion about immigration. One of the criticisms is that people are allowed to enter the UK from other parts of the European Union and undercut the wages of British workers in low paid jobs. Clearly immigrant workers who are willing to work at these jobs have a very different perception of what is a fair return than native British workers.

2. Most of the research carried out to validate equity theory has been carried out in the controlled conditions of the laboratory, not in the more complex environments of work organisations. One of the difficulties of laboratory experiments is that you want to stop other, unwanted factors from contaminating your results. In real world situations, however, you can't control for unwanted variables, so you have to develop a 'rule of thumb' approach which has poor validity or reliability.

3. You may often see a situation as equitable within a restricted context, but see it as unfair if the whole system is perceived as inequitable. You may, for example be receiving a bonus according to a company's policy in the same way as everyone else. However, if you know that most similar companies pay much higher bonuses, then there may well be a sense of inequity. Moreover, such a sense of inequity could well be shared by colleagues.

GOAL-SETTING THEORY OF MOTIVATION

VIGNETTE

The performance review

Every year your manager sits down with you to review your performance over the past year. Depending on the assessment of your performance you will receive your annual salary increase. Performance is usually measured against the achievement of objectives set at the previous review.

At your recent review you were shocked to find that your manager considered that your performance was just about satisfactory and that your salary increase would be in the lower band for this year.

In your view you had performed quite well. There had been a few problems with work received from other departments which had held you back and you had had to help out a couple of younger colleagues who found this a problem. But you thought you had handled this well. You hadn't complained, you had just got on with the job.

Later, as if to rub salt in the wound, one of your younger colleagues told you she had had an increase in the upper band.

What can you do to remedy this situation?

Having many links to the concepts in expectancy theory, goal-setting theory, as the name suggests, focuses on the outcomes of people's efforts. Edwin Locke first developed the theory in the early 1960s. Latham and Locke further developed it in the 1990s.

The theory suggests that appropriate goals will have a positive effect on the performance of a task.

Goal setting is based on the premise that human activity is purposeful and can be directed towards achieving a desired outcome. The theory can be seen as having three dimensions:

1. **The nature of the goals:** whenever we engage in some activity, we usually have either an explicit or implicit intention – that is, a goal we want to

achieve by that activity. As we have seen, when we go to work we have many different possible goals: to earn a living, to progress in our career, to achieve personal satisfaction and many others. Organisations themselves also have goals, of course, and so it is important that the goals of individuals are aligned with those of the organisation. Locke and Latham suggest that work goals should have certain characteristics if they are to enable staff to work effectively for the benefit of the organisation. They should be:

- **Clear.** They need to say exactly what is to be achieved, using what resources and in what timescale. In particular, the outcome needs to be unambiguously measurable.

- **Challenging.** Goals which are easy to attain will not motivate. They need to present a challenge to the person tasked with carrying them out, which stretches their capability.

- **Realistic.** Goals need to be credible and they need to relate to the overall aims of the organisation.

- **Reasonably complex.** Simple tasks appear to be less motivating than complex tasks, although the complexity must not be such as to over-whelm the person carrying it out.

2. **The processes at work which help to achieve those goals:** A number of factors facilitate successful goal achievement:

- **Commitment to the goal.** If the worker is not committed to achieving the goal, then it will either not be achieved or will not be achieved satisfactorily. Commitment to a goal is the key to the motivational properties of goal setting. In this context, we can look at commitment as having two dimensions: First, the goal must be important and make a contribution to the organisation's aims, otherwise why would anyone bother to put in the effort. Second, the person carrying out the task needs to have a high enough level of self-efficacy, or belief in their ability to carry out the task to a successful conclusion. One of the main ways in which managers attempt to achieve commitment is by having the worker participate in the setting of the goals and their parameters.

- **Feedback.** If goal setting is to be motivational, then it is important that staff have information on how well they are performing. This allows them to refocus their efforts on any parts of the task that need to be improved or on things that were not foreseen when the goals were first set. Like goals themselves, feedback should be specific, with suggestions about how to address any problems.

3. **The contribution of the goal achievement:** If a manager and subordinate have spent time and effort on defining clear, measurable goals, then have expended skill and diligence on achieving that goal, only to find that it is not valued, or that it makes little difference to overall departmental or organisational performance, then it is much less likely that there will be a similar level of commitment to achieving future goals.

While evidence is strong for goal-setting theory's ability to motivate, and while the principles are well known, there are nevertheless a number of problems that can arise:

• **Goal conflict:** When the goals that are actually worked towards are not aligned with those of the organisation at large, then there is a problem. Such a problem can arise from several perspectives. For example, a manager may disagree with a particular organisational strategy, and set goals designed to undermine or conflict with that strategy. At a lower level of the hierarchy, the goals of the individual worker may be at odds with those his or her manager wants them to achieve.

• **Employee capability:** part of the goal-setting process needs to be establishing the ability of the person carrying out the task to have a level of competence which will enable them to fulfil the task. If they don't, then the task's success is likely to be compromised. While it is probably a good thing to ask an individual to work at the limit of their capability, support and feedback will be essential.

• **Designing goal parameters:** Designing goals and the parameters that must be achieved is not without its problems. Central to effective goal setting is the ability to measure outcomes. However, many jobs are extremely difficult to express in measurable terms. This is particularly problematic where pay increases are dependent on achieving specific goals. In particular, it is difficult to measure jobs where there is a critical level of interaction with people and where the judgement of the individual worker comes into play. Certainly you can measure, for example, whether they adhere to policy guidelines in the performance of their work, but that alone is often not sufficient for a successful outcome. So should you set goals for successful outcomes as a measure of success? What if the outcome is not under the control of the staff member? For example, in the caring professions each interaction may be unique and successful outcomes unpredictable. There may be variables at work which are not accounted for in the setting of goals, or which are outside of the control of the worker.

• We often know intuitively who is good at their work, who consistently achieves better outcomes than colleagues; we often know who might fall a little short. However, being able to say exactly what it is they do, in a way that can be accurately compared to what others do, is extremely difficult, if not impossible.

Performance-related pay (PRP): Closely linked to goal-setting theory, but with an essentially different perspective on motivation, is performance-related pay. In schemes like this, your pay is not (or not exclusively) linked to your status, length of service or the kind of work you do; it is linked to the achievement of specific targets or goals. Although PRP may look to harness the motivational effects of goals, its principal assumption is that employees will work harder to achieve a goal if there is monetary reward at the end of it.

Most PRP schemes tend to place employees in bands based on performance reviews, with pay, and other benefits, being paid according to which band they are in.

Alternatively some schemes still make use of *piece working*, in which you are paid for the level of output you produce. (This, of course, was F. W. Taylor's preference for rewarding higher productivity.) Yet other, more modern approaches make use of *cafeteria benefits*. This system of reward allows the worker to specify a personalised package of benefits from a 'menu' of what is on offer. Recognising that our needs change as we progress through our work life means that we can structure a package which suits our present needs. Later we can revise our choices as our needs change. This last approach, however, is probably more prevalent in situations where an organisation wants to motivate key staff to remain with the organisation for the long term.

The aim of all these approaches is to improve performance and productivity. They assume that money will motivate staff to greater efforts and that working harder will deliver better performance. This is not yet demonstrated by research. Moreover, it may also be the case that the big financial incentives paid to top earners can have a negative effect on performance.[15]

Pay, according to Herzberg, is principally a hygiene factor; that is to say, if workers perceive it to be inadequate, it will tend to have a demotivating effect. Although there is a small element of motivation in pay in his two-factor model, it tends to be where there is a direct link between performance and pay. There may well be a motivational uplift in performance in the short term from a financial incentive. Over time, however, as the extra pay becomes just another part of the payment package, any performance improvement is likely to diminish and return to the average.[16] However, a salesperson on commission can well find that kind of incentive motivating, providing that the reward is definitely available and its achievement within the capability of the worker – in other words, it fulfils the requirements of expectancy theory. It is also subject to the characteristics of goal setting. As we saw with the sales of sub-prime mortgages in the 1990s and 2000s, the success of commission on sales of loans motivated sellers to make loans which were highly risky. This system played a major part in the economic crash of 2008.[17] Staff were incentivised to sell to anyone, irrespective of whether they would be able to repay the loan.

Obviously not all PRP systems end up so catastrophically. Nevertheless there is little evidence to suggest that they have a major influence on improving performance either. While people are often quite enthusiastic about such schemes initially, it is often problematic. Staff usually see PRP as a way to increase their income, since most of us think we are above average in our performance and so will receive above the average pay award. When we only receive the average (or mid-band) increase we begin to believe that the pay system is inequitable. The process is fine if most of us think we are about average at our work. It is not so fine if most of us think we are a little above average. Moreover, as time goes by, the differentials between individuals doing the same work can increase, leading to dissatisfaction.

PRP is also prone to a potential weakness of goal-setting theory; that is, the problem of ensuring that the goals to be achieved are aligned with the aims of the organisation. Also, while it is quite possible to set goals for work which has an observable and measurable outcome, it is much more difficult for work where the outcomes are less predictable. A probation officer, for example, may work very hard to ensure a client does not re-offend. But in the end, it is the client's choice to offend or not to offend. The probation officer cannot be on hand to control all the problems that might confront a potential re-offender. Should that outcome be part of the PRP goals of a probation officer? It is, after all one of the main purposes of the Probation Service.

JOB DESIGN

If the motivational properties of pay are difficult to assess, what then of the nature of the job? The Hawthorne Studies, Maslow and Herzberg, as we have seen, put factors like achievement, recognition, and satisfaction of higher needs as being among the prime motivators in work. Can we therefore design jobs so that management can exploit these motivators?

This is a difficult question to answer definitively. We can achieve satisfaction from both extrinsic rewards (better pay, status, promotion, recognition from managers and peers, awards, etc.) and from intrinsic rewards (doing a job well, feeling that your skills and values are right for the work and the work is the right fit for you). However, Herzberg has shown that there are certain motivating features of work which are likely to provide intrinsic satisfaction such as the nature of the job, the possibility of development and growth, challenging work, recognition, achievement and responsibility. Herzberg's results have been replicated on several occasions, making his theory one of the more durable and stable theories of motivation. Consequently, if we want to examine the degree to which any job is satisfying or motivating, these are the factors to which we need to pay attention.

Hackman and Oldham developed a model to evaluate the motivating features of a job. They identified five core job dimensions which can be used to identify the key motivational features of any job:

- **Skill Variety:** The range of skills needed to carry out the job. The assumption is that workers prefer to utilise a range of skills, especially challenging skills, than the single, simplified skill set required in work broken down according to scientific management principles.

- **Task Identity:** Seeing the job as a whole entity, rather than as a single, insignificant contribution to a larger whole.

- **Task Significance:** This refers to how important and meaningful the job is for others, either inside or outside the organisation.

- **Autonomy:** The degree of decision making the worker has about the way the job is to be done, the sequencing of activities, the quality of process and output.

- **Feedback:** Feedback is the key to understanding how well you are doing in the job – or how well you are perceived to be doing. It enables you to modify how you are working to achieve improvements. The key feature of feedback, especially critical feedback, is that it needs to be constructive and concrete, with suggestions on what needs to be done to improve.

Hackman and Oldham further develop their model to show how the five core job dimensions lead to three psychological states which are critical to the level of satisfaction or dissatisfaction workers get from their work. These critical psychological states are:

- **The experienced meaningfulness of work:** In other words the job that is done has meaning for both the worker and the organisation. It is important that it is done well. This critical state is mostly influenced by the dimensions of skill variety, task identity and task significance.

- **The experienced responsibility for the outcomes of the job:** This refers to the notion of 'ownership' of the job. That is, the job holder has to take responsibility for the process of carrying out the work as well as for the outcomes of the work. This critical state is influenced by the degree of autonomy in the work.

- **Knowledge of the results of the work:** This is psychologically important since it tells the job holder whether the purposes of the job are being achieved and what needs to be done to make any changes. The main influence on this psychological state is the dimension of feedback.

The first two parts of the model deliver the personal outcomes and degree of motivation of the work. This, according to Hackman and Oldham, consists of four personal work outcomes if the design of the work is right for the individual.

- **High internal work motivation:** Provided that the core dimensions lead to appropriate psychological states for the individual, then the result is likely to be a self-motivated worker.

- **High quality work performance:** We have seen in other aspects of motivation theory that effort and enthusiasm are not necessarily predictors of effective performance. However, Hackman and Oldman suggest that if the job dimensions fit the individual and the appropriate psychological state is achieved, then high quality work can be achieved.

- **High work satisfaction:** As above, if the individual's needs are met by the design of the job, then they will find the work satisfying.

- **Low absenteeism and labour turnover:** Work that is motivating and high quality will tend to be attractive in itself. Consequently, staff will not be constantly seeking other opportunities. Moreover, as long as pay is seen as equitable, staff will not leave for purely financial reasons.

CONCLUSION

From the number and range of theories about motivation, we can see that it is far from straightforward. We may be forgiven for going to the heart of the matter and saying that the principal relationship in a work organisation is between what you do and what you are paid for it. This basic bargain is, after all, why we look for work in the first place and why employers agree to pay us. This, of course, is the end of the story for many of the classical theorists, like F. W. Taylor. This view states that rational-economic workers will work harder and better if financial incentives are properly applied. Such ideas are still prevalent if we look at the present UK government's desire to bring in performance-related pay in public occupations which traditionally don't operate on a system of financial incentives. Yet while there has to be a grain of truth in the notion of the 'rational-economic man' view of workers, studies from the early part of the twentieth century to the present tell us unequivocally that there is more to work than pay.

So if we are capable of getting more from work than an economic benefit, how do we design jobs so that workers are satisfied and employers get the benefit of high quality performance?

We have seen that motivation theories usually look either at *what* motivates people: their needs and wants; or at the process of *how* they become motivated, how they set out to achieve their needs. We have also seen that because we are all different, and there is a huge variety of jobs that we do, then there is no overarching theory of motivation that will apply to everyone in any job.

Moreover, from the point of view of management, there is no guarantee that motivating staff to put in greater effort will in fact result in better performance. Our readiness to be motivated or demotivated may well lie outside of the organisation we work for. It may be to do with our personality, or problems in our lives which have nothing to do with our work. So what are managers to do?

At the time of writing, we can see that there is an element of fear in many workplaces. High unemployment, an economy unable to grow and the decreasing value of wages mean that many people are in real fear of losing their jobs, while many of those in work are finding their pay levels are insufficient to provide more than a basic means of paying their way. In such a context, an upbeat, progressive view of workplace motivation can seem a little hollow. However, even in such straitened circumstances, motivation theory can help us understand what is going on in organisations. Maslow, for example, with his hierarchy of needs, recognises that the hierarchy goes two ways: we can move down the hierarchy as well as up it. So many find that where they used to be at higher levels of need satisfaction, they may well now be much lower in the hierarchy. Expectancies in the workplace may well have been adjusted to make the principal goal that of job retention, so staff will direct their efforts towards that goal.

In short, we cannot divorce motivation from the specific organisational and more general societal context within which work is carried out. Consequently we have to beware of taking a simplistic view of motivation theory. Donald Schön in his work on developing effective professional practice, describe the distinction between what is learned in colleges and business schools as learning 'on the high ground'.[18] Real world practice on the other hand, takes place 'in the swamp'. In other words, problems don't come to us ready formed. We can't say, 'This is a motivation issue'. Or, 'This situation needs a different kind of leadership approach'. Often it is difficult to even know what the problem is. Motivation can often lie in the murkiest waters of the swamp. Its innate complexity, its individual nature, its sensitivity to context, the inability of any one theory to answer all our questions about it challenge our creativity and sensitivity.

Lewis' Difficult Day

The wind blew the cold Autumn drizzle into Lewis' face as he walked along the road to his office. He pulled his coat collar a little tighter. At last he reached his building and gratefully ran up the steps into the atrium. As he walked over to the lifts he ran through in his mind what was in store for him. This was a day he wasn't looking forward to. Yesterday he'd been at a meeting where his departmental head had told him that there would have to be more staff cuts in his team. He had managed to negotiate the number down from two to one, which doesn't sound like a big deal, but from a team of seven (including him), the loss of two would have been disastrous. As things stood, one was bad enough. Especially since the team had originally been 11 before the cuts over the previous two years had taken their toll. Two had been made redundant and two other very experienced colleagues had managed to find alternative work in the private sector. He was not allowed to replace them. The consequences of this had been to increase individual workloads and to lower the morale of a very committed and successful team. No-one felt secure. Lewis knew that some were already looking tentatively for other jobs. This morning he had to deliver the bad news.

Lewis heads the content management team of a large local authority. They are responsible for entering copy and other media onto the authority's websites and making sure that the sites are kept up to date and the material on them is accurate and consistent with the political policies of the authority. When he was taken on originally, his task had been to bring together the various departmental and other websites of the authority, give them a corporate identity and make them user friendly. He thought that he had been very successful in this. His team had developed a professional but friendly house style of writing and regular surveys had told him that users, including members of the public, found the pages they accessed easy to understand and navigate.

When the cuts first began, most of the really tough tasks had been completed. The web sites were unified and integrated; it was now a case of keeping them up to date and slowly developing their uses as well as monitoring references to the authority's activities in the media. There was also an increasing need for the authority to interact with social media, which many of the older staff and the elected members were unfamiliar with and somewhat intimidated by. Fortunately, Lewis' team were competent and enthusiastic and enjoyed working under pressure. They also like to spread their knowledge and expertise to help the more reluctant users to understand the web sites and use them productively. However, the increase in workload and loss of colleagues over the past couple of years had gradually eroded the feelgood climate in the team. Lewis himself felt that he was losing the trust of his staff since he seemed to be permanently asking them to do more with fewer resources. It didn't help that pay had been frozen for over a year, so with the cost of living going up people found themselves working harder for lower value pay.

The chime of the lift arriving broke into his thoughts. The door opened, he stepped in and pressed the button for his floor. As the lift ascended he began to think about his staff. HR would first look for a volunteer to take redundancy. If no-one came forward, they would select by looking at performance reviews and expect Lewis to make a recommendation. Lewis considered his staff:

- **Dora** is one of his more experienced staff. She has been with the team since it was first put together. She is conscientious and considered in her work without being spectacular. She gets work done on time usually but she is occasionally too painstaking. However, she is now very knowledgeable about the technical side of her work and about the needs of the authority. Her performance reviews have ranged from acceptable to good. She does not seem to have any great ambitions, though she has always been positive about the frequent update training the team members have to do. She is a solid and valued member of the team.

- **Jane** comes from the northeastern seaboard of the USA. She has been in the UK for several years and is married to an English man who also works for the local authority, though in a completely different department. She has been on the team for just over two years and, because she was a recent recruit at the time, was lucky to hold on to her job when the first wave of cuts hit the team. She is a great team player and has always had time to help out people who are snowed under – which has increasingly been the case for a long time now. Her own workload seems at times to be getting her down these days. There seem to be more and more errors creeping into her work and she has been heard to snap at people who have asked for her help recently – something previously unheard of. You have heard that she has been looking round for other work. Her performance reviews have been good, with some outstanding features, but you can't see her keeping to these grades this year.

- **Brian** is the youngster of the team. He is enthusiastic and has developed well in the job since his recruitment nine months ago following a successful work placement from university, a case of his being in the right place at the right time. The material he produces for the web site is very good, but he lacks confidence when he has to liaise with people (especially senior people or elected members), which is an important part of the work. Because he is relatively young and inexperienced, he has really been learning the job as he goes along, so is not at the level of competence of the other team members. His lack of confidence sometimes prevents him from asking for help. He has had a couple of interim reviews of his performance. Each one has thrown up parts of his work he needs to improve, and, to be fair to him, he has made progress in these areas. At present, he is the weak link in the chain. However, he shows every sign of developing into a highly competent team member in the fullness of time.

- **Pepe** has handled the workload increases better than any of the others. He is highly competent and seems to have a knack for entering just the right content in the right way very quickly. From conversations with him it is apparent that he thinks he should be in charge of the team. He is very ambitious and has a network of friends and acquaintances in the authority, some at a senior level. He is not really to be trusted and would not hesitate to use his connections to fulfil his ambitions. He always seems to know what is happening before anyone else. He is respected rather than liked by the other team members. He is the only member of the team who thinks that the cuts are necessary and that everyone should be working harder. His reviews show that his work is outstanding, though his potential for progression through to management has been questioned.

- **Gurdeep** was born and brought up in London. He is a good character to have around as he is able to diffuse potential confrontations with his humour and wit. His work is very good and his ability to get information from people outside of the department is uncanny. He is unfailingly helpful and seems immune to the barbed comments of Pepe, who seems to see him as a rival. In fact he is not. He is one of the people who has been looking for a way out of the department. He applied for a research studentship to do a PhD but it appears he has been turned down, so needs to stay in the job for at least another year. He tends to get very good or outstanding grades on his performance reviews

- **Gabby** was on a fast track management trainee scheme with the authority. When it ended it coincided with the second round of cuts, so she found herself without any kind of management position to apply for. As she had been in the Content Management team for part of her training she was asked if she would like to move there permanently. She agreed but was clearly disappointed to find that there would be no management responsibility for her. Nevertheless, she was conscientious and actually found she loved the job and the team work involved. She is, obviously, very ambitious but seems to see working successfully in this job as a platform for her future career. Her performance reviews are peppered with 'excellents' and 'outstandings'. However, even she is finding life tough at the moment. Hopefully she will get through it as she is a real asset to the team.

'This is the twelfth floor', said the voice through the lift speaker. Lewis looked up, exited the lift and went through the double doors into the Content Management team office. 'Okay, you guys!', he said, 'can we have a quick meeting in here at ten. – it's important so if you can't make it let me know straight away please.' The team looked nervously at each other. This was horribly familiar.

Your Task

Analyse the general situation from the perspective of theories on motivation. Do they provide any help as to how Lewis might help them through the coming problems? From the admittedly scant information Lewis has on his team, what do motivation theories tell us about how to encourage each of the team members to continue doing a good job?

GLOSSARY OF TERMS

Content theories Theories which focus on *what* makes people satisfied with their work

Equity A comparison of what one individual receives on completion of a task with what another individual receives on completion of a similar task.

ERG An acronym for Alderfer's motivational needs. It stands for Existence needs, Relatedness needs and Growth needs.

Expectancy This term is used to refer to those theories which are based on the notion that people will put in more effort to achieve something they believe is worthwhile.

Extrinsic needs Needs which can be found in the organisational context, like pay, promotion, opportunities for development, status and so on.

Hierarchy of needs This suggests that our needs are organised into a hierarchy, or progression, in which each lower level need must be satisfied before needs at the next, higher level, can be satisfied. Maslow's hierarchy is the best known of these theories.

Hygiene factors In Herzberg's two-factor theory, hygiene factors (also called *dissatisfiers*) are those things which, if they are absent in the working environment, will create dissatisfaction in the worker. However, if they are present, they will not lead to greater satisfaction.

Instrumentality In expectancy theories, instrumentality is the perceived level of confidence an individual has that the desired reward will be forthcoming on completion of the task.

Intrinsic needs Needs which are found within the individual, such as the need for power, or friendship, or to be challenged, or to self-actualise, and so on.

Needs theories Those theories of motivation (mainly content theories) which suggest that motivation is achieved by meeting important intrinsic or extrinsic needs of the worker.

Process theories Theories which focus on *how* people become motivated to work hard with enthusiasm and commitment

Self-actualisation The higher level need to develop as far as the individual is able and to make use of their talents to the fullest extent.

Skill variety The variability of skills required to carry out a particular job.

Task identity The perception of a task as being integral to the completion of a process.

Task significance How important and meaningful a task is seen to be others within and outside the organisation.

Valency In expectancy theories, valency is the measure of how important a goal is to an individual. It is thought that the stronger the valency, the more effort an individual is likely to put into a task.

KEY POINTS

1. In organisations, motivation refers to processes which encourage workers to strive enthusiastically for the goals of the organisation.

2. There are two groups of theories on motivation:

   a. Content theories, which try to understand *what* motivates people, and

   b. Process theories, which try to understand the processes through which we become motivated.

3. Needs theories are theories which tell us that we are motivated by the satisfaction of psychological and physiological needs. Maslow and Alderfer developed needs theories.

4. Herzberg suggested there were needs which, if not met, would act as dissatisfiers, whilst if they were met, would reduce dissatisfaction. Another category of needs would provide satisfaction if met.

5. Expectancy theories tell us that we will apply effort to achieve things that we value. There are, however, important relationships between how much we want something compared to how much effort we need to put

in, and how likely it is that putting in the extra effort will indeed enable us to achieve our goal.

6. Equity theory compares the inputs we have to make to complete a task and the outputs we receive from its completion. These outputs have to appear equitable compared to the outputs others are receiving from similar inputs.

7. Goal-setting theories of motivation suggest that we will apply effort to achieve goals if we perceive them as appropriate. Appropriate goals should be: clear, challenging, realistic and reasonably complex.

8. Performance-related pay assumes that people will work harder if there is the possibility of improved financial reward. Pay is generally awarded in these schemes if certain goals are achieved. We can see PRP as linked to the principle of the 'rational-economic man'.

9. Theories of job design claim that how work is organised can be motivational. Extreme division of labour is largely demotivating because it requires repetition of very simple tasks. To make a job more satisfying, it has to have skill variety, task identity, task significance, a degree of autonomy and timely feedback.

GOING FURTHER WITH MOTIVATION

Like much of the content of OB, motivation resources are usually one of two types. First are 'how-to' books, which are marketed at managers and individuals who feel they want to improve their own or their staff's motivation. Any web or library search will turn up innumerable resources of this type. Some of these are potentially useful, and attempt to provide a way of applying theory to practice; nearly all of them are based on the work carried out in the second type of book on motivation. These are the books based on rigorous academic research, some of which have been developing the original theories over many years. Of the small selection below, the first three are of the 'how-to' type, the last three deal with some modern ideas which are important to a deeper understanding of motivation.

1. Weinschenk, S. (2013) *How to Get People to Do Stuff: Master the art and science of persuasion and motivation*, Berkley, CA, New Riders.

2. Adair, J. (2009) *Leadership and Motivation: The Fifty-Fifty Rule and the Eight Key Principles of Motivating Others*, London and Philadelphia, Kogan Page.

3. Covey, S. R. (2013) *The 7 Habits of Highly Effective People: Powerful Lessons in Personal Change (25th Anniversary Edition)*, New York, Rosetta Books.

4. Dweck, C. S. (2013) *Self-theories: Their Role in Motivation, Personality, and Development*, Philadelphia, Psychology Press.

5. Ferguson, E. D. (2000), *Motivation: A Biosocial and Cognitive Integration of Motivation and Emotion*, Oxford, Oxford University Press.

6. Bandura, A. (1997) *Self-Efficacy: The Exercise of Control*, New York, W. H. Freeman.

NOTES

1. Discussed in Chapter 1.

2. Taken from http://psychology.about.com/od/mindex/g/motivation-definition.htm accessed, 23 April 2013.

3. Taken from http://www.businessdictionary.com/definition/motivation.html#ixzz2RB3AcOnK, accessed 23 April 2013.

4. See Chapter 1.

5. See for example the report at.http://www.workopolis.com/content/advice/article/2692-global-study-finds-most-people-just-aren-t-interested-in-their-jobs-any-more, accessed 23 April 2013, and at http://www.cwunorthwest.org/docs/News2013/UKWorkersAmongThe MostDissatisfiedInEurope.html, accessed 24 April 2013.

6. Maslow's original article can be read at http://psychclassics.yorku.ca/Maslow/motivation.htm.

7. Maslow, A. H., 1970, *Motivation and Personality*. New York: Harper & Row.

8. Hofstede, G., 1984, 'The Cultural Relativity of the Euality of Life Concept.' *Academy of Management Review*, vol. 9, no. 3, pp. 389–398.

9. Alderfer, C. P., 1972, *Existence, Relatedness, and Growth; Human Needs in Organizational Settings*, New York: Free Press.

10. Vroom, V. H., 1964, *Work and Motivation*. New York: McGraw Hill.

11. Self-efficacy is an *important aspect of* an individual's self-concept. It is based on the confidence in your ability and tenacity to see a task to its successful completion. See for example: Bandura, A. 1977, 'Self-Efficacy: Toward a Unifying Theory of Behavioral Change', *Psychological Review* vol. 84, no. 2, pp. 191–215.

12. Porter, L. W., and Lawler, E. E., 1968, *Managerial Attitudes and Performance*, Homewood, Illinois, Richard D. Irwin, Inc.

13. Adams, J.S., 1963, 'Towards An Understanding of Inequality', *Journal of Abnormal and Normal Social Psychology*, vol. 67, no. 5, pp. 422–436.

14. Huseman, R., Hatfield, J., and Miles, E., 1987, 'A New Perspective on Equity Theory: The Equity Sensitivity Construct.', *Academy of Management Review*, vol. 12, no. 2, pp. 232–234.

15. See, for example, http://www.bos.frb.org/economic/wp/wp2005/wp0511.pdf, pp. 19–21, accessed 22 May 2013.

16. Possibly a 'Hawthorne' effect, as discussed in Chapter 1.

17. The crash occurred because the mortgages were sold to people who could never repay them (ensuring that customers could repay their loans was not part of the incentive system!), so a huge amount of bad debt was brought into the system. Bankers were then incentivised to find ways of getting rid of this debt, which they did by packaging it up with good debt and selling it on in instruments with high credit ratings. It is perhaps one of the best examples of PRP failing to deliver good performance.

18. Schön, D.A., 1995, 'Knowing-in-Action: The New Scholarship Requires a New Epistemology', *Change,* November/December, pp. 27–34.

5

WORKING IN GROUPS

LEARNING OBJECTIVES

- State why effective groups are an important feature of effective organisations
- Define what constitutes an effective group
- Outline the roles group members undertake to achieve effectiveness
- Analyse issues and problems in the management of groups
- Comment on alternative ways of working collaboratively.

INTRODUCTION

A group is a collection of people who:

- have a sense of themselves as a group
- have a common purpose
- interact and combine to achieve that common purpose.

Human beings are social animals, so naturally belong in groups, whether as a family, a local community, a sports club, a work group and so on. The list of possibilities is endless. People who don't belong to groups – loners – are often seen as slightly unusual, and most of us don't want to be loners.

People differ significantly in their abilities, personalities, likes and dislikes. The variety of characteristics which limit the possibilities for one individual provides the group with a rich pool of resources to confront problems, operate effectively in the completion of tasks and to survive as a group. This has been the case since our earliest evolutionary history.

Because the ability – the need – to work as part of a group is so embedded in our human experience then it should come as no surprise that we want to make use of this important characteristic in the work place. The study of how we can work effectively in teams is now an important part of management and Organisational Behaviour programmes. However, this begs the question of why, if being part of a group is so essentially a human characteristic, that we need to teach it on management programmes.

Perhaps part of the answer lies in the history of work since the industrial revolution. The guiding organisational principle of work has been the division of labour – that is the concept of one person, one job, with management and supervisory layers to plan and co-ordinate those jobs. This simplification of task and separation of roles gave us the ability to exploit the new technologies of production to create affordable goods and services for mass markets.

But it came at a price, the loss of autonomy and skill variety in their working lives for many individuals; in other words, the denial of a crucial aspect of human life, the need for individual expression as part of a productive social system. Individuals were now part of the machine, their humanity seen as a disadvantage to efficient production, their co-operation with management demanded and harshly enforced, their ability to contribute beyond the limited skills needed for their job not sought.

More recently, a number of factors have challenged the primacy of rigid division of labour approaches to organising work.

- The growth of service sector jobs at the expense of manufacturing. This has meant a greater focus on solving problems for customers and consequently a need for greater communication across organisational functions. The quickest way to lose a customer is to continually pass them on to someone else because solving their problem is not your job. It also means that you need a strong level of support and interdependence among the work group.

- The tendency over the past 30 or so years for organisations to 'flatten'. The stripping out of layers of management has meant that the individual manager's 'span of control', the number of staff who report directly to him or her, has increased. While it is perfectly possible to closely supervise the work of eight of ten staff members, it becomes a problem if that number rises to 20 or 30 or even more. It means that managers have to be able to trust staff to work effectively without close supervision. An effective way of achieving this is to delegate some of the managerial power to organise work and to solve problems to the work group.

- The specialisation of work. Many jobs are no longer capable of being simplified by reducing them into easily sequenced, simple tasks. In particular, jobs where you need to interact with people, to solve their problems or to gain their co-operation, require the exercise of tact and judgement and success is often dependent on a relationship with a particular individual or group.

- In some professional organisations a manager may be less technically qualified than his or her staff. Consequently staff must be trusted to work effectively without close managerial input.

- The rapid development of information and communication media technologies is enabling groups to work together without physical proximity. This perhaps poses problems for supervision and puts additional onus onto group members to manage themselves. It can also mean that those we have to work with may be remote from us and from each other. Consequently many work groups in modern organisations may have to rely on communication technologies in order to collaborate.

WORK GROUPS AND SYNERGY

Why would a work organisation be interested in organising its staff into groups (or teams[1])? We can identify three reasons why this may be the case:

1. It has become the accepted way of organising staff. This is particularly the case since the UK economy became a predominantly service economy rather than an industrial one. Where organisations are still engaged in

industrial production, much of the repetitive work can be automated, reducing the need for people to do that work. Moreover, many service sector businesses need multi-skilled, multi-tasking personnel with effective back-office support, and so lend themselves to a group-based approach.

2. For human beings, working as part of a group is probably the most natural and satisfying way to work. However, simply putting a number of people in a section or department will not guarantee that they work effectively together. Nevertheless, there are a number of benefits of working in groups for the individual:

- **Sense of belonging** (or *affiliation*): this fulfils an important human need. For many people the time spent at work is greater than time spent on any other activity, so the job, or the work group, can often be their main social activity.

- **Sense of security**: this arises from not being alone when confronted with threats. A 'we're all in it together' feeling in a group can be empowering and help people cope with difficult situations.

- **Status**: membership of a group which outsiders regard as important or prestigious confers importance and prestige on the individuals who belong to it.

- **Self-esteem:** In itself, being regarded as an important member of the group by other members can increase self-esteem.

- **Power in numbers:** groups often find that collectively, they can achieve more than could be achieved by any single individual.

3. Effective groups deliver *synergy*. Simply put, synergy means that the output of an effective group is greater than the sum of the individual contributions. So if, for the sake of argument, five people working collaboratively can do the work of six working individually, the cost implications are obvious and would be attractive to most organisations. However, the issue is not as clear cut as all that. Synergy is not a purely human phenomenon. Achieving it also involves the intelligent application of material and organisational resources. Ironically, perhaps one of

the most extraordinary examples of synergy led to a reduction in human collaboration. This is the principle of division of labour. In Adam Smith's example of pin manufacture, production rose by several thousand per-cent as a result of a simple application of this principle.[2] But in order to achieve this, people specialised in one or two simple jobs and were not required to plan or control their own work; that task was reserved to supervisory managers. The synergy arose not from the collaboration of workers but from the actual organisation of the work. This kind of organisational synergy has been at the heart of labour disputes for more than a century. It has taken a move to more people-centred work for our organisations to remind us of the value of working co-operatively

TYPES OF GROUPS

Formal and informal groups

The Hawthorne studies drew our attention to the existence and importance of informal groups within the formal organisation.[3] Formal groups are part of the organisational design whereas informal groups emerge spontaneously from the formal groups. Wherever members of a workgroup decide to carry out activities beyond the precise remit of their work tasks, then we can see the possibility of an emergent informal group. Table 5.1 summarises the main differences between the two types of group:

Table 5.1 Main differences between formal and informal groups

Characteristic	Formal	Informal
Structure	Part of organisation structure; usually aligned with an organisational purpose	Fluid and emergent; membership often based on formal groups
Leadership	Exercised by a member appointed by the organisation	Unstructured – can be contested; often contingent on what is needed at the time; can be shared

(continued)

Table 5.1 Continued

Characteristic	Formal	Informal
Power and authority	Delegated by the organisation's management; cannot be challenged or changed from within	Emerges spontaneously from the membership; based on consent of members
Discipline	Formal disciplinary processes	Norms of behaviour and sanction arise over time and are based on consent of members
Membership	Members appointed by organisation; members not free to join or leave without formal agreement	Based on personal relationships
Goals/purpose	Formally set and aligned with organisation's goals; accountable to management	Usually implicit and unarticulated, though largely for the fulfilment of the emotional and social needs of members. New purposes can arise, often contingent on events.
Conflict	Subject to formal authority and laid down procedures	Handled according to emergent norms of the group
Relations with other groups	Formalised relationships specified by the organisation's design	No relationship with other groups as a group, though individuals may interact with other informal groups

Organisations need both informal and formal groups to cohere in order to be effective. For example, an informal group which emerged as a protest against what the members perceived as poor management would most probably have an effect on the performance of individuals in formal groups. Moreover, since one of the key features of informal groups is for the expression of emotional and psychological needs among staff, organisations need to be aware of how this can impact on task effectiveness.

Command groups

In a bureaucratic system, these are formal groups which are at the heart of an organisation's design. They are often referred to as sections or departments and have a specific task to accomplish. They usually consist of members with delegated power and authority (managers, supervisors, team leaders, etc.) who take a leadership role along with the other members whose function it is to carry out the tasks of the group. The manager (or whatever term is used for the formal leader of the group) is responsible for the allocation of work, for ensuring that it is completed to the required standard and for maintaining the performance levels of the group.

Each group member is responsible to the group leader for the work that they do while the manager is accountable to senior managers for the group's performance. Members tend to be appraised on an individual basis.

Self-managed work teams

In an attempt to find an alternative to the bureaucratic model of organisa-tion, there has been a trend towards developing self-managed work groups. This trend has been heavily influenced by the Human Relations movement, which stressed the importance of the social and emotional aspects of work as well as the design of the work itself.[4] It has also been influenced by the work on socio-technical systems carried out by Trist and Bamforth[5] in the 1950s. Their work represents an attempt to align the formal and informal aspects of work in groups. In a self-managed work team, key aspects of the management of the team are delegated to the team as a whole. They are often given the freedom to prioritise and organise work tasks, allocate task responsibilities and to be collectively accountable for achieving results. The development of communication and information technologies enables both team members and management to monitor work teams quickly and accurately.[6]

However a number of factors must be present for a self-managed work team to operate effectively:[7]

- Access to available and appropriate resources: Self-managed work groups are just as much at the mercy of resource shortages as any other work group.
- Team membership: It is important that the members of the team bring the right balance of skills to the group. These go beyond the traditional

skills of technical competence in the field of operation to some of the key skills of management, negotiation, positive conflict handling and motivation.

- Supportive management: If you call a team 'self-managed', it needs to be clear to all members what this means. Are the team's objectives clear? Who sets them? What level of consultation is there? In particular, are the lines of accountability clear? What processes are in place when a team starts to become ineffective?

- Team members must be appropriately trained for all the tasks of working in the team.

- The reward system needs to take account of both the efforts of the team as a whole without demotivating individuals. Alternatively, if staff are appraised on their individual performance they may be more motivated towards personal achievement than the team effort.

Cross-functional groups: These are groups of members drawn from different functional areas of the organisation. They are usually formal, with a chair, formal agenda and terms of reference. They can have several purposes:

- Reporting on results and initiatives put in place
- An opportunity to monitor co-ordination of functions
- To raise and solve problems between functions, etc.

These groups (often called committees or liaison groups) tend to be ongoing and can often be identified on the organisation chart. Members of such groups are often members because of their formal position in the organisation.

Task groups: Like the cross-functional groups discussed above, task group membership is usually drawn from several functional areas of the organisation. However, in contrast to the more bureaucratic cross functional groups, task groups will have a specific task to achieve or project to complete. Once their objective has been reached, the task group will be disbanded. Moreover, membership may be variable throughout the life of the group as different skills and knowledge are needed at different times.

This approach to achieving an organisation's goals is often associated with the 'matrix' organisational structure. This structure will be discussed more fully in Chapter 7, but its purpose is to avoid the functional isolation and failure to fully communicate of the bureaucratic organisation. This approach encourages staff who might otherwise never interact with each other to combine their knowledge and skill to solve problems.

Interest groups: An interest group forms because, as the name suggests, members have a particular interest in a topic. In an organisation context, this may be the fostering and support of customer interest groups. Apple have many online interest groups for all of their products. The ability to set up and maintain an interest group is greatly facilitated by the world wide web and people's growing use of social media. Within organisations interest groups may emerge or be appointed to discuss issues which have no clear resolution.

Reference groups: A reference group is a group to which we believe to have power or prestige and to which we aspire to belong. Some reference groups are highly formalised and you often need specialist skills or knowledge to belong to one of these groups. Many professions and occupations can be seen as reference groups. More informally, a prestigious or powerful reference group may emerge within an organisation, but nevertheless be seen as a reference group which confers influence on its members. Often such informal groups cohere around other activities like playing sport or shared outside interests. In these cases access to senior members of the organisation is usually the key to the group's prestige.

CO-OPERATION VS. COLLABORATION

As well as group types, there are also different ways in which groups operate collectively. The main differentiation is between co-operative working and collaborative working. These words are often used interchangeably. However, social scientists, particularly in the field of group learning theory have presented the concepts they represent as differing in important ways. The distinction they propose also happens to be of value in understanding work groups.

CO-OPERATIVE GROUPS

We can see the traditional workgroup based on the section or department as being, at its best, a co-operative venture. It possesses the necessary procedural elements identified by Cuseo[8] for co-operative groups:

1. **Formed by design with a specified purpose.** In an organisational context, this will usually be because of the skill and knowledge mix required to carry out the group's purpose.

2. **Continuity of interaction.** This is normally achieved by locating the group in close proximity to one another (e.g. in the same office, on the same floor, etc.). The consequence of this is to foster a sense of belonging and identity. Where the command and control system of the organisation impedes this development, we can expect to see informal groupings emerge spontaneously.

3. **Interdependence among members.** Members individually have clear roles and responsibilities, but nevertheless are also clear about the contribution their activities make to the overall achievement of the group's objectives.

4. **Individual accountability.** Individual group members are accountable for their own work and their performance is reviewed and evaluated by management on that basis. Although this may be counter-productive to wholehearted group commitment, it has the effect of stopping 'social loafing'. This colourful phrase refers to the potential for any individual in a group to put in minimal effort and allow the other members to do most of the work. Clear objectives with quick feedback can prevent this.

5. **Explicit attention to the development of social skills.** Whilst a co-operative team orientation might emerge from any given group of workers, it is not guaranteed. If management takes teamwork seriously and wants to see its benefits in higher productivity and job satisfaction, then there has to be some investment in training and development. Communication, interpersonal skills, conflict resolution are all critical to effective group working.

Co-operative working is essentially a socio-technical system approach to organising work. It is attempting to overlay the traditional division of labour approach with one that recognises the importance of the social dimension of work. It is, nevertheless, based on the principle of division of labour, even though there may be a greater degree of multi-skilling and members may be expected to master and carry out more than one task.

COLLABORATIVE GROUPS

Collaborative working focuses more on the pooling of labour and skill to achieve a group task. It requires more commitment to the group outcome than to individual ones. Special project groups and task groups largely fall into this category. The norms which each group develops will emerge rather than occur by design, so that it will differ from other groups in important features such as how leadership is exercised, how conflict is handled, how contributions are managed, how new members are socialised, etc.

In the organisational world as most of us experience it, it is very unlikely that any group will exist without features of both co-operation and collaboration. In a co-operative group, for example, there has to be a group outcome, though often the appointed leader is accountable for achieving it rather than the whole group. Nevertheless, some degree of collaboration will be needed even in the most bureaucratic work group. Similarly, even in a collaborative group individuals will be required to take responsibility for specific tasks. It is therefore better to see co-operation and collaboration as existing on a continuum with all groups having features of both to some degree.

HOW GROUPS FORM

Merely putting several individuals together will not of itself create an effectively functioning group. How groups develop to the point of working well together has been the subject of study for many years. The classic theory is Homan's *Social Exchange Theory*.[9]

SOCIAL EXCHANGE THEORY

His friend, the behaviourist psychologist Skinner, intellectually influenced Homan's work. Homan was essentially looking for a set of generalisable principles which could be applied to the study of human behaviour in any group. He thought it was possible (indeed necessary) to look at group dynamics from the point of view of the individual member, since this is how we experience group membership. This also had the advantage of avoiding difficult abstractions about considering the group as a whole.

He developed four propositions:[10]

1. The stimulus proposition:

If an individual finds that a particular behaviour has been rewarded, then in similar conditions the individual is likely to repeat that behaviour.

2. The success proposition:

The more often a successful behaviour is followed by a reward, the more likely a person is to repeat the behaviour. The greater the value of a reward, the more likely an individual is to repeat the behaviour which brought the reward.

3. The deprivation-satiation proposition:

The more often the reward is received, the less value it has to the individual and the less likely that person is to repeat the behaviour.

4. The frustration-aggression proposition:

If an individual's behaviour unexpectedly attracts punishment rather than reward, the individual is likely to become angry and exhibit aggressive behaviour. The consequences of showing aggressive behaviour can themselves become a reward.

The social exchange approach to group formation is therefore essentially a calculative one, based on the perception of each individual member's gain from membership and the ability or willingness of other group members to engage in the behaviour-reward system both from their own personal perceptions and from those of the group as a whole. Homan clearly sees human interaction as a quasi market activity and refers to the nature of any interaction as having a cost and a return. If the return is higher than the cost, the return is seen as a 'profit'.

There may be some value in this when looking at groups in the workplace, since all employment is essentially an economic activity. You are paid for the work you do. The cost of going to work and carrying out your work tasks can be seen as an 'opportunity cost'. In other words, can you find an alternative which would give you a better economic return? However, we have to be a little more sophisticated when it comes to ideas about the costs and benefits of group membership. The reward, or return, may be the satisfaction of non-economic needs: the approval of your peers, the reinforcement of your sense of self-esteem and many other things. The cost can be in terms of whether this reward would be greater if you were part of a different group, or the degree to which you had to compromise some of your own opinions and principles to earn the approval of other group members.

Exchange theory has its critics. Miller[11] sees the process as too reductionist, limiting human interactions to purely rational processes. A further objection is the 'borrowing' of economic theory to explain the complexity of human exchange. Miller further claims that Homan assumes that the aim of any relationship is a degree of intimacy, when this is manifestly not the case. Homan also sees human exchange as an apparently simple linear system, when in fact it usually has much more complexity. This makes the calculation of potential profit from a relationship difficult in practice.

Furthermore, such a theory is embedded in the Western individualistic mindset. How applicable would it be in more pluralistic or collectivist societies?

Finally, Cropanzano and Mitchell have reviewed Social Exchange Theory[12] and conclude that there are key areas where we do not have clear enough formulations of what terms really mean, while in other areas there is little evidence to support the theory.

SOCIAL IDENTITY THEORY

Tajfel and Turner developed the theory of social identification.[13] This theory stresses group membership as a human need. It suggests that membership of groups is a key to a positive self-image and sense of personal worth. According to this perspective there are three mental processes involved in developing our identity in relation to a group:

1. **Social categorisation:** One of the ways in which we help ourselves remember is by grouping things and people in categories. The point

about any category is that its members have important things in common (or at least things which we or they believe to be important). In an organisation we might categorise people according to the job they do, the department they are in, their status in the hierarchy, their relationship to senior members of the organisation and many others. That is fine and useful, but what happens when we experience someone as being, say, unco-operative. We may find that we then label other members of that group similarly – 'Be careful of that lot in IT support, they're an awkward lot.'

We also put ourselves into social categories and define our own behaviour according to the unwritten rules – the 'norms' – of our group.

We also belong to many different groups both inside and outside of the workplace. For example we may see ourselves, or be seen by others, according to our ethnicity, our religion, where we come from, our profession, a club we belong to, our social class, our family, the cultural activities we enjoy and so on.

2. **Social identification:** In this stage of the development of our group membership we begin to take on what we perceive to be the group identity of that group and to behave accordingly. We learn the norms of the group and they in turn become part of our repertoire of behaviour when we act as part of the group. We may, for example, use the technical language and terminology of the group, or we may see other groups as rivals in status and be less co-operative with members of those groups. How this manifests itself is infinitely variable, but taking on these attitudes and behaviours is often key to our sense of belonging and self-esteem.

3. **Social comparison:** This is the final stage of developing our group identity. We seek to compare ourselves favourably to other groups. This is particularly true of groups that we consider rivals. We develop a sense of the 'in-group' – the group to which we belong, and 'out-groups' – those groups we don't belong to or don't want to belong to or which are rivals for resources or prestige. The great danger of thinking in terms of in-groups and out-groups is the potential for prejudice. Because we need to see our group as in some way better or more effective, it can often mean

telling ourselves that the other group is in some way inferior or not good at what they do.

Social exchange theory and social identity theory both apply at the level of the individual member of the group and try to explain the processes and needs of individuals as group members. Tuckman, however, examines the development of the whole group.[14] According to him, groups develop through a four-stage process:

1. **Forming:** This is the first stage of group development; members are unfamiliar to each other and are unsure how to behave. They tend to be guarded in how they express themselves and are busy trying to pick up clues about the other members.

2. **Storming:** After the initial uncertainties and restraint of the forming stage, the group realises it needs to make decisions about how to proceed. Some try to assert leadership roles, some may retreat into their shell, others may argue, while others will try to calm things down. Basically, this stage is a free for all where some members are staking a claim for a role in the proceeding or for influence in the make up of the group, while others are just keeping their heads down. Often, small cliques may form around an individual. Overall, though, there is little communication taking place even though there is sometimes quite a lot of noise.

3. **Norming:** For a group to act effectively, it has to have some cohesion – some way for its members to work together in a consensual way to achieve the objectives of the group. This cohesion begins to emerge at the norming stage. A norm is essentially a rule about how to behave. In all but the most formal groups, like committees, norms are unwritten and often unspoken[15] though they are very powerful. They emerge when people begin to listen to each other, useful suggestions are made and members generally begin to feel comfortable with each other and confident that they can carry out their task. Constructive discussion can take place and any conflict can be managed positively. Put briefly, the norming stage is where the group emerges as an entity, with members understanding and consenting to its internal workings.

4. **Performing:** This is the stage where the group can begin to deliver the synergies of effective teams. Members are focused on the task, problems are tackled and solved, support is given when needed and members understand the degree of personal responsibility they have towards the group as a whole.

5. **Adjourning:** ten years after the development of his model Tuckman, with Mary Ann Jensen[16] reviewed it and added a fifth stage, adjourning. Tuckman and Jensen realised that the growth of project teams and matrix structures in organisations[17] meant that groups had a finite life and would be disbanded when the task was completed. This often brings about a sense of loss to the group members. Tuckman and Jensen suggest that it is important for organisations to recognise this and offer support. However, we need to recognise that, unlike the other group development stages, adjourning does not contribute to the group objective. It is rather a consequence of the objective being reached.

The Tuckman model recognises the important fact that group cohesion is not guaranteed, and that in order to reach that point it may be necessary to facilitate the process. Moreover, we have to understand that while the process Tuckman describes is, at its simplest, a linear one, that may not be the case in practice. What happens, for instance, if members' personal goals change? The relationship with the group may also change and the group may find itself back at one of the earlier stages. If a member leaves or a new member joins, this can throw the cohesion of the whole group off track. New norms may have to be negotiated. The underlying message of this is that, while it is important to an organisation's productivity to realise the synergies of effective groups, those synergies come at a price. There needs to be investment in group skills and group leadership.

GROUP COHESIVENESS

Effective, synergetic work groups are founded on the cohesiveness of the group. By this we mean the degree to which members (and outsiders) want to be members of the group and the degree to which members get on with each other. However, by itself, cohesiveness is no guarantee that the group will strive for the organisation's goals. As we have seen, groups develop and will commit to norms of behaviour. For an organisation to benefit from this collective motivation, the organisation's and the group's goals need to be the same. There are a number of factors which contribute to or inhibit cohesiveness. The effect that any of these factors will have on the cohesiveness of the group will be determined by the group membership and the organisational context:

- **Size:** What is the ideal size for a workgroup? The answer seems to be that it depends on what you want the group to do. It appears that if you want a group to deliver a product or service, then a small group tends to do that best. However, if you are looking for a group to investigate a problem or generate ideas, then a larger group would seem to fit the bill. In other words, a large group may be better at a co-operative task, while a smaller group will perform better collaboratively.

The bank wiring room

Part of the Hawthorne studies mentioned in Chapter 1 was the observation of the workers in the Bank Wiring room at the plant. This was a small group of men, a little isolated from the rest of the plant, who had been working together for some time. Researchers noticed that output from this group remained stable no matter what changes to their working environment were made. When researchers investigated more closely, they saw that the group had its own norms of behaviour, which included producing a satisfactory level of output, but no more.

Moreover, the group had developed sanctions to punish those members who transgressed these norms. These ranged from being ignored to being 'binged', hit violently on the arm.

The cohesiveness of this group appeared to come from its relative isolation and its relatively small size.

VIGNETTE

However, as a group increases in size, a number of problems can appear. The phenomenon of *social loafing* can arise. This is where an individual is able to contribute less than his or her optimum because the rest of the group can carry that person. When this happens you can observe the opposite of synergy. If synergy is defined as the collective output of the group being greater than the sum of the individual contributions, where you have social loafing, you can find that the group's output is less than the sum of each individual's contribution. Studies into social loafing have developed several explanations. Karau and Williams looked at the available published studies in a meta-analysis and concluded that individuals expended effort as a calculus of the reward they expected their effort to bring them, how much they valued that reward and how likely they were to get the reward they desired if they were successful.[18] They suggested that when working collectively the goals of the group may be seen to be less personally rewarding leading to lower expenditure of effort.

> Studies have also shown that as groups get larger, or members are more dispersed, then social loafing is more likely to occur.[19] There is also evidence that culture plays a part. Highly individualist cultures such as we find in the West tend to value individual goals more highly than collective ones. The opposite is true of more collectivist cultures.[20] This study comes with the caveat that whilst we are entitled to make these generalisations of a whole culture, we cannot necessarily make them of every individual member of that culture.

- **Group membership:** Who is in the group has an effect on how cohesive it is. There needs to be a balance between having enough heterogeneity in the team to produce the ideas and skills needed to achieve the team goals and having a membership which is so diverse that they struggle to overcome the differences in perspective and priorities.[21]

- **The status of the group:** A group which is perceived by others and perceives itself as having high prestige (a group often thought of as a reference group) will tend to be more cohesive. Membership which is sought after, possibly because it is difficult to attain, will be seen as a valuable reward in itself and members will strive to retain their membership because the prestige of the group confers prestige on them as individuals.

Membership of professions exemplifies this, as does membership of sports teams. Within organisations, there are groups which are seen to have greater prestige than others.

- **The physical proximity of members:** It is much easier to develop and sustain good relations, or to mend poor interpersonal relations, if group members are in close proximity, all located in the same room or building. Modern ways of working, however, often mean that group members may be geographically dispersed and communicate mainly using internet and intranet technologies. Such dispersal makes social closeness very difficult. It may be even more difficult if group members are also culturally heterogeneous.

- **Nature of group task:** What a group does can have an impact on how cohesive it becomes. Tasks which are inherently collective, like product development or a group based project, demand a high level of cohesiveness. Other tasks, like sales, may require a more individualistic approach, so that, say, a sales team may only be a team in name, because they all do the same job. There may be a need for a degree of cohesiveness in the organisation and allocation of work, but many sales people are incentivised by financial reward and are – or feel that they are – in competition with their colleagues.

- **Technology:** The cohesiveness of any group will be strongly influenced by the kind of technology its members use. Work in a production environment will be highly dependent on the technologies of production and the consequent degree of automation used in that industry. The work may be labour intensive or highly mechanised. The degree of cohesiveness will usually be at the level of co-operating with colleagues responsible for other parts of the production process, or with staff from support functions.

- Some work, for example in education or the caring professions, requires a high level of interpersonal skill and often a high degree of collaboration is needed with colleagues and other professionals. The individuals in these jobs have high levels of personal responsibility and accountability, but nevertheless are often very reliant on the work of colleagues.

- **Management style:** Group cohesiveness depends to a high degree on the ability of the group to develop its own ways of working and its own ways of interacting. This requires a good degree of autonomy, something which management can inhibit or facilitate. A rigid, formal management structure will serve to inhibit cohesiveness because it tends to circumscribe personal relations within its operating and procedural regulations. A more complex examination of the influence on team performance of management style along a number of key variables was carried out by Yang et al.[22] They concluded that there is a positive correlation between the leadership style of managers, team cohesiveness and team performance on project work.[23]

Group performance and cohesiveness are the emergent consequence of a complex human system. The main analytical problem of complexity is the difficulty in identifying which factors cause which consequences. The general contributory factors which can facilitate group cohesiveness are relatively easy to identify. However, for any given group, there may be others which we cannot know. One key relationship among group members can be the making or breaking of that group's effectiveness, while a change of manager or membership can have an unplanned consequence, both positive or negative.

GROUP ROLES

A team is not a bunch of people with job titles, but a congregation of individuals, each of whom has a role which is understood by other members. Members of a team seek out certain roles and they perform most effectively in the ones that are most natural to them.[24]

When teams work effectively it is because there is a balance of behaviours, or potential behaviours, which the team members can bring to situations when they arise. If, say a dispute arises within the group, there will need to be a process of conflict resolution. If a group is tending to focus too much on its internal problems than getting on with its task, then it will need to be led back to a focus on task. If someone leaves, or a new member comes into the group, then they will need to be integrated into the group for it to return to effectiveness.

The roles in a group can be classified as *task* roles or *maintenance* roles. Task roles are those behaviours which contribute directly to achievement of the group's task. Maintenance roles contribute indirectly, though nonetheless importantly, to achieving the task. The people carrying out maintenance roles make sure that the group membership is cohesive, that conflicts are dealt with positively and that members feelings and personal needs are aligned to the group's needs.

Meredith R. Belbin has been researching the roles people play in teams for more than 30 years. The roles he has developed and refined have stood the test of time. At the time of writing Belbin proposes nine team roles, some of which tend to be task focused, some focused on 'maintenance' tasks, such as giving support to other group members, guiding people through conflict, providing motivation when needed and so on, while some deal with both aspects of team performance. The roles Belbin suggests, with their descriptors and a summary of 'allowable weaknesses', are presented in Table 5.2:

Table 5.2 A summary of the Belbin Team Role descriptors. Reproduced with permission of Belbin Associates

Team role	Contribution	Allowable weaknesses
Plant	Creative, imaginative, free-thinking. Generates ideas and solves difficult problems	Ignores incidentals. Too preoccupied to communicate effectively.
Resource investigator	Outgoing, enthusiastic, communicative. Explores opportunities and develops contacts.	Over-optimistic. Loses interest once initial enthusiasm has passed.
Co-ordinator	Mature, confident, identifies talent. Clarifies goals and delegates effectively.	Can be seen as manipulative. Offloads own share of the work.
Shaper	Challenging, dynamic, thrives on pressure. Has the drive and courage to overcome obstacles.	Prone to provocation. Offends people's feelings.
Monitor-evaluator	Sober, strategic and discerning. Sees all options and judges accurately.	Lacks drive and ability to inspire others. Can be overly critical.

(continued)

Table 5.2 Continued

Team role	Contribution	Allowable weaknesses
Team worker	Co-operative, perceptive and diplomatic. Listens and averts friction.	Indecisive in crunch situations.
Implementer	Practical, reliable, efficient. Turns ideas into actions and organises work that needs to be done.	Somewhat inflexible. Slow to respond to new possibilities.
Completer-finisher	Painstaking, conscientious, anxious. Searches out errors. Polishes and perfects.	Inclined to worry unduly. Reluctant to delegate.
Specialist	Single-minded, self-starting, dedicated. Provides knowledge and skills in rare supply.	Contributes only on a narrow front. Dwells on technicalities.

Source: www.belbin.com

If you complete the Belbin Team Roles Inventory, you will see that an analysis of your inventory responses will show that you have a preference for one, or possibly more, of these roles, while your scores for others will be lower. If you have big differences between your favoured roles and the others, we can interpret this as meaning that you will be a little uncomfortable taking on those other roles. However, if your scores are similar for several of the roles this suggests that you are equally capable of taking on those roles when called upon to do so. Because we are all able to carry out different roles Belbin points out that his descriptors are not based on an assessment of personality, but on the self-reported behaviour of people in group situations. Consequently, we should be able to assume other, more uncomfortable roles if needed and become more comfortable with them through practice.

GROUP PERFORMANCE AND DECISION MAKING

There are several factors which influence whether it is better for a group or an individual to make decisions. We can summarise these in Table 5.2.

Table 5.3 Factors influencing group vs. individual decision-making

Requirements of decision	Group decision making	Individual decision making
Speed of decision making	Groups can often be slow to reach a decision. There is the possibility of over-deliberation and sometimes a reluctance to reach a decision which some members don't support.	Individuals can often reach decisions more quickly than a group. However, there may not always be the time to consider all the factors involved.
Knowledge required to make decision	Groups can share knowledge and foresee solutions to problems which may arise.	Unless the individual is an expert on the subject, then groups are able to generate better and more comprehensive knowledge than an individual.
Need for a complete decision	Because an effective group contains roles which monitor both the decision making process and the completeness of the decision, groups tend to produce more complete and feasible solutions.	An experienced and knowledgeable individual can make complete and feasible decisions, especially where they have confronted similar decisions in the past. Where expertise is not needed, then better decisions tend to be made by groups.
Importance of decision for organisation	A group making an important decision may well be subject to the phenomenon of 'risky shift'[25] and decisions may well be riskier than management may accept.	It is easier for an individual to be held accountable.
Need for commitment to proposed solution	Groups, especially those working collaboratively, will tend to gain commitment to their decisions because all group members have been involved in the decision making process.	An individual will have to work very hard to gain the commitment of others to a decision they have made. Without involvement in the decision making process, commitment is uncertain.

Where group action is to be preferred, what then are the characteristics of an effective group and what might be the pitfalls?

We can infer from what has been written above that for a group to operate effectively a number of factors need to be in place:

- The group needs to have developed to the point of operating effectively for both co-operative and collaborative tasks.

- The group needs to have complementary skills and abilities which can be drawn on at each stage of its operations. At different stages of task performance, the skill mix needed may be different. At the beginning of a task, for example, the group may rely on the input of the plant role to generate ideas, and the shaper role to show how those ideas can be implemented. Towards the end of the task the role of the completer and co-ordinator may be more important.

- In its development the group needs to have evolved ways of handling conflict positively.

- The group must be collectively and individually focused on and committed to its task.

- Leadership of the group must be by consent, whether that is the leadership of one individual, or whether leadership is exercised by different individuals in different contexts.

- Group members have to be open in their communication.

ISSUES WHICH MAY ARISE

Given that an effective group needs all these characteristics to be in place before it can perform to its optimum, it is not surprising that there can be problems. If managers and group members wish to improve the working of a sub-optimal group, where should they focus their attention?

Groupthink: Where groups do not operate effectively to work towards organisational goals, various problems can arise. Membership of a group is often a trade off between the personal preferences of an individual and the collective direction of the group. There is often a pressure to conform as the price of membership. Groups may foster conflict or fall under the sway of a dominant individual. They may eventually suffer from the phenomenon of *groupthink*.

The notion of groupthink was developed by Irving Janis[26] when he examined the reasons for the catastrophic failure of events such as the failed US attempt to invade Cuba in the early 60s, the decision of the Nazis to invade the USSR in 1941 and the Challenger space shuttle flight in 1982, where the rocket exploded shortly after launch. in the last case he found that warnings about the performance of a critical rubber seal in low temperatures had been discounted. The reasons for this were not technical or procedural, but were to do with the personal commitment of key individuals to the group and to the other members of the group. He defined groupthink as: 'a mode of thinking that people engage in when they are deeply involved in a cohesive in-group, when the members' strivings for unanimity override their motivation to realistically appraise alternative courses of action'.[27] Janis identified eight symptoms of groupthink:

- Illusion of invulnerability – A highly cohesive group develops extreme optimism that can lead to a sense of always being right.
- Collective rationalisation – Warnings appear as threats to the group's collective view of how things are and are ignored.
- Belief in inherent morality – The group's ends and means are right so moral considerations are discounted.
- Stereotyped views of out-groups – Outsider individuals and other groups are often despised and consequently their views are not considered.
- Direct pressure on dissenters – Members can be pressurised if they dissent from the group line.
- Self-censorship – Individuals are reluctant to show dissent from the group's collective view.
- Illusion of unanimity – The majority view and judgments are assumed to be unanimous.
- Self-appointed 'mindguards' – Members take it on themselves to protect the group from contrary perspectives, so that they do not get discussed.

- **Risky shift:** This is the tendency of a group to make riskier collective decisions than any member would make individually. This phenomenon was
introduced by Stoner[28] in 1961. This flew in the face of received wisdom
at the time, which suggested that a group's decision making would tend
towards the average of the members' individual level of caution vs. risk.
Stoner later modified his thesis to suggest that a group's decisions may
also tend to being more cautious than the average choice of the individual
members.[29] It appears in an organisational context that the risk averseness
or risk acceptance of the organisation in general will have an influence
on whether the shift of group decisions is more towards the risky or the
cautious.

Misaligned goals: When a group feels confident and strong, it will often
develop group-specific goals which are not aligned to those of the organisation. This phenomenon is connected to the phenomenon of groupthink
discussed above. The group members primary mission becomes the maintenance of the group and the comfort of its members. Each of the members
will strive to achieve these goals. Perhaps the most widely publicised example of this is Mayo's study of the bank wiring room team at the Hawthorne
Plant he studied between 1923 and 1933.

When this happens we can often see a demotion of the organisation's
goals to the benefit of those of the group. Naturally, this can be a serious
problem for managers and may be difficult to change.

CONCLUSIONS

Workgroups are seen as being important for successful performance in the
modern workplace. They have advantages for both the organisation as a
whole and for individuals in those workgroups. Human beings are social
animals and we thrive in the company of others. Moreover, the output of an
optimally performing group produces synergy, where the collective output
is greater than the sum of the individual contributions.

However, for this to happen, we need to pay attention to the formation
and management of workgroups. A group of individuals will not become a

high performing work group unless a number of factors are present:

- The group needs to go through a development or forming process in order to develop its own ways of working.
- There must be the proper balance of skills and personal qualities in the group to enable it to perform effectively. Those skills and qualities will encompass both task focused and group support focused activities, with acceptable leadership and conflict handling processes.
- Negative group phenomena must be avoided. Group think can lead to unchallenged assumptions being acted on and a reluctance to accept criticism. Risky shift can lead to a group committing the organisation to courses of action it might not find acceptable. If the group are trying to achieve goals important to them at the expense of the organisation's goals, then there is little hope of delivering synergy at the organisation level.

Humans are social animals. To work with others is as natural (and necessary) to us as using language. The 'revelation' that came from observing the highly effective Japanese methods of group working in the 1960s and 70s was a revelation only in that the division of labour approach to production ran counter to all our instincts as people, in spite of the productivity gains it delivered. In modern organisations, where many of the repetitive, boring jobs can now be automated, it is possible to return to a more satisfying group approach to working. Moreover, most jobs are no longer in manufacturing and many require a much more collaborative or co-operative approach to be done effectively.

Read the case and carry out the task shown below.

The Art Vault

Paula has been made redundant from a major bank. She had worked there for seven years and was happy with the career path she was following. She had risen to become team leader of a small equity and bond trading group concentrating on mineral exploration and

CASE STUDY

mining in central Asia. Her small staff and her manager always found her well-organised, clear about her immediate goals and easy to work with. Her expertise in the field, both financial and technical, had developed over the years. A bright and lucrative future beckoned.

Then came the banking crisis. Her bank was extremely over-exposed to high levels of lending which had little chance of being repaid. The chief executive and other top managers resigned, the government had to inject huge amounts of public money to save the bank from complete collapse and the bank began to shed labour to cut costs. Paula was a victim of these circumstances.

Paula's immediate financial situation was secure. She had been well paid at the bank, with annual bonuses which she had largely saved, or used to pay off part of the mortgage on her flat in the centre of the city in which she lived.

Her immediate plan was to seek out a similar job to her previous one in another bank. However, it soon became clear that no-one was hiring in that field. In fact, most companies were doing what her former employer had done and were laying staff off. When Paula realised that jobs like her old one were not going to be available in the foreseeable future, she realised she needed to re-evaluate her career.

One day, her friend Jaz pointed out an ad in the local listings magazine for a job as an administrator at the local community arts centre, Art Vault. Paula and her friends had often been to the centre to see bands and theatre performances. In fact a couple of her friends regularly attended classes in music and painting.

Art Vault is run as a co-operative organisation. That is, all employees are also members of the co-operative and have an equal say in how it is to be run. Policy is made by the Board, which consists of an elected chairman and five other Board members and the centre staff. Members of the public can also become members of the co-op, and are entitled to come to twice-yearly members' meetings and to elect Board members and officers from their number annually. Paula had become a member of the co-op a few years earlier, knowing that her membership money was crucial to keeping the centre afloat. However, she not been an active participant.

Art Vault has two functions: it is a venue for music, drama and other performances, for which it has a growing reputation; and it is a centre for adult education in arts and related subjects. It has several classrooms, a large and a smaller performance space and a restaurant selling organic food. The restaurant is a franchise run by two partners who are not part of the co-operative. Instead, they pay a rent for the restaurant.

The co-op is a registered charity and is funded by the income it receives from putting on performances, course fees and the rent for the restaurant. It is independent of the local education department, though it does receive grants from the Arts and Culture Department of the City Council, as well as charitable grants from some local businesses. Financially, the centre is always on a knife-edge and recent events in the world economy bode ill for the future. Whoever gets the Administrator job will spend a good deal of time trying to match income with expenditure.

The centre has four full-time staff: the administrator, in overall charge of the day-to-day running of its activities; an assistant, responsible for booking performers and dealing with managing the education activities of the centre; a staff member who takes care of the maintenance and cleaning of the building; and a book-keeper. In addition, there are several part-time and casual staff who are taken on for teaching, bar work, cleaning, helping out at performances and other occasional tasks. As the Art Vault is a co-operative, everyone is paid the same hourly rate, except for the administrator who is paid one third more. There are also several volunteers who can be relied on to step in if extra staff are needed.

When Jaz first showed Paula the ad, she was unimpressed. 'This is no good to me. I've only worked in banks. Anyway, the money's much less than a third what of I've been earning, even without the bonuses.'

'Well, at least think about it', said Jaz. 'You were great at uni, running the gigs. And I know from what you've told me that the money isn't an issue for the foreseeable future. You could live on this easily for a few years – and who knows where it could lead. Think of it as a challenge.'

Gradually, Paula began to take the thought seriously. The more she mulled it over, the more attractive it became and the more she could visualise herself in the job. She knew that the working climate at the Art Vault would be a million miles from what she had been used to at the bank. She knew that it would be an environment which was poorly funded, where people worked for the satisfaction of helping to keep the place going rather than for any expectation of financial reward. Managers could not rely on the acceptance of authority in the same way they might in a commercial environment. In fact, because it was a co-operative, the overt use of authority and traditional management processes would be out of the question.

After thinking it over for a few days, Paula decided to apply, thinking that she would hear no more about it.

Much to her surprise, she had a reply inviting her to come in and discuss the job with the chair of the Board and the staff. The letter included a brief description of the job.

What is Art Vault?

Art Vault is at the cultural heart of our community. We are dedicated to enabling members of our community to develop their own artistic and cultural potential through learning in a relaxed, supportive and collaborative environment. We also give opportunities to established performers from beyond the city to present their work at one of the friendliest and most appreciative venues in the country.

As a co-operative organisation we believe that everyone who comes to Art Vault should be treated with respect and received with friendship. We are a charity which relies on income from our activities and charitable donations to continue to provide our service to this community.

If you feel that you can make a contribution to our work, then please come along and discuss the opportunities we have.

Job Description

Job title: Centre Administrator

Job period: Initially for two years, with continuation dependent on funding.

Responsibilities

The role has three components

- **Day-to-day management of the centre.** this includes ensuring the cleanliness and safety of all parts of the premises; drawing up and publishing termly prospectuses; ensuring teaching staff are recruited and paid; overseeing design and publication of promotional material; dealing with complaints; drawing up exciting programmes of performances and liaising with performers and agents; complying with all legal requirements relating to the running of the centre.

- **Assisting the Board with development of policy.** For this you will work closely with your colleagues and the Board. You may occasionally be required to present reports on the progress of policy matters.

- **Maintaining current income streams and identifying new sources of funding.** As well as ensuring that as far as possible, current income streams are maintained and improved, you will also need to explore new possibilities for generating income.

- You will be assisted by four full time members of staff as well as a number of part-time teaching and domestic staff and a pool of volunteers.

Your Task

Paula has contacted the centre and said that she will accept their invitation. She knows that she will have to convince her prospective new employers of her suitability. In particular she feels she will need to convince them of how she can create and maintain a spirit of togetherness at the centre among a disparate group of people including her full time and part time employees and the many volunteers. The ability of the centre to continue and to thrive depends not only on funding, but also on its attractiveness to potential volunteers and part-time teachers. How might an understanding of group theory help her to set about this task?

GLOSSARY OF TERMS

Collaboration Where members of a group collectively work towards a group goal and are jointly accountable for the group's outputs.

Co-operation Where members of a group are accountable for their own job, but who nevertheless are part of an integrated group to whose output they contribute.

Formal groups Groups which exist as part of the formal organisation structure.

Group A collection of people who: have a sense of themselves as a group; have a common purpose; interact and combine to achieve that purpose.

Groupthink Where group members are so committed to one or more aspects of the group's task that they discount the importance of problems or criticisms.

Informal groups Groups which are often based (though not necessarily so) on formal groups. However, they exist for social rather than operational reasons and are based on shared interests and friendships.

Norms The 'rules' of the group. These are usually informal and unwritten, but in order to be a full member of a group the individual needs to accept them.

Plant One of Belbin's team roles. This role requires the individual to be creative and come up with ideas and solutions to the group's problems.

Reference groups These are groups which have a high level of prestige and to which many people aspire to belong. We often define ourselves according to the reference group we belong to.

Resource investigator One of Belbin's team roles. A resource investigator look outside the confines of the team to link with other teams and individuals and to explore alternative resources which are not accessible within the team.

Risky shift The tendency of a group to make riskier decisions than an individual would make.

Roles For a group to be effective, members need to take on particular roles at particular times during the group's activities. These can be either 'maintenance' roles, which focus on the well being of the group, and 'task' roles, which focus on the required outputs of the group.

Social Exchange theory A post-behaviourist view on group membership which is essentially calculative. According to this theory, we carry out a kind of cost-benefit analysis of our group membership and the level of commitment we are prepared to give it.

Social Identity theory This theory recognises the importance of group membership to the well-being and sense of self-esteem of the individual.

Synergy A phenomenon where the output of a team can be greater than the sum of the output of the same number of individuals working alone.

Team A highly effective group.

KEY POINTS

- Modern jobs, especially service jobs, need people to be able to work collectively.

- Effective groups can be more productive than the combined outputs of individuals in the group.
- Groups satisfy important social and psychological needs of people at work.
- As well as the formal groups designed into an organisation's structure, there are also informal groupings based on shared interests and friendships.
- Formal groups can include:
  - Self-managed work teams
  - Cross-functional groups
  - Task groups
  - Interest groups
- Groups go through a recognisable process in developing their performance levels:
  - Homan's Social Exchange Theory suggests four propositions: the stimulus proposition, the success proposition, the deprivation-satiation proposition, the frustration-aggression proposition.
  - Tuckmann observed that groups went through four observable stages in order to operate effectively: forming, storming, norming, performing.
- Effective teams need a balance of skills, roles and attitudes which are recognised by and accepted within the group.
- Belbin has identified nine team roles: plant, resource investigator, co-ordinator, shaper, monitor-evaluator, team worker, implementer, completer-finisher, specialist.
- Groups may be less than optimally effective for a number of reasons: groupthink, risky shift, misaligned goals.

REVISION QUESTIONS

- Briefly list the groups to which you belong. Which would you describe as formal and which would you describe as informal?
- How effective are the groups to which you belong? What is your evidence?

- To what extent do you agree with Miller that Homan's social exchange theory is too reductionist as an explanation of human interaction with other people? What additional complexities might there be?
- What are the implications for group formation and effectiveness when workgroups are geographically dispersed and rely on communication technology to work with other group members? Can we describe such a network as a workgroup?

GOING FURTHER

There is a lot of material about work groups. This topic has been a subject of intense academic and practitioner research for many years. There are also many resources which provide insights into how group theory may be applied in the workplace. Many of you will have been on training programmes whose goal is to introduce and reinforce skills and behaviours which foster effective group working. As with all OB topic areas, we have to distinguish between the academic work based on research and the prescriptive material which is designed to help managers apply the theories.

- Dale E. Y and Cloyd, H. (1997) *High-Performing Self-Managed Work Teams: A Comparison of Theory to Practice*, Thousand Oaks, CA, Sage.

  A very useful and thorough investigation into self-managed work groups.

- Johnson, D. W. and Johnson, F. P. (2012) *Joining Together: Group Theory and Group Skills (11th Edition)*, Harlow, Pearson.

  Probably the most comprehensive work on groups and group effectiveness. Useful for both the academic and the practitioner.

- Brandler, S. and Roman, C. (1999) *Group Work: Skills and Strategies for Effective Interventions,* New York, Taylor and Francis.

  Useful exercises and games for supporting teamwork.

- 'How To Be Part Of The Team When You Work From Home', http://www.forbes.com/sites/jacquelynsmith/2013/10/30/how-to-be-part-of-the-team-when-you-work-from-home/2/.

An interesting take on how to remain part of the team when you are telecommuting.

NOTES

1. A team is essentially a group of people who operate efficiently and effectively – in other words, an effective group. Since the focus of this chapter is about how to make groups effective, we can use the two terms interchangeably. Many organisations will use the term 'team' for any work group, irrespective of whether it is in fact effective or not.

2. Adam Smith, 1999, *An Inquiry into the Nature and Causes of the Wealth of Nations,* Chapter 1, London, Penguin Books.

3. See discussion on the importance of the Hawthorne studies in Chapter 1.

4. See, for example, Hackman, J. R., and Oldham, G. R., 1975, 'Development of the Job Diagnostic Survey', *Journal of Applied Psychology,* vol. 60 (2), no. 2, pp. 159–170.

5. See Chapter 1.

6. For an example of the issues confronting an actual self-managed work team approach, see. http://mhlnews.com/labor-management/self-managed-work-teams-reality-or-fad, accessed 11 January 2013.

7. For a comprehensive overview of this topic, see: Yeatts, Dale E. and Hyten, Cloyd, *High-Performing Self-Managed Work Teams: A Comparison of Theory to Practice*, Thousand Oaks, CA, Sage.

8. Cuseo, J., 1992, 'Collaborative & Cooperative Learning in Higher Education: A Proposed Taxonomy', *Cooperative Learning and College Teaching*, vol. 2, pp. 2–5.

9. George C. Homans, 1961, rev. ed. 1974, *Social Behavior: Its Elementary Forms*, New York, Harcourt, Brace, Jovanovich.

10. Adapted from Homans, 1987, 'Behaviorism and After', in *Social Theory Today*, pp. 58–80, edited by Anthony Giddens and Jonathan Turner, Stanford, CA, Stanford University Press.

11. Miller, Katherine, 2005, *Communication Theories*, McGraw Hill.

12. *nbu.bg/webs/clubpsy/.../Social%20Exchange%20Theory.pdf*, accessed 14 January 2013.

13. Tajfel, H. and Turner, J. C., 1986, 'The Social Identity Theory of Intergroup Behaviour', in S. Worchel and W. G. Austin (eds.), *Psychology of Intergroup Relations,* Chicago, Nelson-Hall. pp. 7–24.

14. Tuckman, Bruce, 1965, 'Developmental Sequence in Small Groups', *Psychological Bulletin,* vol. 63, no. 6, pp. 384–399.

15. However, even in rule-bound committees if we look closely we will see informal norms emerge. They may emerge, for example about interrupting others when they are speaking; different chairmen or women will have different approaches to the content and tone of how business is conducted.

16. Bruce W. Tuckman and Mary Ann Jensen, 1975, 'Stages of Small Group Development Revisited', *Group and Organization Studies,* vol. 2, no. 4, pp. 419–427.

17. A matrix structure allows organisations to combine expertise across functions by forming project groups. This is designed to foster better communication and collaboration across the organisation and to improve cost, delivery and quality of output. See in more detail in the chapter on organisational structure.

18. Karau, Steven J., Williams, Kipling D., 1993, 'Social Loafing: A Meta-Analytic Review and Theoretical Integration'. *Journal of Personality and Social Psychology,* vol. 65, no. 4, pp. 681–706.

19. Chidambaram, Laku, Tung, Lai Lai, 2005, 'Is Out of Sight, Out of Mind? An Empirical Study of Social Loafing in Technology-Supported Groups'. *Information Systems Research,* vol. 16, no. 2, pp. 149–168.

20. Christopher Earley, P., 1989, 'Social Loafing and Collectivism: A Comparison of the United States and the People's Republic of China'. *Administrative Science Quarterly,* vol. 34, no. 4, pp. 565–581.

21. Watson, W. E., Kumar, K., and Michaelsen, L. K.,1993, 'Cultural Diversity's Impact on Interaction Process and Performance: Comparing Homogeneous and Diverse Task Groups', *Academy of Management Journal,* June, pp. 590–602.

22. Li-Ren Yang, Chung-Fah Huang, Kun-Shan Wu, 2011, 'The association among project manager's leadership style, teamwork and project success', *International Journal of Project Management,* vol. 29, no. 3, pp. 258–267.

23. Ibid. pp. 265–266.

24. Accessible online at http://www.belbin.com/rte.asp?id=, accessed 25 January 2013.

25. See later in this chapter, in the section 'Issues which may arise.'

26. Janis, Irving L., 1972, revised 1982, *Victims of Groupthink; a Psychological Study of Foreign-Policy Decisions and Fiascoes.* Houghton, Mifflin.

27. Ibid., p. 9.

28. Stoner, J. A. F., 1961, *A Comparison of Individual and Group Decisions Involving Risk.* Unpublished Master's Thesis, Massachusetts Institute of Technology.

29. Stoner, J. A. F., 1968, 'Risky and Cautious Shifts in Group Decisions: The Influence of Widely Held Values', *J. Exp. Social Psychology,* vol. 4, pp. 442–459.

6

LEADERSHIP

LEARNING OBJECTIVES

- Give a working definition of the term leadership
- Discuss the part leadership plays in a work organisation
- Explain the differences between leadership and management
- Evaluate the strengths of a range of leadership theories.

INTRODUCTION

In Western organisations the bureaucratic model has been the default position for the design of organisations. It is (or aims to be) a rational way of organising people and resources in a hierarchy of authority and definition of role to deliver the objectives of the organisation. In theory, the bureaucratic way is to create a system of procedures and regulations which define and give authority to all aspects of the hierarchy and its activities. Procedures and regulations are written down and communicated and so are transparent. Everyone knows where they stand and the basis on which decisions are made.

We know that rationality is an important part of the make up of human beings. But it is only part of that make up. We are also emotional creatures. We have different motivations and intentions, we find personal satisfaction in different things and we all have different intellectual abilities and skills. It is these essential differences which cause the complexity in human systems. In contrast, a bureaucracy is premised on the idea that we can all be treated, and will respond, in the same way. So what tends to happen is that when something occurs which the bureaucratic blueprint hasn't accounted for, then you modify the blueprint and make more rules and procedures to deal with it. The consequent proliferation of rules and procedures reaches a point where ensuring that the bureaucracy is followed can result in spending too much time dealing with the demands of the bureaucracy and too little on the core activities of the organisation. At its worst, we see situations where following the rules and fulfilling the goals of bureaucratic compliance becomes an end in itself. Staff are rewarded for being good bureaucrats.

In contrast, leadership operates in the non-rational spaces of the organisation. It engages with the values and emotions of people in the organisation in a way that he formal organisation is not designed to do.

Over the past 30 or so years many organisations have recognised the problem of bureaucracy and have tried to create a balance between using necessary rules and regulations to create accountability with the need for staff to put greatest effort into their core activities.

For instance, we have seen a delayering of organisations which removes levels of bureaucracy and replaces them with more autonomy for the planning and management of work lower down the hierarchy. The greater spans of control which this leads to mean that close management supervision is not always possible.

Organisational design has seen the development of the matrix organisation,[1] which attempts to avoid the rigid bureaucratic delineations of function with a structure that allows different functions to operate together without the potential delays and short-circuiting of information that can arise if the bureaucratic channels are rigidly followed.

A third strand, with which this chapter is concerned, is the opportunity for managers (or others) to exercise leadership. However, if organisations are to encourage and develop leadership, we have to know what it is and we have to be able to recruit and promote individuals who are, or can become, leaders.

WHAT IS LEADERSHIP?

Leadership is one of those slippery concepts which we know when we see it, but because we see it in so many diverse situations it is very difficult to find a simple definition. The definition by Northouse[2] below is as good a starting point as any.

> Leadership is a process whereby an individual influences a group of other individuals to achieve a common goal.

The definition problem arises because we recognise leadership behaviour at several levels: we see it at the interpersonal level where someone will give individual encouragement and support to a colleague or subordinate; we see it at the level of the group where a leader may create unity from conflict, or a drive and determination to achieve a difficult goal; we see it at the strategic level where a leader sets out a vision of change for the whole organisation to commit to. Beyond the organisational level we see national leaders, or leaders who initiate great political or social movements. However, not all leaders do the same kind of thing, nor do they all do it in the same way.

Over time there have been several approaches to understanding leadership. We can place these on a continuum ranging from the view that leadership is something an elite few are born with – trait theories – to the opposite end of the continuum, which claims that leadership is a collection of skills and competences that can be learned. Between the two we find theories which emphasise the functions or behaviours of leaders. Other approaches view leadership as dependent on the situation in which it takes place, and so different kinds of leadership will be required in different conditions. These theories come under the general title of contingency or situational theories. In recent years, many organisations have had to go through fundamental changes in order to survive, so more modern theories have focused on the kinds of leadership needed to move an organisation from its current stage to a radically different one. These theories are referred to as transformational or charismatic leadership theories. They examine the leader's ability to win the hearts and minds of staff to embrace new structures and ways of working.

TRAIT THEORIES

A trait is an inherent characteristic possessed by an individual, usually thought to be genetically inherited. Early thinking about leadership attempted to identify these inherited characteristics. However, if we try to specify what traits a leader should have, we quickly find that there are problems. First of all, we find it difficult to agree about what these traits should be. If we are not careful we can end up with a huge list of characteristics that it would be impossible for any one individual to possess. This is particularly true when we consider leadership in different contexts, where some of the characteristics may well be contradictory. Stogdill,[3] as early as 1948, carried out a review of the literature on traits and concluded that there was no single set of traits that could be confidently assigned to all leaders. He saw that, for example, military leadership required different characteristics from business leadership.

We often begin our study of leadership with an exercise. We consider people generally thought to be great leaders. The problem, however, is that we can only infer their leadership traits from their public persona and this is very unreliable and incomplete. We don't have an intimate knowledge of their personalities. What may appear to be buoyancy of spirit and sureness of action in public may well mask great uncertainty in the private person.

Nevertheless, trait theory has high face validity; that is, it *looks* like it should be true. After all, for a person to be a leader, they must possess some characteristics that non-leaders don't possess. However, there is still the problem of identifying these traits. In 1991, Kirkpatrick and Locke[4] looked through the research and concluded that there were six key characteristics of effective leaders:

1. Drive to achieve; applying high levels of effort, ambition, energy and initiative.

2. Leadership motivation; a clear desire and confidence to lead others in the direction the leader wants to go.

3. Honesty and integrity; a need to be trusted, trusting and open.

4. Self-confidence; a belief in him or herself, their ideas and their ability.

5. Cognitive ability; while leaders do not have to be intellectuals, they have to be able to conceptualise a problem, be able to analyse it and make clear, effective judgements to reach a satisfactory conclusion.

6. Knowledge of business; a leader needs be familiar with the business or field of activity in which the leadership is to take place.

Kirkpatrick and Locke also identify other, less important, leadership qualities such as charisma, creativity and flexibility.

Trait theory is always open to criticism, largely because of the problems of definition. Leadership can be exercised in very many contexts and may well require different characteristics depending what the context is. Although Kirkpatrick and Locke limit their view of leadership to business leaders, we might still argue that business itself is rich in varied context. Both businesses that need to change and those that are stable need leaders. Leadership happens at all levels, from the strategic to the most basic operational level. It is needed when things are going badly, or when things are going well. Small businesses need it just as much as large ones and all those in between. If organisations want to recruit, develop and promote leaders, we need something more substantial to guide the process.

Where trait theorists have tried understand what a leader is like, other theorists have challenged this view and examined the functions, behaviours and responsibilities of leaders.

FUNCTIONAL AND BEHAVIOURAL THEORIES

Theories of this type tend to emphasise the aspects or dimensions of the leadership context to which effective leaders pay attention in their leadership role. Theories of this type often refer to leadership *style* and refer to several dimensions of management behaviour. Mullins identifies three broad categories across a continuum of styles which a leader may adopt:[5]

1. **The Authoritarian** (or autocratic) style in which decision making lies exclusively with the manager. Work is carried out in a climate of threats and sanctions and there is little attention paid to the well being or satisfaction of subordinates.

2. **The Democratic** style, by contrast, finds a much greater focus on the team, with open communication channels, greater collaboration in decision making and a concern for staff well being and group cohesiveness.

3. The **Laissez-faire** style arises where the manager trusts staff to be able to carry out their tasks with a very high degree of autonomy. While that situation occurs and staff are working towards understood organisational and team goals, then the manager will be very hands-off. In some contexts this is a legitimate leadership style. For example, while this may seem an unlikely leadership style, in many professional contexts, the manager may be less qualified or experienced than the specialists they manage. Consequently, close supervision is not possible and the manager needs to trust the individuals to work professionally and effectively.

Although different researchers have given these styles different names, there is an interesting convergence on two important dimensions: task and maintenance. The task dimension relates to the output that a work group needs to achieve, while the maintenance dimension refers to maintaining the drive and motivation of the people in the group. The research has focused on two areas: first, uncovering the centrality of these dimensions and second, on how leaders need to balance these two critical dimensions.

In the 1940s researchers at Ohio State University in the USA began a programme studying leadership. Over many years they developed and refined a series of questionnaires. The responses to these questionnaires by both supervisors and subordinates led the researchers to identify two independent variables in the leadership process: *consideration* and *initiating structure*. Leaders who exhibit high levels of consideration emphasise personal relationships. They develop high levels of trust and pay attention to the welfare of the individuals in the group.

Those leaders who emphasise initiating structure focus on the tasks the group need to perform. Effective leaders on this dimension are clear about what they expect of their subordinates, and are clear about standards of performance and meeting deadlines.

Research carried out by Likert[6] at the University of Michigan from the 1940s on, identified four approaches to leadership:

- **System 1 – Exploitative authoritative:** This system is one in which decisions are made at the top and imposed on subordinates with no consultation. Non-compliance is met with threats and sanctions. There is no concern for the well being of staff, let alone their opinions on the task to be carried out. In such a system staff are unlikely to commit to the goals of the organisation, with a high probability of labour unrest and a low probability of staff doing anything beyond their basic contractual obligations.

- **System 2 – Benevolent authoritative:** This system is an improvement on the 'take it or leave it' approach of System 1. It usually includes an opportunity for some kind of reward system and a low degree of consultation on operational matters. Important decisions are still communicated from the top down, with little opportunity for discussion. Despite the limited opportunity for consultation, threats and sanctions are still implicit in this system.

- **System 3 – Consultative:** The main difference between this system and System 3 is that there is a greater degree of consultation in the decision-making process, at least at the operational level. Consultation will often take the form of discussions about problems, goals and outcomes. In this system, employees are often made to feel more involved and consequently can be more motivated and more committed to the organisation's goals.

- **System 4 – Participative system:** Leaders in this system begin with the belief that skill, creativity and a wish to succeed are widely distributed throughout organisations and it is in the interests of management to make use of these positive characteristics. Consequently, there need to be communication processes that are horizontal as well as vertical in order that open discussion can take place at all levels of the organisation. Means and ends developed in this system bring out greater commitment at all levels of the organisation, and staff are better motivated to succeed.

Likert's work on the four systems resonates with another influential work which come out at around the same time. Douglas MacGregor's[7] *The*

Human Side of Enterprise was originally published in 1961 and has been in print in various editions ever since. In it MacGregor identified two 'theories', Theory X and Theory Y.

Theory X assumes that people are reluctant to expend energy or imagination on their work. Consequently, staff have to be closely supervised and coerced to work effectively by threats and sanctions. Most workers are unambitious, dislike responsibility and are driven by the need for security and want clarity in what they do.

In contrast Theory Y assumes the opposite: that people want work that is satisfying, rewarding and valuable. MacGregor believed that creativity was widely distributed through the population and that work organisations would benefit by harnessing this goodwill and creativity in the pursuit of the organisation's goals. MacGregor further believed that the organisation of work at the time he was writing did not provide any scope for most workers to express their creativity, imagination and ingenuity. Theory Y is essentially a critique of the 'rational-economic man' view of human nature that was prevalent throughout the industrialisation process of the nineteenth and twentieth centuries.

MacGregor understood the difficulties of applying Theory Y in the mass production, labour intensive industries with which he grew up. The need to continually profit from increasing efficiency meant there was little scope for widespread devolution of decision making through the workforce. Managers needed to keep close control of the production process and managers who took a Theory X position achieved this more effectively. However, the need for new products and innovative services which came with post-war prosperity, along with the development of automated production technologies, left the industrial giants behind. It fell to the emerging industrial strength of Japan to show how a more Theory Y approach could pay dividends.[8] Japanese production methods put great emphasis on problem solving by staff at the operational level. Moreover, the development of Total Quality[9] and Just in Time[10] methods, and a culture of continuous improvement showed how a Theory Y approach, even in industrial mass production organisations, could deliver high quality products efficiently and effectively.

A common misunderstanding of MacGregor's work is to think that he categorised workers as either Theory X workers or as Theory Y workers. He did not categorise the workers at all. He categorised the *assumptions of managers about workers*. Theory X and Theory Y tell us about the manager, not the worker!

Using similar conceptual dimensions to those of Likert and MacGregor, which they called concern for people and concern for production, Blake and Mouton[11] developed the Managerial Grid. This was based on a grid plotting leader behaviour over the two dimensions. Blake and Mouton identified five areas of the grid which depicted differentiated leadership behaviours (Figure 6.1).

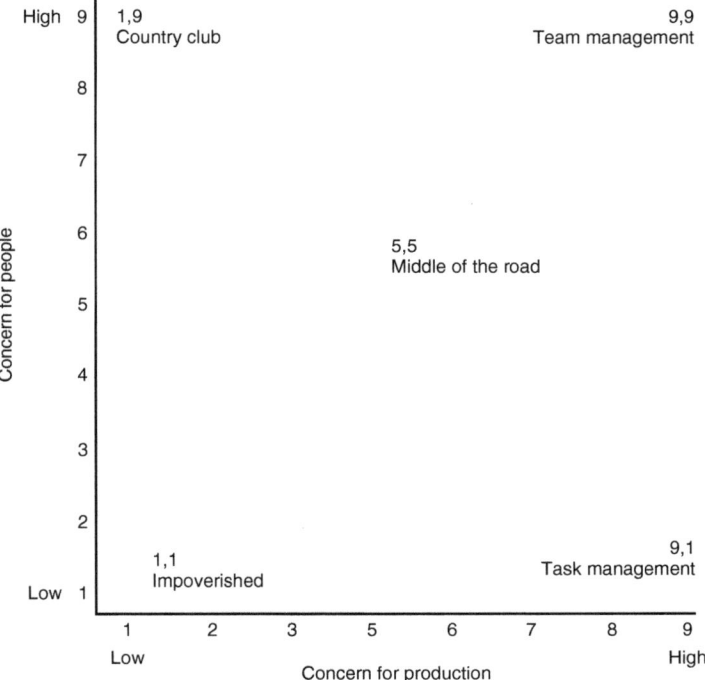

Figure 6.1 Blake and Mouton Management grid. Reproduced by permission of Gulf Publishing Company.

Source: Blake, R. Mouton, J., 1985, The Managerial Grid III: The Key to Leadership Excellence. Houston: Gulf Publishing Co.

The axes of the grid are each divided into nine units. The management behaviours are calculated according the correspondence of managers' behaviour along the x- and y-axes. This gave Blake and Mouton five areas of differentiation which represented distinct leader behaviours:

1. **Impoverished Management (1,1):** This style of leadership is clustered around low scores for concern for production and low scores for concern for people. Leaders who have scores around this point have little concern for their staff and little concern for the task of the group. It is easy to see that such a leadership style would not only produce poor results but would also lead to conflict and disharmony. No organisation would be able to tolerate this kind of leadership style for very long.

2. **Task Management (9,1):** This leadership style is also known as the dictatorial style. This is very reminiscent of MacGregor's Theory X approach. It focuses almost exclusively on the job to be done without paying much attention to developing commitment or trust in the workforce. There is a culture of compliance with the likelihood of poor labour relations and high staff turnover. This leadership style works well in the short term where it is critical that production tasks are achieved, but will fail over a protracted time period.

3. **Middle of the Road (5,5):** This style tends to a style which is just about acceptable to everyone, with no-one being fully satisfied. Production is satisfactory and there are few conflicts or problems with staff. However, it is a compromise in which more could be achieved with better leadership.

4. **Country Club (1,9):** This leadership style is high on trust and the well being of staff. Leaders with this style believe that it leads to self motivation. However, if it does not, then productivity will be very low.

5. **Team style (9,9):** This style is at the maximum score for both task and production concerns. Leaders who are able to develop and apply this style are likely to get the best of both worlds, committed and satisfied staff as well as high levels of productivity.

While the theories outlined above evaluate leadership style and behaviour on dimensions of attention to people and attention to outcome (with a variety of terms they may actually use for these two dimensions), Tannenbaum and Schmidt look at leader behaviour along a continuum from **Manager power and influence** at one end to **Non-manager power and influence** at the other.

They differentiate seven distinct styles along the continuum, with each style having a different mix of freedom of management action and freedom of non-manager action.

1. **The manager decides and announces the decision.** The manager will have an understanding of their department's goals and available resources and will make decisions according those constraints. The decisions will be transmitted to staff who are expected to implement the decisions whether they agree with them or not. This style pays little attention to the needs of staff beyond their ability to carry out orders capably and efficiently. Such an approach may well be quite legitimate in control and command situations. For example, firefighters at an incident need to carry out instructions quickly and effectively; there may not be time to discuss instructions.

2. **The manager decides and 'sells' the decision to the group.** This style shows a little more concern for staff in that the manager will explain why the decision is important and what the benefits of carrying it out may be. As in style 1, there is no room for discussion; the decision, although explained, is still on a 'take it or leave it' basis. Such a style may well be seen as legitimate in situations where non-routine decisions have to be made such as when several staff are unable to get into work, for example.

3. **The manager explains the decision and responds to questions.** This style has a suggestion of more involvement of staff because the manager will explain the background and rationale for the decision. They will also invite questions to discuss the decision and how it was arrived at. In this style the group can feel more involved and valued. The situation given as an example in style 2 can also apply here, though this approach needs more time to allow staff to discuss the decision, so a manager needs to take into account the actual nature of the situation and how much time is available.

4. **The manager suggests a likely decision and invites discussion.**
There is a much greater sense of involvement when this style is used. The decision presented is given as the best in the view of the manager. Staff are invited to discuss the decision and make suggestions for modifying it or for alternatives. Such an approach is appropriate when there is a high level of expertise or experience in the team. The reasons for changing a decision must, however, be extremely compelling to the manager. A situation in which such a style might be appropriate is in the development of a new programme of study at a college. Senior staff may have decided on the structure of the programme, how much time can be allotted to each subject, what the assessment process will be and what the pool of potential students will be. Within this general framework, however, there may well be scope for modifications, and it is likely that there will be exhaustive discussion as to the implementation of the details of the programme.

5. **The manager explains the problem, gets input from staff, then makes the decision.** This style has much greater involvement of staff. The manager identifies the problem, but the staff are expected to understand the problem and its implications and come up with a solution that the manager can accept. The greater involvement of the group can be highly motivational. This style is appropriate where the manager feels that the staff have greater knowledge or expertise in certain areas than they do. The Practice Manager of a medical practice may well need to take this kind of approach when having to implement new regulations or practices.

6. **The group makes the decision within bounds set by the manager.**
In this style the responsibility for the decision is with the group. The manager retains a degree of control by stating the parameters within which the decision is to be made. For such a style to be successful, the group need to be responsible, well informed, willing to arrive at the best solution and capable of understanding the implication of their decision. The manager needs to have a high degree of trust in them since, although the group are responsible for making the decision, the manager is still accountable for that decision. The *quality circle* approach to continuous

improvement of products will usually make use of this style of leader-ship. Problems which arise in the production process are best solved by the team involved in that part of the process, according to the principles of Total Quality Management. So for a group who are experiencing a problem with components, the machinery of the organisation of work will meet to find a solution. The manager will generally accept the solution they come up with provided that it is consistent with general practice and the goals of the organisation.

7. **The group identify the problem and make the decisions.** This style allows staff the most freedom. They identify the problem, examine the options, carry out discussions or investigations and collectively decide what to do. The manager has given them freedom to take on this high level of responsibility because they can be trusted to work towards over-arching strategic goals. This style may well be appropriate where a team of senior staff is charged with arriving at a plan for achieving the strategic goals of an organisation.

All of these leadership styles have their place, even though those of them at the extremes of the continuum may appear at first glance distasteful or potentially chaotic. The point about the continuum is that it shows that different situations call for different leadership behaviours. Tannenbaum and Schmidt present leaders with options for how to lead in these differ-ent contexts. In 1973 they refined the model further[12] by detailing how to analyse the context to help make a choice of leadership behaviour.

They suggest that there are three forces at work which the leader needs to take into account:

1. **Forces in the manager:** The manager is an individual, with their own characteristics and values that differentiate them from every one else. They have different views about leadership, about how far they trust their subordinates and how confident they feel in dealing with situations which arise.

2. **Forces at work in subordinates:** Subordinates also come with their individual differences and value systems. A leader needs to know how ready and willing they are to take responsibility, how committed they are

to the goals of the organisation and what their knowledge and experience about the situation may be. Moreover, the levels of these characteristics may vary between individuals throughout the group. And, indeed, over time.

3. **Forces in the situation:** No two situations are ever entirely the same. The features of any given situation may vary in large or small measure, but will usually call for a leader to make modifications to their behaviour. They need to take into account, for example, the organisation climate, which will expect leaders to act in certain ways, how effective and cohesive the group is, the precise nature of the problem which needs their attention, and the time and other resources that are at hand to deal with the situation.

Clearly, the actual cluster of behaviours and styles available to a leader will be constrained both by the situation itself and the personality of the leader. It would be unusual, for example, for a leader to be able to act comfortably at each end of the continuum. A leader who is happy to operate at the autocratic end of the scale is unlikely be as comfortable at the democratic/ delegation end. However, what the continuum of styles teaches is not only the variability of leadership behaviour, but also the need to take into account the situation in which leadership takes place.[13]

SITUATIONAL/CONTINGENCY THEORIES

While trait theories are looking for the person who has the right characteristics to take a leadership role because of their force of personality and innate leadership qualities (usually because of genetic inheritance) and behavioural theories examine the apparent choices leaders have in how they should exercise leadership in a variety of contexts, contingency theories view the context in which leadership takes place as the critical variable. The situation calls forth the style that the leader needs to adopt and these theories tend to assume that the leader can identify the contingencies (the important variables) of the situation and can alter his or her behaviour to suit those contingencies. Organisations, therefore, need to develop and select leaders with the behavioural repertoire to operate effectively in the context in which they have to lead.

FIEDLER'S CONTINGENCY THEORY

Fiedler[14] developed his Least Preferred Co-worker questionnaire[15] to ascertain whether an individual was more task or people-centred in their approach to management. When you overlay this preference onto a given situation, the interaction gives you the 'favourability' of what style is appropriate to what kind of situation. This questionnaire asked respondents to consider the person they had least enjoyed working with and to score them on a series of about 18 constructs[16].

Respondents with high LPC scores[17] are most satisfied by having good personal relations, whilst those with a low LPC score are task focused. Fiedler regarded the LPC score as relatively unchangeable – in other words, a collection of traits – but only of value as leadership qualities in the most suitable situation. The leadership situation, according to Fiedler, has a number of components:

- **Relations between leader and group members:** This refers to the degree of trust and openness between the leader and the led, and how willing the latter are to accept the leader's role.
- **The structure of the task:** This factor refers to how clear the task is – whether its desired outcomes and the means to achieving those outcomes are known and understood.
- **The leader's position power:** Position power is the formal authority delegated to the leader by the organisation. It defines the extent and limits of the leader's power. The leader's exercise of position power will be backed by the disciplinary system of the organisation.[18]

When these factors are combined we can identify situations which are favourable or unfavourable to a leader's leadership style. Fiedler identified eight leadership styles depending on the combination of the situational variables. He found that the most favorable situation occurs when there are good relations between leader and group members, the task is highly structured and the leader's position power is strong. Figure 6.2 sets out the various combinations:

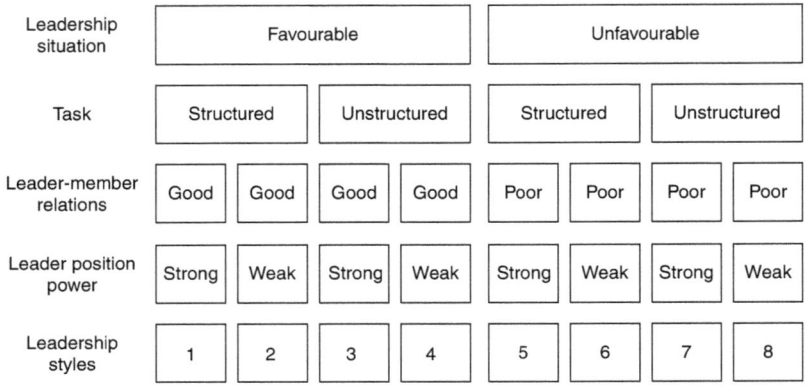

Figure 6.2 Fiedler's leadership styles

The last piece of this rather complicated jigsaw is to overlay the LPC score onto this chart. What research has found is that leaders who have a preference for task achievement are better suited to favourable (1, 2 or 3) styles and to unfavourable (7 and 8) styles. Those with a preference for good relations over tasks fare better in the other styles (4, 5 or 6).

Whilst the Fiedler model is complex and has received some criticism,[19] it nevertheless draws our attention to some of the key variables in an organisation which can have an impact on the effectiveness of leadership. It also implies that there is a sense in which the situation chooses the leader, which in turn suggests that leaders are as often at the mercy of events as the rest of us.

CONTINGENCY THEORY OF VROOM AND YETTON

The contingency model developed by Vroom and Yetton emphasised three key factors in a leader's decision making:

- The *quality of the decision,* or how the decision improved the effectiveness of the group,

- The *level of acceptance* of the decision, indicating the degree of motivation of staff and their commitment to making the decision work, and
- The available *time* to make and implement the decision.

According to this model, these three key variables imply three different leadership approaches to decision making, two of which can be further subdivided:

1. **Autocratic**, subdivided into:

   a. **A.I**, where the leader makes the decisions alone, based on information available to him or her, or

   b. **A.II**, where the leader obtains information from their subordinates and then makes the decision.

2. **Consultative**, divided into:

   a. **C.I**, where key subordinates are asked for their views and the decision is made with or without taking those views into account, or

   b. **C.II**, where the problem is thrown open to the group and their opinions are sought. The decision is then made by the leader possibly, though not necessarily, taking the group's opinions into account.

3. **Group**, giving us:

   a. **G.II**, where the problem is thrown open to the whole group and the leader acts as chair and facilitator to discuss the problem until a consensus solution emerges.

There are echoes of the Tannenbaum and Schmidt continuum in this model, though Vroom and Yetton go further in setting out rules for enabling the leader to decide on the appropriate style of decision making. The rules apply to the quality of the decision and to the group's acceptance of the decision. In order to find the most appropriate style a leader needs to work through a series of yes/no questions, to determine the style to be adopted.

- Is there a quality issue? Is the nature of the solution critical? Are there technical or rational grounds for selecting among possible solutions?

- Do I have sufficient information to make a high quality decision?
- Is the problem structured? Are the alternative courses of action and methods for their evaluation known?
- Is acceptance of the decision by subordinates critical to its implementation?
- If I were to make the decision by myself, is it reasonably certain that it would be accepted by my subordinates?
- Do subordinates share the organisational goals to be obtained in solving this problem?
- Is conflict among subordinates likely in obtaining the preferred solution?

These questions are often converted into a decision tree indicating the best fit style to be adopted from the answers to the questions.

Vroom and Jago later refined this model,[20] which still keeps the five decision making styles but increases the number of situational variables to 12. Moreover, instead of yes/no answers to the presence or absence of these variables, the presence of ten of them are assessed on a scale of one to five. This revised view of the decision making situation leads to the possibility of four decision trees:

1. An individual-level problem with time constraints.
2. An individual-level problem in which a manager wishes to support the development of an employee's decision making capability.
3. A group-level problem where the manager wishes to develop the group's decision making capability.
4. A time-driven group problem.

Like the Tannenbaum and Schmidt continuum, the Vroom and Yetton and the Vroom and Jago theories rely on the ability of the manger to change styles to the situation. Where managers are too set in their ways, there will be little room to change; where they are more flexible, it is still doubtful whether many managers would be capable of moving from highly directive to highly permissive in their management style. The variables of the organisational culture and the personality of the individual manager are not really accounted for in either of these approaches.

HOUSE'S PATH–GOAL THEORY

While the path–goal theory also looks at the style the manager adopts, it comes at the issue from a slightly different perspective. It examines the role of the manager in fulfilling the needs and expectations of followers. It almost looks at management as a service provided to those who are managed. In it we can see echoes of the expectancy theories of motivation.[21] Briefly, expectancy theory says that people will be motivated to achieve a goal depending on how much they value achieving that goal and the intrinsic or extrinsic reward that comes from its achievement. Consequently, a leader's function is to facilitate a subordinate's satisfaction either in the present or in the future as long as: (a) satisfaction is contingent on achieving goals which the subordinate values and which are consistent with the needs of the organisation; and (b) the leader enables effective performance by train-ing and other forms of support and particularly by ensuring that rewards for good performance are available to the subordinate.

House identified four leadership approaches:

1. **Directive leadership:** In this approach the leader sets both the goals of task and the means of achieving them.

2. **Supportive leadership:** A supportive leader sees it as a priority to moti-vate and enable the subordinate to achieve his or her goals.

3. **Participative leadership:** This approach to leadership engages in dis-cussion with subordinates to seek their views and preferences about a task, then the leader makes the decision taking these views into account.

4. **Achievement-oriented leadership:** A leader who takes this approach is looking to challenge subordinates by setting goals which are at the edge of the subordinate's capability in order to stimulate high level performance.

An effective leader, according to this theory, is one who is flexible enough to understand the goals that motivate any individual member of the group and intelligent enough to be able to influence group members to achieve goals which are consistent with the goals of the organisation.

The path–goal theory also stresses the importance of influences on performance from the organisational environment: how structured the task is, how formal the authority system in the organisation is and the dynamics of the work group. In addition, it also emphasises the importance of the individual: their perceived capability, their level of experience and the locus of control. This last factor refers to the degree of control the individual has over the organisation, resourcing, timing and implementation of the task. So, a manager may well be willing to delegate greater control of a task to a subordinate who is motivated by being challenged in this way. A subordinate who has less confidence or capability will need greater guidance and so the locus of control will fall more on the manager than on the subordinate (Figure 6.3).

Provided always that the leader is capable of varying his or her behaviour, this approach to leadership has high face validity. The ability of the leader will depend not only on their own capability to vary their behaviour, but also on the organisational constraints placed upon them. The formality of the authority system in the organisation, for example, may limit their freedom to delegate elements of power to subordinates. The capability of

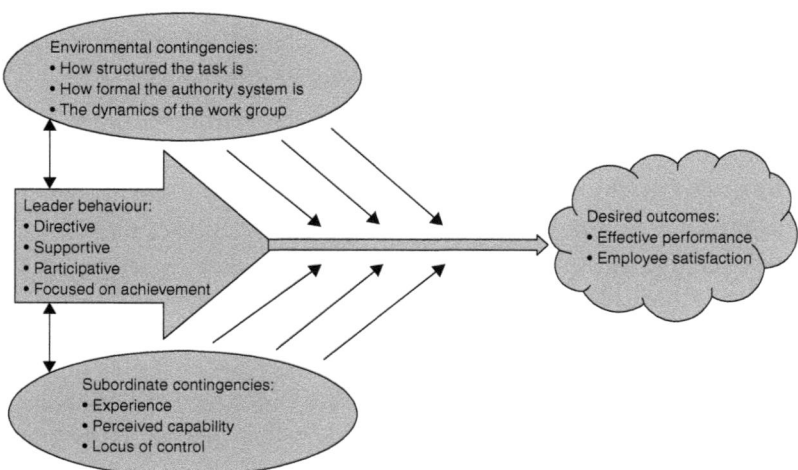

Figure 6.3 House's path–goal theory

individuals may also be a limiting factor on how far a leader would be willing to delegate.

Looking particularly at the relationship between the leader and their subordinates as a key situational variable, Hersey and Blanchard[22] suggest that leaders should adopt a style to fit with a subordinate's *readiness* (sometimes called their *maturity*). Readiness is a combination of the subordinate's competence to carry out the task and their level of motivation to carry out the task. Hersey and Blanchard distribute readiness along a continuum with four key points of differentiation:

1. **R1 – Low readiness:** Subordinates with low readiness lack both the competence and the motivation to carry out the task.

2. **R2 – Low to moderate readiness:** this category of follower is willing or confident about carrying out the task, but does not have the competence.

3. **R3 – Moderate to high readiness:** Subordinates at this level of readiness are competent to carry out the task but lack the motivation or confidence to carry it out.

4. **R4 – High readiness:** Subordinates at this level are both competent and motivated to carry out the task. They also have the confidence to tackle it.

The leader, having identified the level of readiness of the subordinate, then needs to make their leadership style consistent with that level. They do this by selecting behaviours that combine *task behaviour* – the degree of direction as to goals and the means of implementing them – and *relationship behaviour* – the amount of support, communication and training the subordinate will need.

Depending on the leader's estimation of subordinates' readiness, Hersey and Blanchard suggest that there are four styles a leader can adopt. Table 6.1 below shows which of the 'levels of readiness' each of the styles is most suited to:

Table 6.1 A summary of Hersey and Blanchard's leadership styles

Best style	Subordinate readiness
S1 – Tells – High guidance and direction, with low supportive behaviour.	**R1 – Low readiness:**

(continued)

Table 6.1 Continued

Best style	Subordinate readiness
S2 – Sells – High on guidance and direction and high on relationship behaviour	**R2 – Low to moderate readiness**
S3 – Participates – High levels of support and communication, low levels of task direction.	**R3 – Moderate to high readiness**
S4 – Delegates – low levels of both task and relationship behaviour	**R4 – High readiness**

ACTION-CENTRED LEADERSHIP

John Adair developed this approach to leadership when he was advisor on leadership at the Royal Military Academy, Sandhurst in the UK. He continued to expand the model when he became Assistant Director of the Industrial Society.[23] The model is generally represented as three overlapping circles, each circle representing a critical contingency of leadership: *Achieving the task, managing the team* and *managing the individual.* The idea behind this model is that it is the leader's responsibility to achieve the task through the efforts of the group. Therefore, the group needs to act effectively as a team, with each individual making a positive contribution consistent with their talents. Consequently, the leader must keep these critical elements in balance to achieve the tasks of the group, whether those tasks are specific, short-term tasks or longer term, more abstract tasks. Because in work organisations, as well as in military activities, a group will be confronted with a variety of tasks, then it is likely that the leader's focus of attention will shift from day to day, from task to task. Sometimes they may need to energise the group, other times they may need to take account of the needs of an individual who is struggling, while there will also be times when it will be important to push the team to get on with the task.

Adair also suggested the key specific functions associated with each of the action-centred leadership circles. Figure 6.4 below sets these out:

Task functions	Team functions	Individual functions
• Define the task • Devise a workable plan • Brief members on their task and role • Delegate work to team members • Allocate resources • Check quality of work • Control pace of work • Keep team focused • Evaluate progress and modify plan if needed	• Set standards • Maintain discipline • Build team spirit • Maintain morale • Motivate members • Keep open communication • Train in appropriate skills • Resolve conflict • Delegate sub-leader roles • Don't become too focused on task at the expense of group	• Involve everyone in discussion and activity • Work with individual's abilities • Bring in quieter members • Control overactive members • Make use of expertise • Establish previous experience • Offer constructive feedback • Encourage and motivate • Avoid taking sides in arguments

Figure 6.4 Leader functions in action-centred leadership

Such a list of functions is very useful in the training and development of leaders, and, to some extent, in their selection. Like most of the theories that examine leadership from the perspective of function and leader behaviour, it assumes that leaders are able to evaluate situations as they unfold and to adopt the most appropriate style of leadership. This is a credible proposition where there may be relatively slight changes needed to a leader's behaviour, but may be more problematic where changes may call for more radical changes. It is difficult see many people being able to switch from an autocratic approach to a highly democratic one, for example. This is not say that it can't happen, but such a change might well challenge the leader's (and followers') values and assumptions about what the role of the leader is.

TRANSFORMATIONAL LEADERSHIP

In looking at leadership from this perspective, J. M. Burns[24] contrasted it with *transactional leadership*. The latter is based in the bureaucratic approach to organisation where leadership takes place amid the rules and processes of a rationally designed organisation. In such a case there is an interaction – a negotiation or transaction – between the leaders and the led about ways and means of achieving tasks, rewards and responsibilities for carrying out those tasks and the application of discipline when tasks are not carried out effectively. Transactional leadership takes place in the context of the formal authority system of the organisation. Authority, and with it power, are delegated from the top in different degrees to people at different levels in the hierarchy. For example, transactional leadership determines who can hire or fire staff (or authorise the hiring and firing), who holds and allocates the resources the organisation needs to operate. It can be seen in many ways at all levels of an organisation.

Transformational leadership, in contrast, is about enabling followers to accept the new and to thrive in times of radical change. It takes place in a context where the changes to the technologies and organisation of production are so sweeping and continuous that it requires workers themselves to change as well as the material and organisational changes in which work has to be done. You can certainly order someone to change their behaviour, but you cannot order them to be committed to the change. For that you need a kind of leadership that can inspire and give confidence to members.

Moreover, Burns' view of transformational leadership goes beyond the immediate requirements of the organisation to overlay a moral and socially progressive element to leadership. Transformational leadership leads people into change through developing loyalty and trust.

Transformational leadership has been equated to *charismatic* leadership. This was identified by Weber[25] as one of three sources of power in human societies, the others being traditional power (such as that found in feudal societies or under absolute monarchies and aristocracies) and rational-legal power (as found in societies which are based on legal rationality emanating from government or bureaucratic institutions). Charismatic power is based in an individual's personality. Their followers often see them as having heroic or even superhuman gifts. However, charismatic leadership is a two-edged sword; followers are often led to do things they do not want to do, to commit acts which they would find abhorrent if they weren't swept up in the desire to please the leader. Often the focus of the charismatic leader is to benefit themselves or their close associates. We can think of dictators or business leaders who were charismatic, but who persuaded their followers to support aims which were immoral, unethical or not in their best interests.

At the time of writing, the death of former British Prime Minister, Margaret Thatcher had recently been announced. Undoubtedly, she was a very charismatic leader, but her leadership divided the British people, and the reaction to her death shows that it continues to divide them. She habitually referred to people who agreed with her as 'one of us', while those who disagreed were variously describes as 'the wets' or 'the enemy within'. While she genuinely inspired great respect and admiration among her followers, she achieved her goals by the exercise of political and even coercive power. The transformation she brought about in Britain was not one that was embraced by the whole country.

Burns' approach to transformational leadership, while it may well involve a charismatic leader, is inclusive and focuses on building trust and motivation to achieve goals that followers believe in. It is helpful to see Burns' view of leadership as work at the higher levels of human needs.[26] He developed the notion of the 'Four Is':

- **Idealised influence** refers to the need for the leader to be a role model, and to show through their actions that they can build confidence and trust in their followers.
- **Inspirational motivation** gives followers a belief in their ability to achieve high levels of performance and achievement.
- **Intellectual stimulation** is the challenge provided by the leader for followers to be innovative and creative.
- **Individual consideration** is the measure of how well the leader engages with individual followers and shows consideration for their concerns.

Although Burns' notions of leadership have been adopted for work organisations, his reach extends far beyond leadership in the workplace. He was first and foremost a political scientist and a historian. His work suggests he believed strongly in the ability of human beings to improve themselves and his leadership ideas have to be seen in this context. He wrote:

> Transformational leadership occurs when one or more persons engage with others in such a way that leaders and followers raise one another to higher levels of motivation and morality.[27]

Perhaps the key factor in transformational leadership is the notion of *inspiration*.[28] Transformational or charismatic leaders have the ability to enable followers to see a bigger picture and to feel that they not only have a part to play in achieving the vision, but feel a personal commitment to it.

CONCLUSIONS ON LEADERSHIP

Leadership is a mysterious concept. We may feel we can recognise it when it happens, but it is very difficult to reach a consensus on what it is, how it arises or what it achieves. For these reasons it is very difficult to measure. If we take Burns' theory, for example, what are we to measure? Is it whether an organisation performs better as a consequence of having a transformational leader? Or are we somehow to measure how inspired followers are by the vision of the leader?

Any research of this nature will fall foul of complex organisational variables which are difficult for researchers to control for, making it very difficult to ascertain reliably what causes bring about what results.

If organisations want to appoint or develop people to be leaders, how should they go about it? If you accept the trait theory, you must look for leaders with leadership characteristics. If you consider that functional and style theories are valid, then you can perhaps develop leadership skills through training and development programmes. If you believe that the context will deliver the right person at the right time, then, again, you can provide training opportunities so that people can be ready to seize leadership opportunities as and when they arise. If you want leadership to bring about radical change then you need to be able to identify those individuals who possess the ability to inspire followers to believe in the vision they want to aspire to.

At the time of writing there is a major financial crisis affecting the Western world in particular. Wage value is falling; jobs are harder and harder to come by and those in employment are more and more insecure in their work. Such a context is perhaps more demanding of good leadership than ever.

Read the scenario below, which illustrates the limitations of formal organisational rules and an opportunity to exercise leadership which is not taken. Then try to answer the questions.

Louise has just been made supervisor of a small assembly unit in a manufacturing company. She was promoted because she not only worked well and was a reliable employee, but because the production manager believed she had management potential. Her colleagues in the unit were not so sure. She was seen by most of them as too focused on getting the smallest detail right, sometimes at the expense of keeping output to a tight schedule. Moreover, she was intolerant of mistakes made by others.

All the members of this group were in a 'tea club'. Because the unit was located at quite a distance from the company canteen, they had bought their own tea and coffee making facilities. Each of them paid in a small sum of money at the end of the month and this was kept in an old biscuit tin in the locker of the person whose unofficial job it was to look after it. The job usually fell to the most junior member of staff. In this case it was Sanjay, who had taken over the role from a colleague, Phyllis, only a couple of months before. One morning Sanjay noticed that they needed some more coffee, so he planned to get it on his way home that evening. There was plenty of cash in the tin because members had only just paid in their monthly contribution. That evening, as he was about to leave work Sanjay went to the tin to get cash for the coffee. He found it almost empty. As he was looking through the tin to see what money was left, Louise came in and asked him what he was doing. He told her and said someone must have taken the money. She was very angry and told him he should be more careful about keeping the tin locked away. Sanjay was upset at this and said someone had probably borrowed the cash and he would soon have it back. Louise, however, was not pacified. She told him that stealing was classed as gross misconduct and meant immediate dismissal. She would get to the bottom of the matter herself. Sanjay was very worried that he had got one of his colleagues sacked. That night he got an anxious phone call from a colleague, Phyllis, who told him she took the cash as her mother had been rushed to hospital that afternoon and she urgently needed to get a taxi to go and see her. She had discovered that she had no money on her and couldn't easily get to a cash point so she borrowed money from the tea club. She couldn't let Sanjay know because she couldn't contact his mobile and didn't know where he was. She would put it back the next day.

The following day Phyllis returned the money and Sanjay told Louise what had happened and why, and that Phyllis had now returned the money. So everything was sorted out. Louise, however, immediately called in Phyllis and told her she was taking disciplinary action for gross misconduct, and that Phyllis was likely to be dismissed. Phyllis was devastated. The rest of the group were sympathetic and angry that Louise was taking such a narrow view of the situation. They immediately contacted their union representative.

Your Task

Louise seems to be acting like a rule-bound manager. What kind of a leader is she? How might another kind of leader have handled the situation? How do the various leadership theories help us to understand this situation?

GLOSSARY OF TERMS

Contingency The context in which management activity and other organisational behaviours take place.

Continuum A linear concept which links a phenomenon with its opposite, with gradation from one to the other in between.

Laissez-faire A style of leadership where staff have a very high degree of autonomy; some see this as almost an abandonment of managerial responsibility.

Trait An innate or learned characteristic

Transactions The interactions between people; in terms of leadership, we refer to the interaction between leader and follower.

Transformation In leadership studies, we use this term to describe the process of personal change and growth through leadership.

KEY POINTS

- Leadership differs from management in certain important features: leadership engages with the emotions and values of those who are led. It influences followers by making them *want* to follow rather than through the typical power plays of authority.

- Early theories on leadership focused on *traits*; that is, on the personal characteristics of the leader, whether learned or inherited.

- Later theories looked at the skills and behaviours that leaders exhibited and whether these could be learned.

- More recent theories have examined the *context* or *contingencies* of the leadership situation and attempted to identify what leadership characteristics are needed in different contexts.

- McGregor suggested that it is important to focus on the assumptions that managers make about people at work. His Theory X and Theory Y model opposed two sets of assumptions which would lead to two very different leadership approaches.

- Linked closely to the notion of managing change, *transformational leadership* is a process which enables followers to experience radical change

REVISION QUESTIONS

- In your experience, who can you identify as having provided leadership to you personally? Which of the leadership theories you have looked at comes closest to helping you understand the leadership qualities of this person?
- When Burns makes the distinction between *transactional* and *transformational* leadership, is he talking about anything more than a distinction between management and leadership? Why have you reached that conclusion?
- To what extent does the economic climate and the culture of an organisation influence the leadership approaches adopted in that organisation?

GOING FURTHER

Leadership in business and other work organisations has been an important topic for many years and it is still an important area of study for both researchers and practitioners. Consequently, even a brief online search will turn up innumerable resources on the subject. We can see that more recent work has concentrated on transformational leadership and the interactions between leaders and their followers.

For an informed and readable article on modern leadership, look at Bill Miles work, downloadable at: http://works.bepress.com/cgi/viewcontent.cgi?article=1001&context=bill_miles.

A similar evaluative article, focusing on German organisations (for a change) can be downloaded at http://www.bertelsmann-stiftung.de/cps/rde/xbcr/SID-0D7A7B67-75DF353E/bst_engl/xcms_bst_dms_34409_34410_2.pdf.

In the 'how to' category on leadership, there are lots of books by well known entrepreneurs and business leaders, but an interesting one comes from a US navy officer: David Marquet, 2013, *Turn the Ship Around!: A True Story of Turning Followers into Leader*, New York, Portfolio.

NOTES

1. See Chapter 7.

2. Northouse, G., 2007, *Leadership Theory and Practice (Third Edition)*, Thousand Oaks, Sage Publications.

3. Stogdill, R. M., 1984, 'Personal Factors Associated with Leadership: A Survey of the Literature', *Journal of Psychology*, vol. 25, p. 64.

4. Accessible online at http://sbuweb.tcu.edu/jmathis/Org_Mgmt_Materials/Leadership%20-%20Do%20Traits%20Matgter.pdf, accessed 19 February 2013.

5. Mullins, Laurie J., 2006, *Essentials of Organisational Behaviour*, Harlow and New York, FT Prentice Hall, p. 314.

6. Likert, R., 1961, *New Patterns of Management*, New York, McGraw-Hill, p. 233–234.

7. Douglas MacGregor, 2006, *The Human Side of Enterprise, Annotated Edition*, New York, McGraw-Hill.

8. Accessible online at http://www3.uma.pt/filipejmsousa/ge/Nonaka,%201991.pdf, accessed 27 March 2013. This article looks at how Japanese companies have approached innovation.

9. TQM is a system of building quality into the manufacturing process. Teams of workers on the production line take responsibility not only for the quality of the product, but also for continuous improvement.

10. Just in Time (JIT) manufacturing is a system where components in the production process are delivered to the production area as an when they are needed. This avoids keeping expensive stocks of components.

11. Blake, R. Mouton, J., 1985, *The Managerial Grid III: The Key to Leadership Excellence*, Houston, Gulf Publishing Co. The grid was further refined in McKee, R.; Carlson, B., 1999, *The Power to Change*, Austin, TX, Grid International Inc.

12. Tannenbaum, R., Schmidt, W., 1973, 'How to Choose a Leadership Pattern', *Harvard Business Review*, May/June, pp. 3–12.

13. The word 'situation' is often used interchangeably with 'contingency' or 'context'. All refer to the fact that leadership (or any other management activity) has to happen in a given set of circumstances which will vary and so call upon different behaviours.

14. Fiedler, F. E., 1967, *A Theory of Leadership Effectiveness*, New York, McGraw-Hill.

15. A version is accessible online at http://www.sagepub.com/northouse 6e/study/materials/Questionnaires/03409_06lq.pdf

16. A construct is usually shown as a continuum between two opposite concepts. The continuum is seen as a scale on which you can score a person's tendency to act nearer to one of the opposite than to the other, as in the example here, the construct of 'Friendliness':

    Friendly 8 7 6 5 4 3 2 1 Unfriendly.

17. If you want to have a go at taking the LPC you can access it at http://www.practical-management.com/Analytics/Fiedler-LPC.html, accessed 2 April 2013

18. See Chapter 9 for more detail on position power as well as other sources of power in organisations.

19. See, for example, a relatively early critique: Terence R. Mitchell, Anthony Biglan, Gerald R. Oncken and Fred E. Fiedler, 1970, 'The Contingency Model: Criticism and Suggestions', *The Academy of Management Journal*, vol. 13, no. 3, pp. 253–267.

20. Vroom, Victor H., Jago, Arthur G., 1988, *The New Leadership: Managing Participation in Organizations*, Englewood Cliffs, NJ, Prentice-Hall.

21. See Chapter 4.

22. Hersey, P. and Blanchard, K. H., 1969, *Management of Organizational Behavior – Utilizing Human Resources*, New Jersey, Prentice Hall.

23. The Industrial Society began as a welfare society after the First World War. It developed its activities into research, training and consultancy after the Second World War. In 2002 it changed its name to The Work Foundation and is now part of the University of Lancaster.

24. Burns, James M., 2010, *Leadership*, New York, HarperPerennial

25. Weber, Maximillan, 1947, *Theory of Social and Economic Organization*, translated by A. R. Anderson and Talcott Parsons, New York, The Free Press. Originally published in 1922 in German under the title *Wirtschaft und Gesellschaft*, chapter III, § 10 (available online at https://archive.org/stream/wirtschaftundges00webeuoft#page/n5/mode/2up).

26. See for example Maslow's Hierarchy of Needs in Chapter 4. The higher level needs refer to the need for social satisfaction, the need to develop self-esteem and the need to self-actualise.

27. Cited in Rost, Joseph Clarence, 1993, *Leadership for the Twenty-first Century*, Greenwood Publishing group, pp. 95–127.

28. Compare Burns' work with that of Bass in Bass, B. M., 1990, 'From Transactional to Transformational Leadership: Learning to Share the Vision', *Organizational Dynamics*, (Winter), pp. 19–31.

7

STRUCTURING THE ORGANISATION

INTRODUCTION

When we want to understand the key relationships and functions of an organisation, we study its structure. Structure serves a number of purposes:

- It shows the authority relationships in the organisation.

- It shows how resources are allocated across the organisation.

- It highlights the key functions and the supporting functions.

- It provides a formal communication system.

• It sets out group and individual responsibilities.

• It can give clear guidelines on career progression.

Typically, the structure of an organisation is shown in an organisation chart, or organogram. This is a way of showing graphically the important features of the structure, such as the functions of different parts of the organisations, their relationship to each other, responsibilities and accountabilities.

However, not all organisation structures are there by design. In small organisations particularly, the structure may emerge over time in response to changing circumstances. A one-person business requires little structure, as long as the person running the business is able to organise their time around the important activities they need to carry out. If that business expands, then the new people may be allocated certain areas of the work to be responsible for. When this happens, we are seeing the beginning of an emergent structure. The more people a business takes on or the more it expands its activities, the more apparent the structure becomes. However, there comes a time when the emergent properties of the organisation may no longer suit the activities of the business. At this point, management is likely to attempt to design a structure from the top down.

ORGANIC VS. MECHANISTIC STRUCTURES

Burns and Stalker,[1] in developing their ideas on contingency, recognised this process and classified organisational structures as either *organic* or *mechanistic*. In doing so they were using two metaphorical opposites: the metaphor of the organism, which adapts when faced with new situations, and the machine, which is designed to behave consistently and efficiently no matter what the circumstances.

We can summarise the main difference between organic and mechanistic structures by comparing them along key dimensions as shown in Table 7.1.

As laid out in the table, these types of organisation appear to be polar opposites. Organic organisations tend to have emergent structures, while mechanistic organisations tend to be designed. However, we will rarely find organisations which are at the extremes of organic or mechanistic.

Table 7.1 Organic vs. mechanistic structures

Dimension	Organic	Mechanistic
Environment	Unstable and dynamic. Organisation frequently faced with new challenges which cannot be solved by traditional responses	Stable and predictable. Problems usually routine and can be solved by following standard procedures
Formalisation of procedures and work processes	High levels of multi-functional working. Adaptable, non-specialised workforce.	High levels of specialisation and standardisation. Organised mainly by function.
Communication	Information travels vertically and horizontally. Open communication, both verbal and written.	Mainly vertical, within functions. Strict protocols for communicating across functions. Emphasis on written documentation.
Centralisation	Highly decentralised. Strategy and policy decided at the top, managers and other staff trusted to make decisions to further strategic goals.	Centralised decision making, including standardisation of operational tasks.
Scalar chain	Few levels of hierarchy.	Many levels of hierarchy.
Span of control	Wide. Many day to day management activities delegated to operational level.	Narrow. High levels of supervision.

As with many human systems, the reality is more complex. A highly mecha-nistic organisation will find it difficult to achieve the integration it needs to operate effectively without there being good relations between people who work in different functions. Consequently, we see the development of the *informal organisation*.[2] This is where relationships develop between people who often find ways of circumventing rigid hierarchical rules to make work-ing simpler. Favours get done and trust develops. Where structures are more organic and cross functional working and communication is encouraged, informal aspects of working will already exist.

Whether structure emerges or is designed, it must concern itself with certain key elements. These are the drivers of structure. Every type of organisation has functions that it must carry out. Any commercial organisation, even if it only consists of one person, has to carry out the operations it was set up for. It has costs which it has to account for and revenue that it has to take in. It needs to make sure that, to be viable, revenue exceeds costs. Therefore there has to be a means of financial control, however simple. If staff are employed, there has to be a way of finding the right people and employing them productively. Even the smallest businesses may need to advertise. These basic, necessary functions are the drivers of structure. The bigger and more complex the organisation, the more drivers of structure there are likely to be.

Clearly, structure is needed when running the organisation is too big a job for one person. Sharing the tasks with other people requires there to be agreed areas of responsibility. This differentiation of tasks has to increase as more people operate in the organisation, or as the activities of the organisation expand. At its most basic, then, structure is a response, first to the need to ensure basic functions are carried out, and second, to increasing workload and expanding activities.

THE HIERARCHICAL STRUCTURE

In Western societies, we are probably most familiar with the hierarchical structure, though that has a wide range of variation. A hierarchy is a series of levels of authority and task. It is broadly in the shape of a pyramid, since there are more people at the operational (lower) levels than at the top, where there are very few. The hierarchical structure has to incorporate several key features:

- Ownership (or the main controlling body in the case of public sector or not for profit organisations).
- Top management, often in the form of a CEO and board of directors.
- Various levels of management responsible for the implementation of policy and day-to-day operations and functions.
- The operational level.

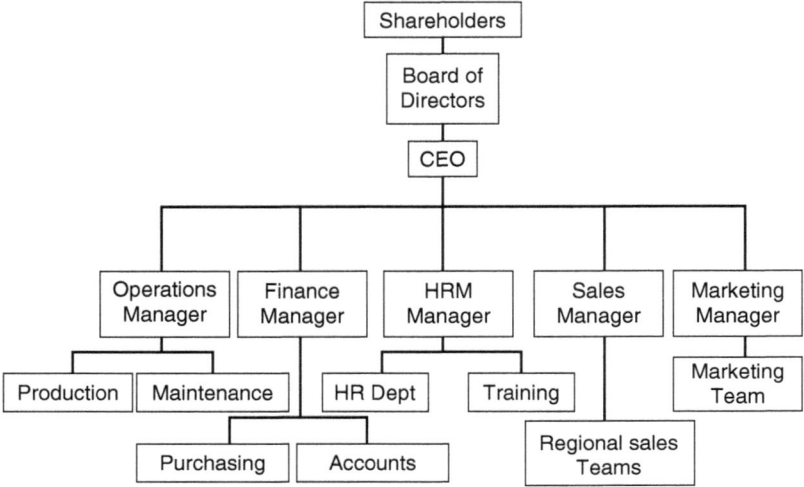

Figure 7.1 Simplified hierarchical structure

A hierarchical organisation is one in which staff at each level have progressively more authority and, usually, more responsibility as they progress up the hierarchy. There is a *line of command* (sometimes called a *chain of command*) which runs from the top of the hierarchy to every individual in it. We can see three key relationships in hierarchies:

- **Line relationships:** This is the relationship between a senior and a subordinate who reports directly to them. A line manager allocates work, evaluates performance, and is entitled to exercise authority and discipline over direct subordinates and others further down the same line of command.

- **Functional relationships:** These describe the relationship between a particular function, such as training and development or HRM, and other functions in the hierarchy. There is no line relationship between a training manager, for example, and the staff of another function, even though the trainers have a responsibility to ensure that everyone is trained to do their job effectively.

- **Staff relationships:** Many organisations have a small pool of staff who provide assistance and services directly to senior managers. They often carry out special projects, or need information from other parts of the organisation. Again, they have no line responsibility over staff in other functions, although being the assistant to the CEO is likely to carry a significant degree of influence!

The individual at the top of a hierarchy is responsible for all the operations of the organisation and is accountable – that is they have to answer for the success or failure of the whole operation – to a board of directors, or to the owners of the business. Normally in a hierarchy, your pay rises as you progress through the various levels and take on more responsibility.

TYPES OF HIERARCHICAL ORGANISATION

The notion of a hierarchy goes hand in hand with our concept of a bureaucracy.[3] It is an example of a 'rational-legal'[4] organisation. As we discussed in a previous chapter, Weber believed that a bureaucracy was a fair and rational way to organise people. Everyone knows what their job is, whom they report to and how decisions are made, at least in principle.

Any hierarchical structure needs to strike the right balance between differentiation (separating tasks so that they can be carried out more efficiently) and integration (ensuring that all parts of the structure contribute to the overall goals of the organisation). The example in Figure 7.1 shows a hierarchy differentiated by function. This is probably the most basic form of hierarchy, but it is by no means the only one. A hierarchical organisation can be structured according to:

- Function,
- Product,
- Client group or
- Geographical location.

We often describe hierarchies as *tall* or *flat*. A tall hierarchy is one that has many levels within it, whereas a flat hierarchy is one where levels have been removed, so there are not many levels between the staff at the lowest level of the hierarchy and the person at the top. When we discuss levels in a hierarchy, we refer to its *scalar chain*. This simply means the number of separate levels of seniority in a hierarchy.

DIFFERENTIATION BY FUNCTION

Although there are fundamental functions that all organisations will share (operational purpose, control of finance, organisation of staffing) there will also be others, depending on what the organisation actually does, its size and the industry sector it operates in, for example. There will be a correlation between the range of activities the organisation carries out and the complexity of the structure. As organisations grow, it is common to begin the differentiation process by organising according to function. Consequently, we will find a departmental structure, with each department working on one function. So you will find, for example, a finance department, an operations department, marketing, HRM, research and development and other functions appropriate to the needs of the organisation.

Each of these departments will usually be structured as mini-hierarchies, with a manager at the top and managers at other, lower levels, in charge of further differentiated activities.

DIFFERENTIATION BY PRODUCT

Organisations which produce more than one product or service will often find it more efficient to structure themselves by product or service. This enables the organisation to appoint staff who specialise in their various outputs. Automotive manufacturers will often differentiate by vehicle type, for example. So, you may well find a truck division, a commercial van division, a car division and so on. Each product group will have a different customer base, potentially different production processes, different distribution and marketing needs from the other divisions, so it makes sense to organise production accordingly.

DIFFERENTIATION BY CLIENT GROUP

Where customers or clients have very different needs, then we often find organisations structured specifically according to those needs. We frequently find this approach to structure in public sector organisation. So if you have a social services department in a local authority, it will usually be structured so that one section deals with children's needs, another with the needs of older people, yet another with disabled adults, and yet others dealing with other client groups.

Such a differentiation often comes about because the training and expertise required to carry out these services are themselves very specialised, and are difficult to transfer to other client groups, so there can be little crossover between activities.

DIFFERENTIATION BY GEOGRAPHICAL LOCATION

Many organisations are by chance or necessity located in different places. The organisation may be a group of shops, for example, or organisations which have merged may well find that the new organisation now has plant in different locations. With increasing globalisation of trade, we often find that even similar products may have very different marketing requirements and production processes in different parts of the world. Consequently, it may make sense to organise according to local conditions.

As well as the expected differences we may find that when organisations find themselves in different countries they have to pay attention to the legal and political frameworks under which organisations have to operate. We find in some countries it is not possible to operate without finding local partners. This may require a very different structure to the one preferred in the 'home' country.

CENTRALISATION VS. DECENTRALISATION

Since structure is intended to make an organisation as effective and efficient as possible, one of the key decisions in creating or developing an organisation's design is how centralised or decentralised it should be. A highly centralised organisation will have all its decision making carried out by senior staff at the top of the hierarchy. This will include the strategic direction of the organisation, operational policies such as budget allocation, staffing levels, management of human resources and control of sales. It will make decisions as to financial incentives and pay structures which will apply across the whole organisation. No key decisions will be left to local managers. Their role is to implement centrally ordered policies and procedures.

At the other extreme is the highly decentralised organisation, in which many key decisions are left to local managers. The centre decides overarching policy and strategy and trusts local managers to implement it using their discretion and knowledge of local conditions. Such a decentralised structure may well exist in chains of shops, for example. What sells well in one region may not be very popular in another. Pay levels may vary through a country and a strictly enforced level of pay would not attract good staff in one area, whilst in another it would be regarded as a good salary. Recently in the UK, some national supermarket chains have given local managers discretion in sourcing some locally produced foods, rather than buying centrally (and more cheaply) in bulk.

THE FLATTENED HIERARCHY

In recent years managers and researchers have criticised the hierarchical structure on several counts:

- It can become too rule-bound. That is, when there is a problem, the typical bureaucratic way to solve it is to modify current regulations or develop new ones. This approach is known as 'boxing the problem', since what often happens is a new committee or section is set up and appears as a box in the revised organisation chart. This approach results in a proliferation of rules which staff find difficult to keep abreast of. Moreover, individuals are discouraged from taking the initiative in solving new problems without having their actions legitimised by the organisation.

In 1987 there was a fire at Kings Cross underground station in London. Thirty-one people lost their lives. The problem was that there were no clear rules about what to do in the event of fire – or even what constituted a fire. This is in spite of London Underground issuing every member of its staff with a rulebook.

Part of the problem lay in the proliferation of rules to the extent that no operational staff could understand the totality of them. Every staff member was given an A5 size rule book on joining the organisation, along with 13 appendices. They had to sign for these documents and by signing were deemed to have read and understood them.

Every week a bulletin came out with details of operational matters for the forthcoming week. It was also the vehicle for communicating changes to the rules and appendices. Staff were expected to cut and paste (literally – hardly anyone used a computer back then!) these changes into their copy of the rule book and appendices. Add to this that the regulations were written in 'officialese', a quasi-legal style of writing difficult to understand, and that many staff did not have a high enough level of education or command of the English language to grasp the meaning easily, and we can see that the confusion ensuing from the fire is not so surprising.

The safe and efficient working of a railway system demands a detailed system of rules. However, if rules are not understood and staff are not trained in applying them, there is little value in them.

The communication channels in hierarchies tend to run vertically, that is, from managers to subordinates and back within the same department. There is often little lateral communication between staff in different departments at the same level of the organisation. This can be a problem when it is necessary for people to work across functions. We refer to people in this situation as 'working in silos'. Each department can give the impression of being sealed off from other parts of the organisation.

- Hierarchies respond slowly to change. It is in the nature of a hierarchy to discuss and evaluate potential changes at various levels before arriving at a decision. This can take time; it has to be done according to laid down procedure. When the organisational environment becomes less stable, it results in rapid change. The hierarchical structure tends to respond poorly to speedy change.
- Human systems are complex and it is not possible to regulate absolutely everything without the regulatory system becoming untenable (as we saw in the London Underground scenario). People need to be able to respond appropriately to new challenges. In a rule-governed hierarchy this may be difficult.

One of the responses to the rigidity of the hierarchy was to 'flatten' organisations. This meant that you reduced the number of levels in the scalar chain. As well as trying to make hierarchies more responsive to change, there were also other drivers to this move.

The development of computerised Management Information Systems (MIS) was important in allowing organisations to flatten. The storage of key information about all aspects of the organisation enabled people who needed that information to obtain it quickly and accurately. Before the advent of MIS information had passed down the chain of command, with the danger of it being interpreted and glossed at each level it passed through. Consequently there was a danger that the information received by staff who needed to make use of it was not the same as the information that was originally transmitted. The interpretation and glossing of information is not necessarily carried out deliberately or with any intention to change its meaning (although that can happen), it just seems to be a property of information that passes through several hands before it reaches its destination. The message that leaves the desk of person A and passes over the desks of persons B, C and D is not the same message that reaches the person at desk E.

Another driver was the goal of encouraging teamwork in organisations. Division of labour under Scientific Management meant that each individual worker was responsible for one job. The bureaucratic model was, in a sense, the Scientific Management version of administration. Each staff member had a job specification which described the job, the outputs required and the reporting process. Working outside of the job description was frowned upon by both workers and management.

However, the successful rise of the Japanese economy in the 1960s and 70s came as a serious challenge to Western managers, who saw that Japanese companies produced things on time, on budget and of very high quality. When Western researchers and managers went to see how the Japanese achieved this, they were struck by the commitment of Japanese workers to their companies and their products. The Westerners put this down to an ethos of teamwork in Japanese companies, which encouraged problem solving and quality assurance at the operational level. Consequently, Western managers believed that the way to bring about an improvement in productivity in their own companies was to develop a team-based approach in their organisations.[5] This, it was believed, would develop motivation and commitment to the organisation and deliver higher productivity. In a sense it was a victory for a human relations approach over a classical rational approach to management.

Such an initiative led to changes that many managers brought up in hierarchical organisations found difficult to commit to. In effect, it meant a new approach to management:

- The shorter scalar chain meant that managers had more staff reporting directly to them. The technical term for this is *span of control*, which means the number of staff who report directly to an individual manager. Where previously there had been levels of management and supervision involving smaller spans of control, now some of these had been removed. The consequence of this was that because managers had more staff to manage, close supervision of staff was no longer possible. Consequently, managers found they had to delegate more of their authority and decision-making further down the line of command.

- Staff who previously had had little input into decision making and problem solving now found that this was part of their day-to-day work.

- Because operational problems could no longer be passed up the line of command for a solution, workers had to rely more on each other. So it was important that individuals learned to work in teams.

- Because job specifications now contained skill and task variety that had not previously been the case, HR departments needed to recruit staff with different capabilities. They also had to support existing staff through training and development so that they could carry out their changed roles.

- Greater decentralisation became necessary because of the delegation of management tasks to the work group.

THE MATRIX ORGANISATION

However, a flattened hierarchy is nonetheless still a hierarchy. In spite of the changes to approach needed when stripping out levels of the organisation and developing staff into teams, many organisations still found it difficult to develop teams whose members came from different functions of the organisation. Particularly in complex long-term project-based industries where there were high levels of investment and where it was critical to compete effectively to safeguard the investment, organisations needed to come up with a different structural approach.

One of the earliest organisations to develop the matrix solution was the National Aeronautics and Space Administration (NASA) in the USA. Because of the complexity of the projects it was developing, and because they were all safety critical, it was important that teams from a range of disciplines and functions were able to work effectively together.

A matrix is essentially a grid. When we discuss organisational matrixes we see a combination of vertical, functional structure with a lateral, project team structure. This means that staff are still members of a functional line management system but are 'loaned out' to one or more projects so that they can contribute their functional knowledge and expertise.

University courses are often run on a matrix. Academic staff are members of a functional department, usually containing staff who are specialists in the same subject areas. They have to work alongside staff from other functional areas to deliver teaching programmes. So a matrix of academic business programmes might be shown in a figure such as in Figure 7.2.

Pro gramme	HR	Strategy	Marketing	Finance	Operations management	Organisational behaviour
Degree Level 1	X		X	X		X
Degree Level 2	X	X	X	X	X	
Degree Level 3		X		X	X	X
MBA Level 1	X			X	X	X
MBA Level 2	X	X	X	X	X	
MBA Level 3	X	X	X	X	X	

Figure 7.2 A matrix of academic business programmes

The 'X' in a box indicates that that function needs to carried out at that time. The key to a matrix is its flexibility. Projects need to be able to draw on functional expertise as and when it is needed. It also requires a grasp of complex organisation, since allocating staff time across different projects can place stresses on a functional department.

The advantages of a matrix are:

- It enables staff from different functional areas to work together outside of the functional structure without having to continuously refer to the functional line manager.
- It allows individuals to develop their skills and knowledge and to contribute to a larger project.
- It improves the speed and accuracy of inter-functional communication.
- It can be more cost effective by deploying resources more efficiently.

However, there are also some potential disadvantages:

- Fayol's principle of Unity of Command is broken because an individual reports to both a functional line manager in the normal way, but also to one or more project leaders. This can lead to friction between functional managers and project leaders, leaving the staff member uncertain as to their responsibilities.

• Sometimes the matrix structure will coexist with the traditional functional structure. This can cause tensions with divided loyalties.

• Staff accustomed to a traditional structure may find the relative uncertainties of working in a matrix difficult.

The matrix has been adopted by many large organisations. It seems to have the advantage of being based within a traditional functional structure which people understand, but the capability of being flexible enough to cope with a variety of organisational challenges where staff needs to work across functions.

CORE-PERIPHERY STRUCTURES

In the late 1980s and the 1990s many organisations, both public and private, faced difficult economic conditions. For the first time since the 1930s workers in the UK faced large scale unemployment as the manufacturing base of the economy contracted. The keyword for managers became *flexibility*. As we have discussed, the hierarchical organisation struggled with flexibility. The matrix had been a partial solution, but was not applicable to all organisations.

In 1982 Peters and Waterman published *In Search of Excellence*. This is still the most widely read of any business book and was very influential in developing management thinking, though it is not without its critics.[6] Peters and Waterman evaluated the performance of 43 major global corporations that they categorised as excellent. From the data they got from this investigation, they developed eight principles which an organisation wishing to become or remain excellent needed to embrace.[7] The two that concern structure are 'Stick to the knitting'; and 'Simple form, lean staff'. The first was interpreted as encouraging firms to focus heavily on the core purpose of their organisations, contracting out as many other activities as possible. This means that activities such as recruitment, IT services and several others, depending on the organisation's needs, could be run on a contractual basis by outside suppliers. The second largely follows from the first: if you are not having to expend resources on non-central activities, you can slim down the structure of the organisation and with it your manpower needs.

Most organisations have always had contracts with external suppliers for many things, but, partly as a consequence of Peters' and Waterman's book and partly as a response to the spirit of the times, many more organisations began to outsource more and more services. In the UK local authorities were required by law to put many of their traditionally in-house services out to competitive tender. Often their own service providers were turned into autonomous profit centres or even privatised so that the expertise, which had been built up over years, could still be available to the local authority.

This model came to be referred to as the 'Core-Periphery' model. The core of the organisation is a relatively permanent entity, offering long-term, permanent employment to staff involved in the delivery of the goods and services the organisation was set up to run. The periphery element of the model contains several kinds of organisation and individual supplier who were taken on to fulfil specific contractual purposes.

The key to understanding this model is the term *flexibility*. We can identify three types of flexibility that the core-periphery model can address:

1. **Functional flexibility:** This refers to the ability, especially of core workers, to undertake a range of work activities. It goes beyond the traditional view of 'one person – one job' to developing staff to be able to work across functions. It means that staff can be reliably allocated different responsibilities as they are needed.

2. **Numerical flexibility:** Numerical flexibility occurs when an organisation is able to increase or reduce the number of people working for it. You may, for example, need more staff at busy times, fewer at slack times. The core-periphery model allows this to happen by:

   • Employing staff as casual workers on short-term or zero hours contracts;

   • Contract staff can be taken on for specific one-off or occasional purposes such as maintenance, IT installation or similar needs;

   • Consultants or other experts can be contracted in similar ways for areas of expertise that the organisation does not possess itself and which would be too expensive to keep in-house;

- Many businesses such as coffee houses and restaurants make use of part-time staff with only one or two permanent staff.

3. **Pay flexibility:** Probably the main driver of the core-periphery model has been its perceived cost effectiveness. If you don't have to pay staff when the organisation is not busy, or you are able to negotiate pay rates with companies supplying temporary workers below those you would be paying permanent staff, and if you can avoid on costs such as pension contributions, sick pay and holiday pay, then using peripheral workers is a good deal for management.

Figure 7.3 shows the main features of the core-periphery model:

Figure 7.3 The main features of core-periphery model

The core organisation contains staff who are permanent employees, who are key to delivering the main outputs of the organisation and who give management functional flexibility.

The periphery consists of a range of different possibilities:

- **Outsourcing companies:** these are companies which carry out a whole range of functions for the organisation, such as payroll. Some outsourcing companies, like Experian and Capita, are now much larger than many of the organisations to which they supply their services. Outsourcing allows organisations to slim down many of their support activities and focus on their main priorities.
- **Sub-contracting companies:** These differ from outsourcing companies in that they usually work at the operational sites of the organisation to which they are contracted. They carry out such work as safety and security, plant maintenance, cleaning and consultancy services of various kinds.
- **Self-employed sub-contractors:** These are usually one-person, or very small, businesses which carry out similar tasks to the larger sub-contracting companies. They may at times even be contracted by the sub-contracting company rather than by the organisation itself. Because of their size, they usually deal with small-scale operations.
- **Agency temporary staff:** Many organisations achieve their numerical flexibility by taking on staff supplied by employment agencies. These agencies may also act as recruiters for permanent staff. Where temporary staff are concerned, the supplying organisation deals with tax and other costs so that the employing organisation simply pays the agency a flat rate for the services of the temps.
- **Other peripheral workers:** As already mentioned, some businesses employ almost exclusively part-time staff. These staff are usually taken on directly by the employer for a certain number of hours per week. This arrangement is typical in catering businesses. Often the employees are students or others who can't commit to full time work but want to earn some money.

The degree to which the core-periphery model has been a success is disputed. Legge[8] identifies three major flaws with the theory:

1. 'Sloppiness in conceptual specification'. There is a lack of rigour in the qualitative and quantitative advantages proposed for the model
2. We cannot use the model as a description of what is going on in the workplace because it lacks empirical support.

3. The model serves a covert ideological agenda. That is, the benefits of such a model accrue principally to the owners and controllers of capital at the expense of wage levels and job security to labour.

However, for many organisations, especially in the public sector, it has been a prevalent model which continues to develop. For example, in the UK we see a growing trend to outsource health service activities, prison security, information technology and many other traditional public sector activities to the private sector.

THE NETWORK ORGANISATION

The importance of knowledge as a competitive asset has been recognised in recent years. The rapid development of technologies and the reach of globalisation has demanded a response from organisations that want to exploit new markets with new products. The key to this is the uncovering, sharing and application of knowledge found both within and outside of the organisation. However, the traditional, and even matrix and core-periphery models of organisations will find it difficult to find and harness this knowledge since these structures are premised on the production and delivery of goods and services already in existence. Innovation is typically restricted to research and development departments or consultancies.

The knowledge and 'know-how' possessed by people in an organisation at any level are often ignored or, worse, not even known about or discussed. However, the need to exploit new technologies and emerging markets demands new approaches to innovation, and new approaches to innovation inevitably lead to changes in the way organisations structure their activities.

We already understand how an informal structure co-exists with the formal structure, and the power of the informal relations in an organisation.[9] We now recognise that the informal organisation also contains untapped knowledge, which is frequently shared informally, but rarely surfaces in the formal structures. People who are experienced at their work often pass on their know-how informally in a work setting, without needing to set up specific training sessions. Others interest themselves in technology and new opportunities it presents. Often groups spontaneously arise to develop interests in a topic away from the organisation. Such interest groups can become highly knowledgeable and skilled.

The challenge facing organisations is how to use these informal groupings to develop new assets and products. Traditionally, we have seen capital, labour, enterprise and land as the main factors of production. We now need to add a fifth – knowledge. For example, a couple of decades ago someone had the simple idea of creating a grid on a computer into the cells of which could be put information. This information could be manipulated in various ways. Such an apparently simple idea developed into the hugely powerful and useful tool of the spreadsheet which we take for granted today. Similarly, we find commonplace the use of the World Wide Web and its various offshoots. Writing this book, for example, relied heavily on information and ideas accessed on the web. Previously, a writer would need to travel to a library, spend long periods searching through paper based indexes, jot all ideas down on paper and organise ideas using a card index – or in some cases, disorganised scraps of paper! Then they would return to base, formulate their notes into a coherent whole and write them up on a typewriter. Computer technologies, combined with access to the web make such activities unbelievably more productive.

All of these technologies are relatively new, and they needed inspired insights and a determination to develop and market them to bring them to the point where they have become indispensable. This is the challenge facing modern organisations.

Work done by Rob Cross and others has emphasised the need for a corresponding growth in informal networking in organisations which have restructured by delayering. He cites an example of this by comparing the organisation chart of a department in a petroleum company with the real world communication patterns in that department revealed by Organisation Network Analysis (ONA).[10]

What can be seen from a comparison of the formal structure chart and the analysis of the informal structure chart is that certain people act as 'hubs' of communication, whilst others are peripheral to the process. Moreover, those at the hubs are not the more senior staff, who tend to be more peripheral to the communication web. Such an analysis does not tell us whether the contribution of individuals at the hub or at the periphery is more or less

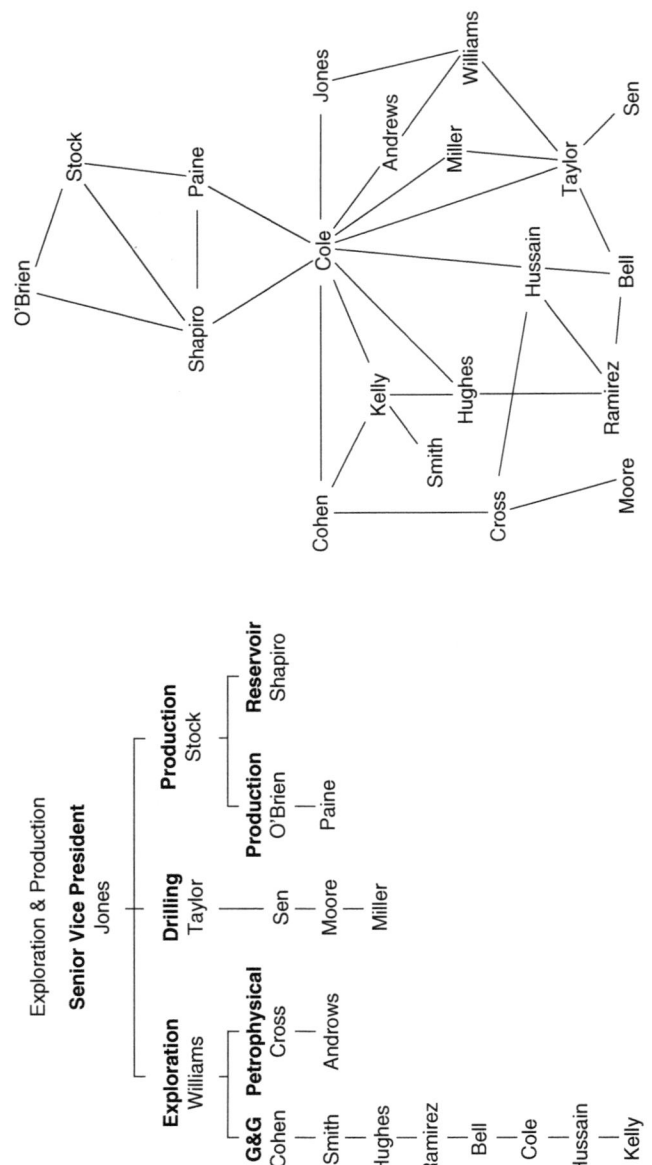

Figure 7.4 Comparison of a petroleum company's organisation chart with its real-world communication patterns. Adapted and reproduced with permission from Elsevier Publishing.

valuable, but it does show that managers need to be aware that, where spans of control are large, communications networks will emerge and if an organisation wants to optimise the working of these networks, managers have to be able to intervene positively and sensitively.

The network approach is particularly crucial in 'knowledge' organisations. These are organisations which depend on bringing the knowledge held by individuals within the organisation to the attention of others who can develop innovative products and services. Such organisations are often staffed by a range of people with high levels of experience or expertise, often possessing greater knowledge than the people who manage them. Consequently, there needs to be a level of professional trust between managers and the managed. Staff have to take responsibility for managing themselves and for acting with integrity in using the knowledge they have. Managers, for their part can ensure that there is a an appropriate reward system in place and that accountability for achieving goals is clear.

THE VIRTUAL ORGANISATION

As the name suggests, such an organisation can only come about because of the existence of a 'virtual' world. Technology has provided the means for organisations to network not only within their own boundaries but beyond them so that they can harness the capabilities of other individuals and organisations. There is a real sense in which the virtual organisation is an example of a core-periphery organisation taken to extremes.

A virtual organisation is one which uses internet technologies to form online alliances and collaborations with other, geographically dispersed, individuals, groups and organisations. Such an organisation can be very fluid, changing its alliances rapidly in response to market changes. Although we can argue that organisations have always done this with travelling salesmen, subcontracting and so on, modern technology means that we no longer have the barriers of time, travel, distance or availability of personnel to contend with.

Staff can be located anywhere in the world and can communicate with other elements of the network through synchronous (communicating with others when all are present) or asynchronous (when it is not possible to communicate with others present at the same time) technologies.

The advantages of virtuality are:

- **More expertise:** There is a much wider pool of expertise available.
- **Greater flexibility:** Changes can be made more rapidly by developing new collaborations. Staff can operate at times and in ways more convenient to them. Quality of life issues can be addressed more flexibly.
- **Cost reduction:** Outsourcing functions and having fewer buildings and other sites can reduce cost. An organisation can reduce its exposure to financial risk by outsourcing production and setting up franchises for sales.

However, there are also problems with such a structure, often brought on by the same features which give advantages:

- **Expertise:** Individuals or organisations which provide expertise can just as easily change partners as any one else in the network. This can make an organisation vulnerable unless they have comprehensive contracts enforceable in whatever jurisdiction is being used.
- **Flexible staff:** Flexibility does not always improve quality of life for staff. The social advantages of working with others are not fulfilled for staff whose contact with each other is restricted to online communication. Moreover, working in the virtual organisation is only as secure as the length of the contract, making it difficult for workers to make long-term plans.

Probably the best known virtual organisation is Amazon. Amazon uses collaborating organisations for warehousing and delivery and its payment system is automated.

Many organisations now have an online presence for many of their operations, though the degree to which any individual organisation is virtual in the sense discussed above has to be evaluated on a case by case basis.

CONCLUSION

As we can see, organisation structure can take many and varied forms, from the rigidly mechanistic to the almost chaotically organic. Structural forms are usually of their time. The mechanistic hierarchical structure reflects developments in scientific management. It was an attempt to be just, legitimate, transparent in its expectations of people and rational. However, human systems are complex and constantly resist attempts to classify and order behaviour in a one size fits all way. What the rational, mechanistic organisation omits is the psychological and social aspects of work, which are just as important as the economic contract at the heart of a work relationship. In other words, people don't just go to work to work.

The Hawthorne Studies made clear these other needs from work. Organisational structures were slow to follow, however, although many organisations instituted social and welfare policies. Organisations tend to be more responsive to economic and financial demands. When Western firms were challenged by the rise of the Japanese economy, they brought in many initiatives such as teamworking, quality circles, total quality management, employee involvement programmes and so on. Nevertheless, organisations remained hierarchical, and responses to the need for change tended to be bureaucratic. The matrix organisation is an attempt to find a means of keeping the functional differentiation of the hierarchy, whilst creating critical cross functional working.

The recessions of the 1980s and 90s forced organisations to delayer their hierarchical structures, leading to greater autonomy and decision making at the operational level because of the reduced scalar chain and increased spans of control. At the same time the trend towards focusing on the core operations of the organisation led to increased outsourcing and the evolution of the core–periphery model of structure.

The increasing availability of new technologies allowed even greater flexibility in organisations and in the 1990s and 2000s we see the emergence of organisations based around internal networks. Much of this development is driven by the need to leverage knowledge as an important asset in the organisation, and knowledge tends to be in the minds of individuals, so individuals need to be able to communicate and the organisation needs to be able to manage knowledge for competitive advantage.

Finally, in recent years the technological revolution has enabled the coming of the virtual organisation, a flexible, dynamic, boundaryless entity within which there are shifting patterns of collaborations and contractual relationships.

Of course, the structures described and discussed are 'pure' forms. How they are put into operation is different from one organisation to the next.

Indeed, many organisations are hybrids, with some functions being hierarchical, others forming a network and yet others making use of autonomous team working. In the virtual world, some are more virtual than others, with some operations carried out mainly online and others carried out in more traditional ways. Many retail organisations, for example, still have a chain of stores while also having a big online presence. The balance between the two operational forms is a matter of understanding the market and the importance of tradition versus innovation.

Cottswell Computing

Cottswell Computing is an IT consultancy company based in the town of Evesham in the centre of England. It was set up in 1995 and provides specialist IT services from software design through hardware installation and systems management. It serves a wide range of clients, primarily in the public sector and, up to now, based mainly in central and southern England.

Cottswell Computing currently employs around 300 staff. While the majority of these staff are employed on a permanent full-time basis, 35 staff (approximately 20 full-time equivalents) work part-time. Some of these are technical experts and some provide administrative support. In addition, at any one time between five and 15 specialists are contracted in on a short-term basis to provide specific skills.

The company currently operates on a predominantly project basis. Depending on the nature of the contract, a project team is usually set up for the life of the contract. These teams may be of only three or four people for a four-month installation contract, but can grow to 20 or 30 at some points for larger system design and maintenance programmes. An employee is likely to be working on two or three different projects at any one time. This matrix organisation has so far worked well; staff are respected for their unique contribution to their particular projects, formal hierarchy is kept to a minimum and the management operate a 'light touch', with project leaders taking responsibility for team functioning. However, there is a recognition that the company has outgrown this fully flexible model and the HR manager is in the process of reforming its employment policies and procedures, trying to balance the need for flexibility with the requirement for greater order and predictability demanded of a larger organisation.

Cottswell Computing is now facing a new challenge. Over the last 12 months, it has been running a project for the Bristol regional office of a government agency which has involved designing, installing and managing a new IT network for the southwest region. This project has been spectacularly successful. The initial specification and installation came in on time and under budget, and Cottswell Computing's subsequent support facilities have been very favourably received. It is held up as a model collaboration between a public agency and the private sector, a field where IT contracts have notoriously been unsuccessful and very expensive.

As a result of this project, the Environment Agency and Cottswell Computing have been in negotiations for Cottswell Computing to take over the management of the entire agency's IT systems, initially on a three-year contract, using the Bristol model as a template. This represents not just a huge expansion for Cottswell Computing, but also a major change of direction. For the first time, a large group of staff will be working permanently and on a full time basis for one client organisation. The project itself will form approximately one fifth of Cottswell's projected turnover for the next three years and will require initially an additional 20 staff, rising to 30 by year two, to operate the contract. The work for the government agency will require a lot of travel; as well as the six main regional offices (of which Bristol is one) agency staff are based all around the UK. Many of them work from home and appropriate technical support and training will need to be provided for these staff.

At the same time, Cottswell Computing will continue with its regular shorter and medium term contracts. Those staff not dedicated to the Environment Agency contract will continue to work flexibly on multiple projects.

A number of key managers have expressed concern that these developments should be handled sensitively in order to minimise disruption to the company at large as well as to maintain the productive dynamic that is the hallmark of Cottswell's culture.

Very few of the Cottswell managers have undertaken management training of any formal nature and management initiatives have been taken on a largely intuitive basis, which up to now have been successful. However, there is a perception that managers have to become more up to date in their knowledge of how organisations work and the management implications of the challenge facing them change.

Your company, Broadlands Consulting, has been commissioned to help remedy this situation.

Your Task

> Outline the salient factors of organisational structure as it applies to Cottswell, with recommendations as to how the company might initiate structure change in order to enhance company performance and help facilitate the expansion taking place.

GLOSSARY OF TERMS

Centralisation The degree to which important decisions are made at the centre of an organisation.

Differentiation The way in which work is divided up in an organisation

Hierarchy The levels of authority in an organisation.

Matrix Literally, a grid. This is a way of organising cross functionally.

Mechanistic structure A kind of structure which is dominated by rules and procedures, designed to be stable and predictable.

Network A relatively informal grouping of people brought together to complete a specific task.

Organic structure A kind of structure which allows for change and variability.

Organogram A graphical representation of the organisation's structure.

Scalar chain The number of levels in a hierarchy.

Span of control The number of people reporting to a manager.

Structure The way in which functions, tasks, accountabilities and responsibilities are allocated in an organisation.

Virtual organisation An organisation whose activities are carried out using web technologies.

KEY POINTS

- Structure, and the organisation chart which represents it, shows the different relationships in the organisation. The key ones are: line, functional and staff relationships.

- Most organisations have some form of hierarchy, even if it is very 'flat'. The hierarchy represents the levels of authority in the organisation. There are many different forms of hierarchical structures, depending on the key functions of the organisation.

- Organisations are human systems, which means they are complex. Consequently, it is very difficult to design a structure which will cope with the unpredictability of this complexity. To counter this, we see the emergence of informal groupings within the formal system.

- Organisations can be flexible in several ways: functional flexibility, numerical flexibility, pay flexibility. Each of these forms of flexibility challenges the rigid hierarchical structure.

- Matrix organisations are designed to short-circuit the rigid functional differentiation of traditional hierarchies by allocating staff from different functions to work collectively on operational tasks.

- The core-periphery structure is an approach to structure which encouraged companies to outsource all but their key functions (the 'core') to contractors of various sorts (the 'periphery').

- Network structures arise because of the need to uncover, disseminate and exploit new knowledge. Organisations have to look beyond the traditional hierarchy find ideas. So the idea of the network has arisen, in which informal relationships and emergent communication networks are encouraged.

- Virtual organisations are an extension of the organisational network approach. It is totally dependent on computer and web technology. In such a structure, it is often possible to cut back on buildings, staffing, transport and so on.

REVISION QUESTIONS

- Think about your college or a place where you have worked. Try to draw an organisation chart for it. How would you characterise the structure? Would any other structure be more effective?

- Would you agree that organic structures are more appropriate for modern organisations? What are your reasons?

- What in your view are the challenges facing managers of increasingly virtual organisations?

GOING FURTHER

Most recent work on structure tends to focus on organisational forms influenced by new technologies. An interesting discussion of the main issues can be found in:

- Malone, T. W., Laubacher, R. and Morton, M. S. S. (eds) (2003) *Inventing the Organizations of the 21st Century*, Cambridge, MA, Sloan School of Management.

- Burton, R. M. (2006) *Organization Design: The Evolving State-of-the-Art*, New York, Springer Science and Business Media.

- A very useful discussion on how traditional theories of structure stand up to modern challenges can be found in: Daft, R. L. (2009) *Organization Theory and Design 10th edition*, Mason, OH, Cengage Learning.

NOTES

1. Burns, T., and Stalker, G. M., 1961, *The Management of Innovation*, London: Tavistock.

2. See Chapter 1.

3. See Chapter 1.

4. According to Weber's classification of organisation types. The rational-legal type is to be preferred for its transparency of power relationships, clear work standards and meritocratic fairness.

5. Of course, there is arguably much more to it than this. Many western observers overlooked, or discounted, the role played by Japanese companies in providing things like healthcare for employees, support for education and other welfare facilities. But perhaps the most important feature of all was the 'job for life' that was guaranteed to any employee in return for their commitment to the company. Western employers weren't going to guarantee job security to their staff, but it is believed by many observers that the root of commitment to the Japanese company lay not in the fact of the organisation of work, but as a quid pro quo for job security.

6. See, for example, David Collins, 2000, *Management Fads and Buzzwords: Critical-Practical Perspectives*, New York, Routledge, Chapter 5.

7. Waterman Jr, Robert H. and Peters, Tom, 1982, *In Search Of Excellence: Lessons from America's Best-Run Companies*, New York, Harper and Row.

8. Legge, K., 1995, *Human Resource Management Rhetorics and Realities*, MacMillan Business.

9. *See the example of the* Bank Wiring Group in the Hawthorne Studies, discussed in Chapter 1.

10. Cross, Robert L. and Parker, Andrew, 2004, *The Hidden Power of Social Networks: Understanding How Work Really Gets Done in Organizations*, Boston, MA, Harvard Business Review Press.

8

CULTURE IN ORGANISATIONS

LEARNING OBJECTIVES

- Discuss what is meant by the term 'culture'
- Outline the main theories on organisational culture
- Critically discuss their applicability to the effectiveness of an organisation
- Examine approaches to the management of culture.

INTRODUCTION

The term 'culture' has two meanings. The first is the technical term used for the growing of organisms. So we have agriculture and horticulture and various other words which incorporate the term. In medical language a culture refers to growing organisms in laboratory conditions for research purposes. These meanings of the term all refer to the controlled growth of organic material.

The second usage is metaphorical. It is used at the societal level to indicate the shared set of values and behaviours in a given community. It incorporates the rituals of a society at important moments in the life and death of its members as well as its artistic, linguistic and literary forms and tastes. Its cultural values determine things like how that society is governed, the relationships between groups and individuals, what kind of education people receive and what constitutes acceptable behaviour. All human behaviour can be said to be influenced or determined by a society's culture.

Culture in this metaphorical sense is perhaps the archetypal complex human system in that it is made up of countless interactions, negotiations, decisions and challenges at the level of ordinary people over long periods of time. From all of these activities emerges a set of values, beliefs and behaviours to which we attach the term culture. The flavour of a society's culture can be inferred from observing its rituals and preoccupations, though it is unlikely that we can ever encapsulate with any certainty the totality of any one culture. Moreover, to add to the complexity, culture changes over time. Sometimes it changes very slowly; sometimes a major event, like a war or conquest or a huge natural disaster, forces a society to change rapidly to survive.

Culture is also variable within a society. We can often discern cultural differences between communities of the same society which are geographically dispersed. Different groups within a society, having a sense of their difference, will develop values and behaviours which are not the same as those of people outside the community. These differences show themselves in linguistic variations, differences in art or leisure activities and in many other ways. We refer to these varieties within a culture as sub-cultures. We also find groups within a culture who don't accept the norms and values of that culture and rebel against it, with their own cultural features emerging. In the 1960s, for instance, the hippy movement evolved as a rejection of the perceived materialism of the post-Second World War economic boom.

It is this second, societal, metaphor of culture that we generally use when discussing culture at the level of organisations. As with societies, so with organisations, the sheer complexity and lack of agreed criteria about what constitutes culture makes it difficult to describe. We have an intuitive sense that it is important. Some writers consider it the most important contributing factor to an organisation's success. We have seen in other chapters the emergent properties that organisations display when organisational design cannot deal with the inherent complexity of human systems. Moreover, organisations, especially large ones, will also see the presence of counter-cultures and sub-cultures. The National Health Service in the UK is a vast organisation, containing a wide range of jobs and professions. Often these professions will have a strong professional culture of their own. Managing such cultural diversity is never going to be easy.

Consequently, the big issue when we study organisation culture is: How do we develop and sustain a culture that will allow an organisation to flourish? Like leadership, culture engages with people's emotions and values, and these things are, by definition, not susceptible to planning, measurement or management in a technical-rational sense. Consequently, many managers are reluctant to engage with issues so difficult to understand, let alone to control.

There is, however a great deal written on the topic. There are both academic works trying to understand and describe the culture of organisations. There is also a great deal of published work which is designed to present managers with heuristic tools for managing and changing culture.

The notion of culture is now so embedded in the minds of both academic observers and of members of organisations that it is commonplace to hear the word attached to a key feature of an organisation or industry. We talk of bankers and other highly placed executives having a 'bonus culture'. Other people, we find, work in a 'blame culture' or a 'risk-averse culture'. You will find terms like this cropping up with great regularity once you become attuned to looking for them. Such terms suggest how embedded the notion of culture has become within our organisations. These terms usually refer to a single aspect of the organisation which is seen to represent one of its main features in some important way. However, we have to remember that, useful though these terms are as a shorthand for talking about one aspect of an organisation, the truth is usually much more complicated.

THE WORK OF EDGAR SCHEIN[1]

Schein is generally considered to be the main precursor of interest in the study of organisation culture. He referred to culture as an 'empirical abstract'. That is to say, we can clearly observe the elements of an organisation's culture, even though we may find it difficult to describe or measure it in its entirety.

We can envisage Schein's concept of culture as an inverted pyramid (Figure 8.1). The levels at the top are those aspects of culture which are

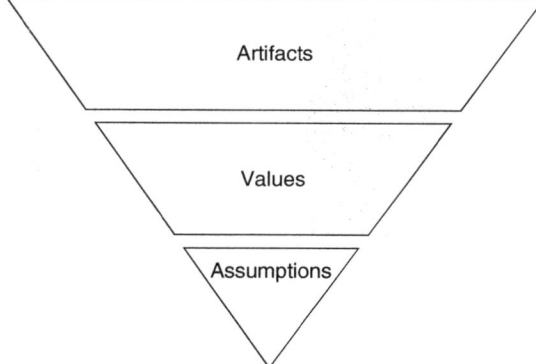

Figure 8.1 Schein's model of organisational culture

most apparent to the observer, with those lower in the pyramid being less easily observed.

ARTEFACTS

The most obvious indicators of an organisation's culture to the outside observer are what Schein calls 'artifacts'. This refers to the material objects we can see in an organisation: whether the building is open plan, how modern the furnishings are, the types of clothes people wear and so on. However, Schein uses the word not only to denote physical objects, but also the observable behaviours of the members of the organisation: the formality of speech among members, the relations between peers, as well as those between seniors and subordinates, the kind of jokes told by staff. In fact whatever someone from outside the organisation would notice can be categorised as an artefact.

VALUES

These are the values that the organisation lays claim to promote, the values it *espouses*. They may well be written out as a mission statement or be found in policy or training documents, or promoted within and outside of the organisation through publicity as being those values it wishes to be known by and against which it should be judged. Examples of such values are: having a customer focus as a priority, the professionalism of its staff, an open and trusting environment. There are, of course, countless other values an organisation may espouse, but they are only an accurate representation of an organisation's culture so long as they are honest. It is, after all, easy to make an untrue claim about the organisation to outsiders – customers, suppliers and the general public – but much more difficult to get members of the organisation to accept those values if they are not experienced by them as real on a day-to-day basis. So if, for example, the reward system incentivises rule adherence, but claims to value creative thinking, the mismatch is apparent and is likely to be resented.

The values element of organisational culture occupies a smaller segment of the model since, compared to artefacts and behaviour, it is a little more difficult to observe. Those outside and inside the organisation would want to see a consistency between the declarations of members of the organisation and its actions. You can't directly observe an organisation's values, you have to infer them from what you see and experience.

ASSUMPTIONS

The assumptions held about the organisation, its purpose and the way it carries out its activities is the least visible of the elements in Schein's model. Consequently, it occupies the smallest segment. There are two reasons for this:

- Assumptions are mainly tacit. That is to say, they are rarely articulated (and then only with difficulty) but remain part of the unspoken way of seeing the world which influences individuals and groups to act in a particular way. We saw a similar phenomenon in Chapter 2 when we discussed schemata. A schema is a set of assumptions which guide our actions. Groups will develop collective schemata over time through collective action, informal conversations and by sharing problems.

- Our assumptions are dynamic. That is, they are constantly developing as we interact with our environment. They will either be reinforced or challenged by day to day events. At the level of the organisation what we infer about its collective assumptions at any given time may be subtly different at a later date. Radical organisation change will often force a revision of long-held assumptions. We can see such a shift in assumptions as public services in the UK have gradually been privatised over the last three decades. The public service ethos has had to be replaced with a much more market oriented approach to the work. Focus is often on compliance with contractual obligations and cost reduction.

The Schein model is a useful way of getting us to look at organisational culture. It suggests a linearity leading from our basic assumptions, which in turn influence our value system, which in its turn influence our behaviour. The implication is that culture emerges from the causative interactions of these three elements. At its heart is the notion of corporate values. If members of the organisation buy into these we can suppose that the culture of the organisation will be supportive of the organisations goals and its means of achieving them.

THE FOUR CULTURAL TYPES OF DEAL AND KENNEDY

Deal and Kennedy[2] suggest that there are a number of influences which contribute to an organisation's culture:

- **Values and beliefs:** None of us goes into a job without a set of values and schemata with which we make judgements about everything around us including matters relating to the organisation and the work it does. Those with authority will also have beliefs and values which they will express in the way they manage the activities of the organisation. Over time we would expect to see an alignment between the value system of leaders and those of subordinates. The organisation will tend to recruit staff with complementary values, while beliefs about what an organisation is like will attract some people, but put others off.

- **Rituals:** These are the regular ceremonial activities we find within an organisation. They may involve the whole company, like the sending out of a company bulletin every week, or be highly local, like ways of celebrating someone's birthday, which might vary from one part of an organisation to another. Recent years have seen the emergence in the UK of rituals like 'dress-down Friday' where staff leave off their normal, traditional workwear and go to work in less formal clothes. Rituals serve to give people a sense of belonging and togetherness, provided always that the ritual is acceptable. Many trades and occupations have ritualised ceremonies for initiating people into the job. Most organisations will have some kind of induction process, which, although introducing staff to the formal aspects of the organisation, also provides clues about the organisation's values.

- **Heroes:** We like heroes. We use them in several ways: as figures of admiration whom we would like to emulate; as examples of sacrifice for something good; as super beings who rise above the mundane and achieve great things. Organisations, and the groups within them, promote their heroes for just the same reasons. Often the founders of the organisation will be promoted as heroic figures. Smaller groups will also have heroic memories of key figures in that group.

- **The informal cultural network:** As we have seen information passes around the organisation in informal ways, through channels and relationships that we don't see on the organisation chart. From this emerges the informal culture of the organisation. In this informal system, Deal and Kennedy identify key roles that disseminate the culture, interpret events in the context of the culture and reinforce the values of the culture. They classify these as:

  - **Storytellers:** These people interpret events and convert them into coherent stories that relate to and reinforce the culture of the group. This category also includes 'gossipers' who put their own spin on events. Generally, we tend not to take gossip too seriously, though it can be destructive of relationships.

  - **Whisperers:** These are people who can communicate directly and informally with those at the top of the organisation. It is a way of getting messages to the top, bypassing the formal communication process.

- **Spies:** Whether deliberately placed or self-appointed, we sometimes find that there are people in the organisation who provide informal information to senior managers about things which formal reports do not communicate. If the spies are reliable, then they provide a way of letting managers know what is really going on.

- **Priests:** These tend to be members of the organisation of long standing, who identify strongly with the organisation, and who consequently interpret events according to the organisation's values. They play an important part in reinforcing those values.

These cultural elements can be said to be in a reciprocal relationship to the organisation's culture; they are both its causes and its consequences.

However, Deal and Kennedy look beyond the indicators of culture. They suggest that the organisation's operating context is the key to a typology of cultures. Within the general context, they identify two important variables which determine a culture 'type' for an organisation. These variables are: the degree of risk inherent in the organisation's activities and the speed with which an organisation learns whether its activities have had their intended consequence or not. This leads to a four element matrix, each element of which has its own identifiable culture type.

1. **Low risk – slow feedback**: Deal and Kennedy characterise this as a 'Process culture'. Examples of this kind of culture are found in large retail chains, public planning departments or retail banking and similar organisations. These organisations make many decisions, which, individually, carry little risk to the organisation. Moreover, it can be a long time, in some cases years, before they know how successful their decisions have been. Such cultures focus on consistency and slow development of procedures. Employees will tend to concentrate on how things are done since it may be a long time before they find out how successful they have been.

2. **Low risk – fast feedback:** Typical of this culture type are sales driven environments. Staff know quickly how successful they have been, but no individual transaction carries too high a risk. Such a culture, the 'Work hard, play hard' culture in the words of Deal and Kennedy, demands

high levels of energy, lots of individual initiative, but also a supportive structure to enable people to function effectively.

3. **High risk – slow feedback:** You find this combination of features in organisations like aerospace, architecture and pharmaceuticals. There is large scale investment in products which will take a long time to get to the marketplace. It can be many years before an organisation finds out whether it has been successful. This is a 'Bet-the-company' type of culture since failure can ruin the organisation in the long term. Members make sure that they do as much detailed research as possible on both what they produce and on the potential market they are aiming the product at. Thinking tends to be long term, with a focus on high quality technical abilities.

4. **High risk – quick feedback:** Deal and Kennedy have characterised this type of culture as a 'Macho/Tough-guy culture'. It is to be found in industries such as sport and investment banking where individuals take high risks, but can also suffer rapid failure. Such a culture tends to foster the individual who is prepared to accept the possibility of failure to achieve high rewards. There is strong competition among members with acceptance that colleagues may quickly fall by the wayside.

As with all attempts to classify or describe culture, we may find that no single type represents our own organisation, or that we may see elements of several different cultures in the same organisation. The main lesson from Deal and Kennedy is that culture emerges from a context. And while we may be able to identify broad typologies of culture we need to remember that context is different, even in organisations in the same sectors. So culture will be specific to that organisation. The value of a broad brush approach is that it gives us a starting point from which to try to understand the main features of a culture so that it may be more effectively changed and managed.

THE CULTURAL WEB

Johnson and Scholes,[3] in their work on organisational strategy, describe the 'cultural web', in which we can see parallels with the work of Schein and echoes of the Deal and Kennedy model.

However, rather than modelling culture as an inverted pyramid, like Schein, they recognise greater complexity in culture by visualising it as a web. In this sense they are in the tradition of Deal and Kennedy. They see culture as a collection of phenomena which are interlinked and which influence each other. The overarching source for the characteristics of these phenomena is 'the paradigm'.[4] An organisation's paradigm is rather analogous to a schema in human individuals. It is a view of how the world ought to function that leads us to our values and beliefs about what is the right way to do things. Consequently, it powerfully influences the other phenomena that Johnson and Scholes identified. To the observer, these phenomena in turn give us an insight into the assumptions which underlie the paradigm. These phenomena, which are similar to Schein's 'artifacts', are both formal and informal aspects of the organisation. Control systems, organisational structures, symbols and power structures are mainly formal. They are put in place by the leaders of the organisation in order to solve particular problems and deliver predictable outcomes, such as the flow of authority, allocation of resources, who does what in the organisation, how activities are accounted for and so on. Rituals and stories tend to be (or have the appearance of being) more informal.

Johnson and Scholes developed the cultural web as an analytical tool, but one with a purpose beyond simple analysis. It is a way of seeking consensus about the culture of an organisation in order to facilitate organisational change.[5] Radical change in an organisation often depends on the ability to change the paradigm, which is difficult since the characteristics of a paradigm are largely unspoken assumptions. Consequently, it is important to capture and agree on the other features of the cultural web in order to understand and capture the nature of the paradigm. What then do we look for in analysing a cultural web?

- **Organisational structures:** These set out the formal relationships within the organisation. They tell us who does what, who is responsible for what and what their relationship is to other parts of the organisation. They tell us the degree to which the structure is centralised, formalised or bureaucratic, or whether the structure has grown mechanistically or organically.[6] However, as we have already seen, the formal organisation is usually complemented by an informal structure which grows out of individual relationships and tends sometimes to short-circuit the formal processes. It also has the effect of satisfying some of the emotional and psychological needs of staff members.

- **Control systems:** These are the procedures an organisation uses to understand how well or badly it is doing. The most important one for a commercial enterprise is controlling finance. Put simply, it needs to know that its costs are under control and its revenue sufficient to cover costs and deliver a surplus. Other control systems will relate to how efficient the operations of the organisation are. The control systems of an organisation are a useful indicator of various cultural aspects of the organisation; for example, does the organisation reward good work or apply sanctions to poor work? How important is quality? How is it ensured? We might also want to look at any informal control systems which exist within the formal system. For example, individual managers may well consider certain aspects of control more important than others. Some may be very rigorous about controlling costs, while others may be more interested in improving performance of staff. There are many subtle ways in which control systems can be varied by an individual.

- **Power structures:** Who holds the real power in the organisation? Does power actually reside with those who should have it according to the formal organisation structure? If you examine members who, formally, should have equal power, do you find that certain individuals seem to be more powerful than their peers? We can never forget that although the structure of an organisation presents a picture of the power structure of particular posts or roles within the organisation, individuals occupy those posts, some of whom may be more adept at using power than others. We can also examine how power is exercised. How consultative or coercive is it? Even when groups discuss situations and reach decisions, not everyone in the group is listened to equally. Moreover, those who understand the dynamics of group decision making are often skilled in lobbying and in preparing the ground so that they achieve what they want.

> Hewlett Packard employees all know about the founders' development of an oscillator in their Palo Alto garage. A bell was rigged so that they could be called to meals, otherwise there was a danger that they would not notice the time and just continue working. A bell is still rung in HP plants to this day to indicate coffee breaks.

- **Stories:** Many organisations have stories associated with key figures in the organisation's past. Occasionally, these reach legendary status. They show us what people in the organisation consider important about it as well as what outsiders think are the salient features of the organisation. Often they are stories about the founding of the organisation, usually from very humble beginnings.

  Often stories circulate among customers. These may be trivial stories or even just impressions about an organisation, but they can lead to important opinions being formed about what a company is like to work for, or how it treats its customers. Such impressions can be very important. The Czech car manufacturer Skoda has suffered from this. Skoda has a long tradition of making cars – it was among the first half dozen companies in Europe to manufacture automobiles. During the Communist era, it was owned by the Czech state. After the fall of Communism it found its cars were far behind those of Western European manufacturers in both quality, design and desirability. This gave them a reputation in Western markets as being cheap but unreliable. In the 1990s the German Volkswagen group became partners with Skoda, eventually taking them over in 2000. In contrast to Skoda, Volkswagen are known for producing reliable, well engineered modern cars. Skoda cars became, in essence VW cars. They shared engines and other components with their German parent company. Nevertheless, the reputation they have in the public's mind for being poor quality has been difficult to change.

- **Rituals and routines:** Organisations tend to have certain routine ways of dealing with situations which arise regularly. Often these are formalised procedures, though they do not have to be. They can emerge over time through the sharing of experiences and storytelling. These situations can be events which relate to the operations of the organisation, such as the launch of a new product, or something relatively trivial such as the birthday of a member of the team. Most organisations in the UK tend to mark the occasion when someone leaves with a presentation. The tradition is that when you retire from work, your organisation presents you with a clock! These rituals are both formal and informal. Often informal socialising is encouraged because it is believed to help with team bonding. In many European organisations, you begin and end the day by shaking hands with your colleagues.

Rituals and routines can also be used to indicate status. A senior member of the organisation, for instance, usually carries out the award of prizes for good performance. The award forms a ritualised representation of the reward and resource power of that individual. Similarly, whether or not you are expected to knock before entering someone's work space can be an indication of relative status.

- **Symbols:** Closely related to routines and rituals are the symbols found in organisations. Where rituals and routines are based on behaviour, symbols are embedded in the 'look and feel' of the organisation. They may indicate status, like a bigger, more comfortably furnished office, or titles given to particular roles. They can be seen in the way that an organisation presents itself to the outside world through its logo, slogans and colour schemes. We can also include aspects of language as symbolising the culture of an organisation. Most organisations use jargon as a general communicative currency. Jargon is a specialised use of words and phrases used in a particular occupation or organisation. It is understood by members of that occupation or organisation, but may be less clearly understood by outsiders. The use of jargon to outsiders will have the effect of making the job or the organisation seem remote and formal. Perhaps the most well known example of this is law. Lawyers need to use language which is specialised and often difficult to understand at first glance. They need to do this to avoid ambiguity and misinterpretation. However, that kind of language is of little use to their clients. When they come into contact with the law, they need to be able to understand what is happening and what the implications are for themselves.

VIGNETTE

Perhaps the most potent symbols of organisations are their logos. These tend to encapsulate the purpose and values of the organisation or its products.

Look on the web for the logo of the Citroën DS car. It is a stylised 'D' and 'S', but put together to resemble a flying figure. This figure is intended to remind us of a goddess. The name of the car, the DS, is pronounced in French as Déesse, the French word for – goddess. There was also a DS model many years ago, so the logo also harks back to an earlier, very popular car.

The Johnson and Scholes model is a useful way to try to get to grips with an organisation's culture. It invites us to examine some of its crucial features. However, we need to remember that culture is an emergent complex system. It arises from countless small interactions.

CULTURE AND STRUCTURE

As we saw above, Deal and Kennedy identified risk and speed of feedback as key variables in determining the general nature of an organisation's culture.

Roger Harrison's[7] work implies that the key component of a culture is the organisation's structure. He classified cultures according to the two variables: formalisation and centralisation.

Handy developed Harrison's ideas and describes the culture types suggested by Harrison's variables:

1. **High centralisation – Low formalisation:** This produces the 'power culture'. Such cultures tend to be small, with a powerful individual at the centre who intervenes at all levels of the organisation. This culture is usually shown as a web. The radiating lines are the organisation's key functions, though functional responsibilities may be rather loose. There are unlikely to be things like job descriptions. Allocation of work is communicated from the centre and may be quite fluid. Managers and

other members of staff could be asked to take on other roles at short notice. People who enjoy variety and flexibility can flourish in this kind of culture. However, survival in the organisation can be precarious; the personality of the person at the centre has the greatest influence on the climate within the organisation.

All key decisions (and possibly many that are not so important) are made at the centre. Those closest to the centre tend to have most power and are in the best position to influence central decision making. If the person who holds power at the centre is professionally capable and managerially competent, a power culture can be a dynamic and rewarding place to work. However, if the central personality has poor interpersonal skills, or is unclear about the organisation's direction, they tend to be much less successful. Moreover, disagreements and conflicts with the central power, or with those close to the centre, can lead to demotivation.

Power cultures can respond flexibly to changes in their environment – always provided that the person in power recognises that changes are needed. Jobs and roles can quickly be changed and resistance to change can be overcome using the authority from the centre.

If an organisation with a power culture is successful and expands, there will come a time when the central power will no longer be able to intervene effectively in all parts of the organisation. Then the structure may well have to become more formalised – a change that would have implications for its culture.

2. **High centralisation – High formalisation:** This is known as the 'role culture'. In this combination of characteristics, the centre still makes all key decisions. However, in contrast to a power culture, the organisation is careful ensure to that jobs and roles are clearly defined. Everyone knows who they report to and what the outputs of their work should be. There will not be sudden changes of role unless in an emergency. Standard operating procedures are developed and enforced, and staff know exactly what is required of them. The role culture is the quintessential bureaucracy.[8] Role cultures flourish in stable, predictable environments but might be slow to respond in times of rapid or radical change.

This culture is often characterised by a Greek temple. The top represents the overall management structure. It is shown as the typical bureaucratic pyramid, with layers of seniority flowing from the top. This is held up by the columns, which are the functions of the organisation; these will be things like: operations, research, finance, human resource management and marketing. This metaphor for a role culture also highlights its greatest potential failing; there may be a lack of direct communication between functions. In a formal bureaucracy, communication tends to travel vertically. Lateral communication is formalised in meetings and committees. This can make for slow and inadequate decision making. In such rigid situations, as we have seen, informal communication patterns emerge, just to make work flow more efficiently.

Because of the structure of a role culture, it attracts people who like to specialise in a particular job or role. Moreover, people who like to feel secure in their jobs or like predictability will feel at home in such an environment. Others who embrace change and want a more dynamic workplace will often finds those needs unmet.

3. **Low centralisation – High formalisation:** This combination has been characterised as the 'task culture'. It is an attempt to overcome one of the main drawbacks of the role culture, namely its lack of communication between functions. It is shown as a grid or matrix, sometimes a net. This structure is effectively a development of the role structure. We see the top management structure and the functional 'pillars'. However, we also see cross-functional relationships. This is in effect the culture that arises from the matrix structure. As we saw in Chapter 7, it arose as a response to the problem of cross-functional working in bureaucratic organisations. The difference a person would find between working in a role culture and a task culture is that they would be expected to work closely with members from other functions on specific programmes or projects. So imagine, for example, if you were a tutor in OB, you would be in the OB Department of your college. Your boss would be the head of that department. However, you would have to work on several different programmes with staff from other departments. The leadership of those programmes would vary from programme to programme.

This kind of culture suits people who like working as part of multi-function teams and who are happy to belong to several teams, at different stages of task completion, at the same time. They will see their expertise used for a direct input into a complex project. One of the more difficult aspects of the task culture is the potential problem of reporting. You will have several bosses: your line manager in your department and the leaders of various programmes you are allocated to. However, organisations which use the matrix structure are aware of these potential difficulties. The situation is known and staff are recruited and trained accordingly.

4. **Low centralisation – Low formalisation:** This is known as the 'atomistic' or 'people culture'. It is seen in organisations in which the goals of individual members are the paramount concern. There is no organisational strategy or purpose other than to support the individuals who work in it. Those individuals generally make a financial contribution to maintaining the structure, such as it is. They may also form a management committee to oversee the general working of the organisation. We can often see this kind of structure/culture in traditional professional settings. The individual professionals within the organisations have their own work, their own clients and are often self-employed. The organisation provides premises, administrative support and can operate as a central clearing house for work coming in to the organisation. Any work coming in this way is offered to members according to rules set by the members. In such a culture, the management are also the operating staff. More recently, with the growth in working through online networks, we are likely to see more and more of these organisations. They are beneficial for people who have an expertise to sell, but who don't want to be employees in the traditional sense. Such a culture shows how the culture attracts different individuals, albeit with the same professional expertise, but with perhaps different ways of working and with their own client base. The surrounding organisation is fluid and, because of the growth of working in cyberspace, increasingly nebulous. A modern version of such an organisation may well have no physical building, but communicate with other members online, via a communication hub,

where work leads, finance and other administrative matters may be dealt with.

CAN CULTURE BE MANAGED?

Interest in organisation culture arose because leaders of organisations became convinced that a strong, unifying culture would be to their competitive advantage. Behind such an assertion lies the assumption that culture can be managed. If that is the case, then managers can bring about changes to an unsatisfactory culture so that an organisation can reap the competitive rewards of such a change. However, there is little agreement about what the term really means.

- **Culture as an emergent property of an organisation:** So far, this chapter has, if anything, taken the view that an organisation's culture is a self-organising, emergent property of a complex human system. In other words it is the observable manifestation of the values, beliefs and interactions of all its members between themselves and with outsiders. As such, it represents what the organisation *is*. There is reciprocity between the influence on the culture of the activities of the organisation's members and the influence of the culture shaping those same activities. So if over time an organisation has developed, say, habits of open communication and high levels of delegated decision making, those activities will probably be reinforced and valued. Because of its complexity, it is difficult to be sure of what effect interventions by the leaders of the organisation will have. In addition, each group and individual experience and perceive the organisation in their own ways. Consequently, there can be little agreement about culture as an objective, measurable phenomenon. The culture that managers engage with is management's perception of what the culture is and is no more valid than the perceptions of the culture among other members of the organisation.

- **Culture as an organisational resource:** If, on the other hand culture is something that an organisation *has*, like its structure and policies, then these are subject to change at the behest of managers in just the same way as those structures and policies. This is the 'functionalist' view of culture. In this view, a culture is an organisation's asset (or liability) and needs to be maintained, nurtured and controlled to deliver competitive advantage. If managers view culture in this way, the consequences of management interventions are considered to be largely foreseeable, the link between cause and effect more straightforward. Moreover, such a view of culture can be measured, so that managers wishing to instigate cultural change can know their starting point and see when they have reached the desired state.

So the change of verb from *is* to *has* represents a rather important distinction. If culture is a property[9] of an organisation (the *is* version) then management interventions may have the potential to modify a culture, but won't be able to determine its precise final character. After all, they are only one contributory input to the cultural whole. The exemplar of organisational culture is culture at the societal level, which changes slowly and organically, often in unexpected ways. As members of our society, we don't expect our leaders to decide that we all need a different culture and then begin an implementation process to achieve that change (however much they may wish to).

On the other hand, if culture is another organisational resource (the *has* version), then it is as much subject to management control as other elements of the organisation. It can be seen as an asset, if it is the right 'fit', or as a liability if it isn't. It can also be measured[10] and it can be changed.

At the same time, the lack of certainty about what precisely are the levers of culture change must be unsettling. Consequently, there are many books, guides, consultants and other resources available which attempt to reduce this uncertainty. A web search for 'changing organisational culture' will bring up many links to works on how to achieve this, some more tried and tested than others.

According to the work of Gareth Morgan, this uncertainty about the nature of culture arises because of how we as individuals frame our understanding of an organisation. Moreover, if this framing is different for different members, then there will be little agreement about what the organisation is really 'like'. Morgan proposes several metaphors which we use to understand organisations. By exploring these metaphors, we might be able to arrive at a more general consensus about an organisation. These are:

- **Machines:** We have already seen this metaphor used in understanding the structures of organisations. The concept of the *mechanistic* organisation is using this metaphor. It suggests a rational, designed approach, where each part of the organisation contributes to the overall organisation goals. It also suggests that deviation from intended activity is a problem that managers must solve to bring the mechanism back into full working order.

- **Organisms:** Comparing organisations to living organisms is also a concept we met in Chapter 7. This metaphor sees the organisation as being located within its environment, and needing to respond and react to its environment in order to survive. This means that there can be no fixed, detailed blueprint for the organisation, because it needs to constantly adapt to environmental changes. In such a metaphor, managers need to be adept at spotting environmental challenges and opportunities, and to be able to change elements of the organisation quickly to respond effectively.

- **Brains:** Visualising the organisation as a brain suggests that there is a central, controlling command structure, which is constantly communicating with its limbs and organs. It takes information from these limbs and organs through a complex neurological system and rapidly evaluates the information so that it can order an appropriate response. While such a metaphor initially seems to suggest a sophisticated, centralised mechanism, we also have to remember that brains learn, and from their learning they themselves change. We know that real, human brains have 'plasticity', that is, their structure changes as we build and reinforce some neural circuits, while others, less used, can decay. The brain metaphor therefore requires the senior managers in organisations to trust and learn from the information they receive. Based on this information, they can direct the activities of the organisation, but perhaps more importantly, they may need to adapt themselves.

- **Cultures:** We have discussed above whether culture is metaphorical, and therefore essentially subject to differing interpretations, or whether it is a measurable, objective thing, albeit difficult to conceptualise. Morgan unequivocally takes the former view. Culture emerges through the interpretation of symbols and the perception of meaning. These are likely to differ between individuals and groups within the same organisation. Management activities are one of the contributory factors to the culture, and, while they are important, they are not necessarily decisive in shaping it.

- **Political systems:** A political system is one where there is disagreement and competition about both the goals of the organisation and how to achieve them. Different groups and individuals have differing interests and use the organisation's processes and practices to try to realise them. Political systems are characterised by the development of ad hoc and semi-permanent coalitions; by attempts to control the organisation's agenda and direction and by the growth and demise of small 'empires' around powerful individuals.[11]

- **Psychic prisons**: Imprisonment is the removal of personal liberty. When Morgan uses this metaphor for an organisation he is implying the loss of psychological freedom that individuals can experience in an organisation. This can come about when there is a mismatch between an individual's personal values and those of management. An individual in this situation may feel that their views are never listened to or taken account of, or changes are made with which the person is unhappy. We can also find ourselves imprisoned without realising it. We can become accustomed to acting and thinking in a particular way, so that we are unable to act or think differently. This can apply throughout the organisation. Change programmes are often necessary because the old ways of doing things are no longer applicable. This can bring about resistance when people are reluctant to leave what is known for something that is unknown. We are familiar with the notion of institutionalisation for people who have been in prison or similar institutions for a long period. When this occurs, an individual can sometimes feel that prison (which he understands) is preferable to an outside world he doesn't understand. Our familiarity with an organisation's way of going about things can also institutionalise us so that we are reluctant to abandon what we know for what is threatening.

- **Flux and transformation:** Our world is changing very rapidly. New markets, new technologies, developing power blocs and powerful economic presences force organisations to look carefully at how they are to survive. The metaphor of flux and transformation is one that chimes well with our times. It implies an environment that is almost chaotic in its unpredictability and requires organisations to be endlessly adaptable merely to survive. The degree to which this is possible, or even desirable, is uncertain. The self-organising properties of human systems are observable only in retrospect and no management can afford to let things develop without trying to influence the outcomes they desire.

- **Instruments of domination:** This metaphor sees organisations acting as instruments of domination in their outward-facing organisational activities and as instruments of domination in their internal structures. As actors in the world, we can see organisations from powerful economies dominate those from weaker economies. Cheap, insecure work in developing countries adds to the profits of the owners of those organisations, whilst doing very little for those whose labour produced those profits. Moreover, many international organisations are so powerful they can defend their interests beyond the national jurisdictions of their home countries or of those countries in which they operate. Clever exploitation of the complex tax laws in the UK, for example, have allowed large, highly profitable companies to avoid paying tax on the profits made in the UK.[12]

  Within the organisation, the power plays we see carried on internationally are reflected inside the organisation. Workers who have high, necessary skill levels have strong bargaining power and are well rewarded. Less skilled staff are poorly paid in comparison and their jobs are less secure. Moreover, in periods of high unemployment wage rates fall since the supply of labour increases.

Morgan differs from other writers on culture because he sees it as a phenomenon experienced by individuals and evaluated according to their own value systems. As such, interventions by management to align (or realign) an organisation's culture will be understood and interpreted by each individual according to the various metaphors he has outlined. However, he does not see his list as exhaustive, or that we merely interpret our organisational experience in one metaphorical dimension. He is, rather drawing our attention to comparisons we make about our experiences which metaphors can intensify.

A stark contrast to the work of Morgan is Peters and Waterman's very influential book *In Search of Excellence* of 1982. In this book, they examined the characteristics of several Fortune 500 companies which they believed made those companies successful. Using the organisation analysis tool of the McKinsey consulting group[13] they developed eight themes related to an organisation's values and assumptions:

1. **Bias for Action:** Make clear decisions and act on them.
2. **Close to the Customer:** Keep open communication with customers and learn from them.
3. **Autonomy and Entrepreneurship:** Give people space to innovate and take risks.
4. **Productivity through people:** Influence staff to want to work productively and develop their skills.
5. **Hands-on, Value-driven:** Have a clear management philosophy, which managers are committed to, that is communicated and acted on.
6. **Stick to the Knitting:** Focus on the core activities of the business.
7. **Simple Form, Lean Staff:** Keep the structure simple and uncluttered, with the staff needed to carry out the work, but no more.
8. **Simultaneous Loose-Tight Properties:** Keep overall strategies and values at the forefront of the organisation while allowing staff to respond autonomously to day-to-day problems.

What Peters and Waterman were doing was to suggest a cultural 'recipe' for being an effective and successful organisation. Peters has since revised his claims for the universality of the recipe. In a later interview, Peters stated that these eight values were right for business at the time, but were not applicable in all times and in all situations.

CONCLUSIONS

Culture is a difficult concept. There is general agreement that it is related to beliefs, values and assumptions we make about what is right or wrong, good or bad, attractive or repellent, the right way to do things or the wrong way to do things. These beliefs, values and assumptions influence our behaviour; they tell us 'how things are done round here'. There is, however, little agreement about what precisely a given culture is made up of. How do we assess the beliefs, values and assumptions of a group, or several groups which make up an organisation? And even assuming we can do this, how do we make it what we want it to be? Morgan, as we have seen, claims that culture is interpreted by each individual for themselves. Consequently, different people will experience and evaluate the culture in different ways.

At the same time, many studies suggest that it is the organisation's culture which lies at the heart of competitive advantage. Consequently, managers are encouraged to manage the culture, so that in some way, they control the beliefs, values and assumptions of their staff and are able to drive through the organisation's goals.

Different writers have attempted to do slightly different things to help us understand culture: Schein and Johnson and Scholes, for example, have tried to highlight the main features which comprise an organisation's culture. Deal and Kennedy, along with Harrison, have provided a typology of cultures for managers to work with, linking the culture with different aspects of the organisation's environment. Morgan, on the other hand, views culture as one of several metaphors we use to interpret the culture of our organisations to ourselves. This approach is important because it engages with our individual interpretations of events we experience. Morgan suggests that we can get a deeper understanding of an organisation's culture by exploring the metaphors that people use.

In contrast to Morgan, Peters and Waterman provide a list of cultural values which will deliver success. For them, culture is, by implication, decided on and created by managers. The two approaches couldn't be more different.

What then are we to make of this uncertainty? From the perspective of academic study, the complexity of the notion of culture is itself interesting.

It can be discussed in a variety of ways, from the disciplines of psychology, social psychology, critical theory and anthropology. Such perspectives are not there to help businesses to be better businesses, they are there to understand the role of organisations in other contexts – psychological, societal, political and ideological.

The study of management, on the other hand, is specifically there to find ways of helping organisations to be more effective. How successful it has been in relation to the concept of culture is debatable.

Read the information in the case below and then carry out the tasks.

The Jesperson's Case

Jesperson's is a family-run firm specialising in art restorations. Through various owners, it has been in existence for about 150 years. The Jesperson family bought it in the 1920s when the previous owners went bankrupt in the Depression. Robert Jesperson, who originally bought the business, retired in 1952. He died in 1968. He had no children of his own so passed the business on to his nephew and niece Andrew and Katherine Jesperson.

In the 1950s and 60s the business under Andrew and Katherine became very successful. It focused on two related activities. First there was the frame making and frame restoration work. This was carried out for private art owners as well as for museums and galleries. This side of the work grew rapidly so that the firm became known worldwide.

The second activity was developed and promoted especially by Katherine. This was the cleaning and restoration of the artworks themselves. This was a very specialised type of work with very few people skilled and knowledgeable enough to undertake it. Katherine's strength was in forging and maintaining relationships with fine art schools, universities and galleries throughout the world. This ensured that the Jesperson name was known in the art world and led to steady, well paid business.

Andrew's two children, Tony and Tara, came into the business in the early 1970s, at a time when the economic situation meant that the art boom of the 60s was no longer sustainable. When Andrew retired in 1975, Tony and Tara were made junior partners in the business. Katherine took overall control and kept the business afloat through difficult economic times. Her only child, Oscar, didn't want to enter the family business, so when Katherine retired in 1985, Tony and Tara took joint control. They still enjoy overall control of the firm, though both are contemplating retirement.

Some years age Tony and Tara took on Oscar's daughter (and Katherine's granddaughter), Bella Hawthorn to manage the company day to day. She is now equal partner with Tony and Tara, and expects to take sole charge when they retire. She came into the business in 2008, having had some useful business experience in auction houses in the USA. As she has gradually taken over the operational control of the business, she has attempted to modernise the organisation (at least as she sees it.) She has developed the two parts of the business as stand-alone divisions responsible for generating their own profits and covering their own respective costs. She is also planning to expand the business into auctioneering, in which she has experience and expertise.

Over the past four years, Bella has presided over a significant expansion of both sides of the business. The business as it currently exists can be seen in the organisation chart shown in the next page.

Jesperson's has survived for more than a century as a family business and over that time has largely prospered. It has remained small but has a worldwide reputation. However, the art world is becoming more corporate. Rich individuals, corporations and financial companies are increasingly seeing pictures as investments. Jesperson's are seeing more and more of their work going to large, corporate arts services companies who use their size to undercut Jesperson's.

Recently, one of these companies, Hudsons, based in New York, approached Jesperson's offering to take them over. Hudsons has largely focused on East and South Asian artefacts, but now wants to expand into Europe and has chosen Jesperson's as the most likely way to do this. Hudsons is a highly professional organisation, with all staff subject to the setting of challenging performance goals against which they are measured and which determine their level of pay. The highest paid people are the sales staff, most of whom are highly qualified in business, possessing an MBA or similar qualification, and have a globetrotting, sophisticated lifestyle. For all staff, however, the rewards for good performance are high.

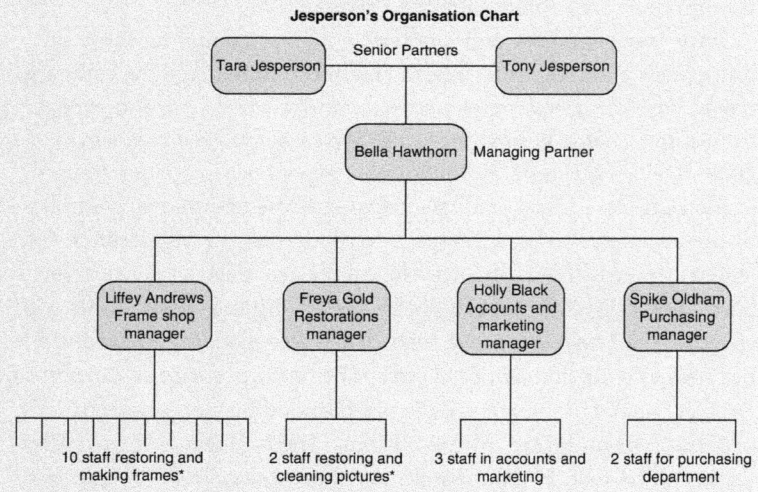

Jesperson's Organisation Chart

Senior Partners
Tara Jesperson — Tony Jesperson

Bella Hawthorn | Managing Partner

Liffey Andrews Frame shop manager

Freya Gold Restorations manager

Holly Black Accounts and marketing manager

Spike Oldham Purchasing manager

10 staff restoring and making frames*

2 staff restoring and cleaning pictures*

3 staff in accounts and marketing

2 staff for purchasing department

* Work is also farmed out to outwork contractors for specialist work or when the workshops have too little capacity.

Hudsons' offer was a very good one. It enabled Tony and Tara to retire very comfortably. Bella would be kept on to run the new European division of Hudsons and was to become a Vice-President of Hudsons worldwide with attractive stock options and a salary way beyond her present earnings.

Hudsons' core business is selling works of art to individual and corporate clients. Jesperson's is attractive to them because of its reputation, not because of its expertise. In fact Hudsons employ very few staff outside of their core selling operations. They contract restoration and frame making work out to small workshops and studios. They also tend to have several trusted agents in key parts of the world who are paid a commission for finding art which Hudsons can sell on at a profit through its private sales or its auctioneering operations.

The three partners agreed to sell. However, there were stipulations. Hudsons agreed to maintain Jespersons framing and restoration staff provided they could show that they were competitive with the craftsmen and women that Hudsons contracted with, many in other countries with much lower wage rates. The admin staff would be increased slightly to support the European operation. These staff would be brought in from other Hudsons divisions to oversee the transition to doing things the way the Hudsons board wanted. In any case there would be a few redundancies, with two staff from the framing division opting to retire as well.

Clearly life at Jesperson's was never going to be the same again. The staff in the framing and restoration divisions were all very uneasy and few of them felt confident of thriving in the new competitive world that Hudsons had thrust upon them.

Jesperson's was being propelled from a relatively comfortable small expert culture where the business model had provided good if unspectacular profits and incomes for many years, into being a small, expendable part of a global corporation which looked for high returns and a low cost base. Moreover, the emphasis was now on sales and the expertise of Jesperson's was now relegated to a support service for the core business.

Your Task

1. Using the frameworks discussed in the chapter, how might you characterise the culture change the staff of Jesperson's are facing?

2. What kind of initiatives might help smooth the transition?

GLOSSARY OF TERMS

Artefacts Physical manifestations of a culture, including objects and behaviour.

Culture The values and beliefs of members of an organisation which influence their way of doing things.

Empirical abstract A term used by Schein suggesting that features of culture are observable, although its deeper sources and complexity make it very difficult to measure or describe.

Metaphor A figure of speech where words used to describe a situation or person are not the literally true of them, though they convey powerful symbolic meaning. E.g. where an organisation is describes as a 'psychic prison'.

Paradigm A pattern, or template, which guides how we behave (or think we should behave).

Rituals Repeated behaviours which have a symbolic meaning to the participants.

Values Deeply held moral beliefs about the world.

KEY POINTS

- Organisational culture refers to the behaviour of people in an organisation which captures their values and beliefs about the organisation and which influences how they act.

- Schein developed a way of understanding culture by observing the artefacts of the organisation and inferring the values and beliefs of the organisation from these.

- Like Schein, Deal and Kennedy used observable behaviour as indicators of an organisation's culture. However, they used the two variables of risk and feedback inherent in the organisation's activities as guides to four types of culture.

- Johnson and Scholes developed the 'cultural web' as an aid to understanding a culture. Their purpose was to use this model to help initiate strategic change.

- Harrison's typology of culture is based around the organisation's size and structure. He identified four culture types.

- Culture as an emergent feature of an organisation suggests that it emerges organically form the many interactions and groupings we find in an organisation. In this view, management is an important intervening variables, but not the only one.

  This suggests that culture is not within the control of management though it can be influenced by them.

- The view that culture is a resource suggests that it is a manageable thing to be controlled and changed to the advantage of the organisation.

- Morgan developed the idea of seeing the organisation through the filter of metaphorical images. His suggested metaphors are: machines, organisms, brains, cultures, political systems, flux and transformation, instruments of domination and psychic prisons. He cautions that his is not an exhaustive list, nor should we see organisation only through these metaphors.

- *In Search of Excellence* is a widely read book which purports to identify the eight important cultural features which will make an organisation 'excellent'. It has been very influential, though it also has received a lot of criticism.

REVISION QUESTIONS

- 'Culture is simply too complex, too ill-defined and too difficult to manage, so managers should just stick to managing what people do, not what they are like.' Anon. How far do you agree with this view?

- Think of an organisation you are familiar with. How helpful are the theories on culture in understanding the collective values of the people in that organisation?

- In what management function is an understanding of organisational culture a useful tool?

GOING FURTHER

Culture is still very much a hot topic, particularly in the field of management. This is not only because it is seen as a 'difficult' subject for managers to engage with, but also because the financial turbulence of the past years has tended to put pressure on some of the 'softer' issues in OB, replacing them with more of a crisis management perspective. The first two publications below deal with this aspect of culture.

We also have to be aware that most of the OB work has been on Western organisations. However, increased globalisation has meant that more and more of our organisations have to deal with companies and institutions in other parts of the world. So can we make the same kinds of assumptions about those organisations? The last two publications listed below suggest not.

1. Kotter J. P. and Heskett J. L. (2011) *Corporate Culture and Performance*, New York, The Free Press.

2. Deal T. E. and Kennedy A. A. (2000) *The New Corporate Cultures: Revitalizing the Workplace After Downsizing, Mergers and Reengineering*, London, Texere Publishing.

   An examination of cultures in a period of radical change.

3. http://blogs.hbr.org/2011/10/the-problem-with-chinas-busine/. Accessed 4 December 2013.

   An article that draws clear distinctions between Western and Chinese approaches to doing business.

NOTES

1. Schein, Edgar H., 2004, *Organizational Culture and Leadership, Third Edition*, San Francisco, John Wiley & Sons.

2. Deal, Terrence E. and Kennedy, Allan A., 1982, *Corporate Cultures: The Rites and Rituals of Corporate Life*, Reading, MA, Addison-Wesley.

3. Johnson, G. and Scholes, K., 1997, *Exploring Corporate Strategy, Fourth Edition*, New York, Prentice Hall, p. 70.

4. The notion of the paradigm comes from the work of Thomas Kuhn. Kuhn suggested that science does not develop in a rational, linear way, through the accumulation of evidence. It develops 'paradigm shifts', where new insights and ways of thinking which were previously not thought appropriate are accepted by consensus of the scientific communities.

5. See Chapter 10.

6. See Chapter 7.

7. Harrison, Roger, 1972, *Understanding Your Organisation's Character*, Harvard Business Review. See also the work of Charles Handy in Charles Handy, *Gods of Management: The changing work of organizations*, Oxford, Oxford University Press, 1995. Handy uses the imagery of Greek gods to highlight the differences between the cultures.

8. See Chapter 7.

9. The word property is here being used in its technical and scientific sense, meaning a defining quality or attribute of something. So flight is a property that most birds possess.

10. For a review of the measurement instruments used see: http://www. uclouvain.be/cps/ucl/doc/iag/documents/WP_53_Delobbe.pdf, accessed 8 July 2013.

11. For a more detailed discussion on this, see Chapter 9.

12. At the time of writing, the avoidance of tax by very large companies is a hot topic. See, for example: http://www.bbc.co.uk/news/magazine-20560359, accessed 4 December 2013..

13. McKinsey's 7-S model, which looked at structure, strategy, systems, style of management, skill sets, staff and shared values, was the tool used to understand and raise issues in companies.

POWER AND POLITICS IN ORGANISATIONS

LEARNING OBJECTIVES

- Describe what is meant by the term 'organisational power and politics'
- Examine the paradigms which underpin different approaches to understanding power in organisations
- Discuss a variety of theoretical perspectives on organisational power
- Analyse the political processes which are used to obtain, hold and exploit power in organisations
- Critically discuss managerial strategies of empowerment.

INTRODUCTION

We have seen in previous chapters that there is a tension between the planned, well thought out attempts to understand, manage and change organisations – the rational approach – and the more unpredictable, sometimes chaotic, emergent characteristics that all organisations experience. The latter can often complicate, or even undermine, the former.

One of the features of human systems which muddies the waters between the planned and the emergent is the fact that individuals and groups won't always agree about what the organisation's goals should be or how they should be achieved. The disagreements may be about details, but they may also be about more important issues, like the strategic development of the organisation. This is the field on which power and politics come into play. The question is, how do you make your voice heard and influence people to act in a way you believe to be right?

How are these key decisions arrived at? Who are the key players in driving a particular point of view? How do we get people to commit to carrying out these initiatives?

We may be tempted to think that clever, well-informed people sit down together and thrash out the problems they want to solve, and that the correct solution emerges from these discussions. Certainly, that is the way that organisations often present the outcomes of their deliberations – as if they have arrived at the only logical decision that could be made. However, nothing could be further from the truth. There is rarely any but the sketchiest agreement about either ends or means. Players in the organisation have to make their case, find support for it and ensure that it is implemented in the way they want. The way that they go about this is what we mean by exercising *power* in the organisation. We can refine the notion of organisational power a little more:

What is power? There are several meanings to the word 'power'. When we think about the meaning of the word in the context of organisations, we usually mean one or more of the following:

- The ability to direct the behaviour of other people in the organisation.
- The capacity to influence or direct the events in an organisation.
- The authority that is delegated to a person or a role by senior management in the organisation.
- A person who exerts influence in a given situation.

We can see from the above list that power comes from the assumed authority of those who run the organisation, but that it may also come from an individual who finds power from some other source. We shall enter into a fuller discussion of sources of power below.

Individuals who want to exert influence in the organisation need to confront certain questions in order to understand the ways in which influence is gained and used. How can you be taken seriously by others? How can you overcome opposition to your views? How can you make sure that your voice is the one that is heard and the one which prevails? How do you overcome opposition to your point of view? How do you ensure that rival claims to power are overcome? The strategies we use to gain and use power we refer to as *politics*.

What do we mean by 'politics'? The word politics also has several meanings. In general use it refers to government, but we can also use it analogously when we talk about the governing of organisations. In that context it can mean:

- The methods or tactics employed in the running of an organisation.
- Manoeuvring within an organisation to obtain control or power.
- Dealing with conflicting relationships and views within an organisation to ensure an outcome that you desire.

People in organisations engage in political behaviours for a variety of reasons. Among them are:

- To promote a view of what goals the organisations should aim for and how those goals should be achieved.
- To further personal ambitions.
- To promote sectional interests
- To resolve personal antipathies.

PERSPECTIVES ON POWER AND POLITICS

The assumptions we make about how an organisations should work have a profound influence on how (and whether) we engage in political behaviours in our organisational lives. We can summarise the assumptions we make under three headings:

1. Unitarist assumptions.
2. Pluralist assumptions and
3. Radicalist assumptions.

UNITARISM

The principal underlying assumption behind unitarism is that the interests of all stakeholders coincide. In particular, owners, managers and employees all have the same investment in the success of the organisation and consequently, there should be general agreement about means and ends. Consequently, there is no need for unions, since staff only need a union when they have ongoing differences of interest.

The authority and competence of managers is unquestioned (particularly the former) and managers control the context of any discussion. Where this assumption is the accepted one, there is general acceptance of the 'right to manage'. That is, there is no questioning of the authority delegated to managers not only to control and co-ordinate work, but also to prescribe the organisation's values and priorities.

Where there is a lack of agreement, this is seen as disruptive and counter-productive. It becomes a management 'problem' to be solved by managers. Where this cannot be solved by early management intervention, it can often escalate until it becomes a formal disciplinary or grievance issue.

PLURALISM

The pluralist perspective, in contrast, accepts that different stakeholders have different interests, and that those interests can often be in conflict. Consequently, in this context, you would expect to find a strong emphasis on negotiation, building positive relations and compromise. Its adherents see such a perspective as healthy and natural. The main concern in such an organisation is to ensure that all interests can be met as far as possible. In many organisations such a perspective is made official through the presence and acceptance of trade unions representing the interests of the workers. There are often formalised negotiating processes to thrash out wage rates and conditions of employment. Members of organisations who are also members of unions have a voice to air grievances and are protected from the more oppressive actions of management.

The potential disadvantage of pluralism, whether with or without worker representation through unions, is that disputes can become entrenched and work against the success of the organisation.

Differences in interests are not only present between management and workers, however. In large, complex organisations, where there are several different professional groups, we can often see conflict between groups. In the British National Health Service, for example, there are many clinical professional groups, like physicians, surgeons, different specialisms among nursing staff, paramedical professions and many others. Conflict may arise between these groups and need to be managed.

RADICALISM

Radicalists believe that organisations, as part of a wider society, reflect the struggles and divisions which we observe in that society. For those who see things in this way, sectional interests in society are not left at the door of the workplace, but are taken inside and form part of the organisational context.

Radicalism differs from pluralism in one important respect. A pluralist perspective assumes that differences arise from disagreements about means and ends regarding the organisation's operations and strategies and the effect of these on sectional interests. These disagreements can be resolved through negotiation or compromise. However, in a radicalist perspective, the differences come about because of more deep-seated differences in society. Therefore they will not be resolved in the workplace, but only through changes in the wider society. Consequently, they will remain unresolved, or resolved only through the application of coercive authority.

Arguably, most management theory is premised on a unitarist perspective. Managers presume that their staff's efforts can be aligned with the goals of the organisation. Organisation theories and management initiatives such as motivation, leadership, total quality management,[1] empowerment[2] and commitment are concerned with promoting the goals of the organisation over those of other sectional interests. Performance related pay is designed to ensure that effort seen to be contributing to management goals is rewarded.

Table 9.1 Summary of characteristics of differing perspectives across three key parameters

Perspective	Stakeholder interests	Conflict handling	Management authority
Unitarist	Assumed to be the same for all stakeholders. The success of the organisation is what everyone wants and should be committed to.	Conflict seen as unhealthy and to be avoided. Where it occurs it can quickly become a formalised disciplinary or grievance issue. Conflict is often seen as a challenge to management authority.	Accepted as paramount. Where there are forms of consultation, management decisions are final. Staff participation schemes are bounded by what management see as acceptable.
Pluralist	Stakeholders are assumed to have differing interests and priorities. This is seen to be healthy and normal. Interests often cohere around occupational or professional differences. Staff are often represented by unions or professional bodies.	Because there is broad acceptance of different interests, we usually find a sophisticated system of negotiation and compromise in operation. This happens at both a formal and informal level.	Accepted but subject to challenge in particular situations, where the interests of one or more groups are threatened.
Radicalist	Seen as irreconcilably separate. Differing interests arise from conflicts embedded in society and cannot be resolved in one organisation.	Because conflict, or the potential for conflict are ever-present, no lasting solution can be found in the organisation. Sectional interests may for a time reach a way of working together, but the possibility of conflict recurring is always present and will remain until societal conflicts are resolved.	Challenged at every level. Management authority cannot be accepted unless it recognises and tries to rectify the imbalances that exist in society.

Although the approach is rarely presented to staff as crudely as a 'take it or leave it' option, at the heart of the unitarist perspective is the fact that making persistent challenges to the right of managers to manage is to risk being removed from the workforce. Within such a framework, managers exercise power through control of what is or isn't legitimate to discuss. Issues which support or promote the management agenda are discussible, issues which don't are not. Managers control the discourse of the organisation.[3] Moreover, individuals who persistently raise matters of concern to them which management find uncomfortable or challenging can often be ignored or sidelined. Of course this doesn't prevent others from having an opinion or discussing it informally, but their discussions will have no forum in the official decision making process.

SOCIOLOGICAL PARADIGMS

Whether we take a unitarist, pluralist or radicalist view of power, we base our assumptions on certain beliefs about human communities. We follow what are called *paradigms*. Often the paradigms we adopt are tacit; that is to say, we don't always consciously realise that we hold them. Nor do we always understand that there may be other, competing and equally strongly held paradigms which others hold. Moreover, as we shall see later in the chapter, part of the exercise of power is persuading people to believe that the only paradigm which has any validity is the one underpinning the actions of the powerful.

However, when we examine human systems, from the level of a whole society down to a single organisation, we need to uncover the underlying paradigms that people bring to that understanding. Looking at human systems from the perspective of social theory, Burrell and Morgan have attempted to confront the key questions that are posed when we try to understand human systems and phenomena like power.[4] Those key questions are:

- Is reality an objective fact that exists outside of us or do we 'construct' the world in our mind from our knowledge and experience of it? This, of course is the key question when we try to understand the complexities of human perception.

• Do we have to experience something to understand it, or can we draw our understanding from scientific investigation? This can often pose problems. For example, we all know that the world is round – this is scientifically demonstrated. However, we all live our everyday lives as if it were flat, which is what was generally believed for centuries. Our experience[5] told us that we lived on a flat surface because we could not physically experience the spherical structure of the world.

• Can human beings make free choices about what courses of action to take or are those choices determined by circumstance and environment? Much of the time we feel that we are making choices based on our evaluations of a situation. We tell ourselves that the outcome we have chosen is the best from our understanding of a situation and that we would come up with a different solution if the situation differed in key features. But is that really true? Are our solutions based on tacit assumptions and understandings about the world that we may not be aware of?

From these key questions Burrell and Morgan have developed a two-dimension matrix which is formed from intersecting continuums and shows four paradigms which we use for understanding human systems.

The intersection of these continuums gives us four quadrants, each representing what Burrell and Morgan refer to as paradigms of social theory and which can, in various combinations, inform our assumptions about the world. The horizontal dimension ranges from a theoretical perspective in which all our understanding of human systems is constructed in our minds (subjective theories), to the opposite, which claims that there is an observable, quantifiable objective world which is capable of discovery through scientific investigation (objective theories).

The vertical axis ranges from a perspective which says that the important feature of a human system is that it is regulated and controlled so that it is stable and predictable, to its opposite, which propounds the belief that human systems are exploitative, limiting of human potential and inherently unstable. Consequently radical change is needed to bring about situations in which people can flourish.

When we combine the two dimensions, we arrive at four key paradigms:

1. The functionalist paradigm (regulatory/objective):

This paradigm arises from two assumptions: that the reality of organisational life is an objective, observable entity which exists independently of our individual perceptions, and that the principal organisational goal is stability and order. Burrell and Morgan call this paradigm the *functionalist* paradigm. Like unitarism (discussed above), functionalism seems to be the preferred model for studying and managing organisations. It assumes that organisations are capable of being understood and run by rational people making rational decisions. In such a model, for example, we will usually see change coming about based on investigations which reach conclusions and make recommendations for action. Those recommendations are then tested for their resource implications and a programme of implementation decided on. In OB, topics like scientific management, change management, motivational theories like expectancy and performance-related pay tend to make functionalist assumptions. Because of the reliance of the functionalist paradigm on rationality, it is easy to see the link between it and unitarism. In both belief systems, proponents claim that the proper investigation and application of scientific methodologies will lead to a right answer. Consequently, there is no room for alternative views.

2. The interpretive paradigm (regulatory/subjective):

This paradigm is based on the belief that organisations (and society as a whole) should be stable and ordered, whilst understanding that each individual perceives the organisation and their role in it in their own unique way. Consequently, there is no 'one right way' to manage, but managers need to take into account the individual needs and motivations of their staff. Motivation theories like equity and needs theories, and change processes like organisational development come mainly from this paradigm. Proponents of this view accept that there is more to running a successful human system than a reliance on rationality. People have strong, though differing, opinions and values about work and work organisations which are not susceptible to a reductionist rationality. We can see that an interpretivist paradigm would foster a pluralist approach to managing.

3. **The radical structuralist paradigm (radical change/objective):**

Radical structuralists believe that society is riven with conflict between its constituent parts. This leads to constant instability and change through political and economic crisis. They believe, moreover, that these conflicts exist beyond the perceptions of individuals in an observable, objective world. The conflicts in the outside world cannot be left at the factory gate or the office door, so are played out in our organisations whether we like it or not. Traditional Marxism is based on this paradigm, which is very much out of favour in modern Western thought (including most of the field of OB studies). However, radical structuralists would counter by saying that although this paradigm is not discussed,[6] its constituent elements are nevertheless present and observable in society.

4. **The radical humanist paradigm (radical change/subjective):**

Radical humanists believe that organisations, along with other societal features, prevent most people from fulfilling their potential. There is no objective reality, merely a set of structures imposed on people which serve to promote a view of the world according to the powerful, but which is not in the interests of most individuals. These structures can include work organisations, medicine, education, law and political institutions.

The radical example set by Ricardo Semler at his company in Brazil, Semco, is potentially enlightening as an example of radical humanism. In Semler's factories, staff and managers set their own pay and conditions of work, and there is complete transparency about the company's performance. A comprehensive review of the Semco case can be downloaded at http://www.divaportal.org/smash/get/diva2:16517/FULLTEXT01.pdf

VIGNETTE

However we wish to classify the tacit assumptions we make about organisations and power, the important thing to accept is that some theory of the organisation and its relationship to its members is at work in both employees and managers. This theory will influence how each behaves towards the other. We can see, for example, how the functionalist and interpretive paradigms are played out in the OB theories we have looked so far. It is less easy to see how the remaining two can be applied. The radical structuralist paradigm is unlikely to be entertained in a market-orientated capitalist context since it holds capitalist organisations responsible for the societal ills it is concerned with. The radical humanist paradigm looks equally sidelined in modern Western and Western influenced organisations.

SOURCES OF ORGANISATIONAL POWER

In the late 1950s, and subsequently,[7] French and Raven developed their influential analysis of where power in organisations comes from. Raven has systematically developed this since. French and Raven defined power as the ability to change the belief, attitude or behaviour of another person using the resources available to them. Throughout French and Raven's work, the person using the power is referred to as the *agent,* while the person being influenced is referred to as the *target.*

They identified six sources (or *bases*) of power:

1. **Informational power** – People in senior positions in organisations have access to more, better and more relevant information than their subordinates. When this information is explained to subordinates, they can then see the need for any changes that may be needed. The change brought about is influenced by information from the agent, but the target makes the decision to bring about the change.

2. **Reward power:** Managers are in a position to provide incentives to staff to make changes. These may be financial incentives, potential for further promotion or development opportunities. In this instance, the target does not need to believe that the change required is necessary, but they

need to want the incentive on offer. This kind of power source is reflected in expectancy theories of motivation.

3. **Coercive power:** This kind of power uses threats of negative consequences to influence changes. Coercive power, like reward power, achieves compliance because of the actions of the agent. Coercive power can often lead to resentment, since the target is obliged to comply whether or not they believe the change is necessary. Moreover, the application of coercion requires the agent to monitor the target to ensure that they do what is required. Consequently, there is the possibility that non-compliance may be hidden from the agent to avoid the threatened sanctions.

4. **Legitimate power:** In this situation, the target believes that the agent has, by right, some power to influence change.8 Usually, this is because of the position of the agent in relation to the target. So, a subordinate is likely to take this view in relation to their line manager, or towards a senior manager in the organisation. Moreover, in the UK, there is a presumption in the laws that regulate employment contracts that a subordinate should carry out any reasonable instruction from their employer.

5. **Expert power:** This comes into play when a subordinate believes that someone has superior and reliable knowledge and understanding of an issue, either through their professional expertise or because of their experience of similar situations. This power source differs from information power in that the target does not need to understand the complexities of the situation to be persuaded that they should make the changes required. Information power relies on the target being persuaded by taking in, understanding the information and agreeing that changes should be made.

6. **Referent power:** Sometimes called *personal power*, or *charismatic power*, this power source relies on the target identifying strongly with the agent as a role model, or as encapsulating important personal qualities that the target finds attractive. Such power makes that target want to please and be accepted by the agent.

The French and Raven approach, which looks at power in terms of where it comes from, is a useful start to understanding power in organisations.

When we come to define each of the power sources, it becomes clear that the exercise of power is a two-way street. There must be a willingness on the part of the agent to make use of their power resources, but these cannot be successfully used to bring about changes in attitude, values or behaviour unless the targets accept their role in the power interaction. In other words, the target has to agree to power being exercised over him. That is not to say that a target is necessarily happy with this state of affairs. However, they have to be willing to recognise either that they have no choice (as in the case of coercive power) or they are willing participants in the power interaction (as, for example, in the case of referent power).

Rather than examining where power comes from, Barach and Baratz[9] tried to understand the context and consequences of power interactions. They posed the question: When we look at the uses of power in society, who participates, who wins, who loses? Such an approach can provide a very useful analysis of power, provided, of course that the person carrying out the analysis has access to sufficient information to draw clear conclusions. They would need to know the positions of the principal protagonists, what agreements and disagreements were aired and by what means the final conclusions were achieved – in other words, what sources of power were brought to bear.

However, the exercise of power is not only about who has power and how they apply it. Nor is it only about who benefits and who loses out. These things are obviously important, but power is a more complex phenomenon, according to Lukes.[10] According to his analysis, what Bachrach and Baratz describe is what he refers to as the *visible* face of power. In other words, these are the aspects of power that we can observe. Other aspects of power are less easy to observe. Lukes calls these the *hidden* face of power and the *invisible* face of power.

THE HIDDEN FACE OF POWER

The face of power which is hidden is the ability of the powerful to control the agenda. So they determine what the problems are, how they are to be solved and who is to benefit from their solution. They control the *discourse* of the situation. A discourse is a communication process. In linguistics, it refers to the language and communication processes used in a particular context. The French philosopher Michel Foucault suggested that people in positions of power control the discourse of a situation and thereby exclude discussion of topics which they find challenging or contrary to their interests.[11] They create a climate where certain topics are simply not discussed. People who attempt to broach such topics are not listened to, are made to feel that what they are talking about is not relevant, or are excluded from decision making forums. We find this in many situations. Professional groups may use their professional discourse to exclude non-members from participation in discussion, even in cases in which the non-members have a direct interest.[12] Feminists, for example, have long complained that they struggle to access traditional male preserves in politics, the professions and many other arenas. Women find that they can be ignored, patronised, excluded and talked down to. Their concerns are belittled as of no importance. These are all key tactics in maintaining control of a discourse. Discourse in this context is part and parcel of exercising power, since those who determine the discourse are determining what is or isn't true.[13]

THE INVISIBLE FACE OF POWER

In addition to the hidden face of power, Lukes has also identified another, perhaps even more pernicious, the *invisible* face of power. Here, we find people without power who have internalised and accepted that condition. They believe that their situation is normal and cannot be challenged. People in power are there because of some kind of right or superior ability which the powerless cannot hope to achieve. Such a situation is, of course, very much in the interests of the powerful since the powerless will do nothing to change the status quo. This is achieved through the processes of accultura-tion (people being assimilated into a culture and gradually adopting it as their own), indoctrination (persuading people to accept uncritically a set of beliefs) and socialisation (taking on values and beliefs in return for being accepted). These processes are reinforced by institutions like the mass media, religions and education systems and by the prevailing espoused orthodoxies about the relations between bosses and workers, about the role of government and the nature of economic reality.

Writing about this phenomenon, Hinson and Healey say:

> When those who have the power to name and to socially construct reality choose not to see you or hear you … when someone with the authority of a teacher, say, describes the world and you are not in it, there is a moment of psychic disequilibrium, as if you looked in the mirror and saw nothing. It takes some strength of soul – and not just individual strength but collective understanding – to resist this void, this non-being, into which you are thrust, and to stand up, demanding to be seen and heard.[14]

Power, then, is a complex thing. It involves issues about the right to exercise it, the context in which it is exercised and, perhaps most importantly, the acceptance and consent of those over whom it is exercised. Moreover, as with many other topics in the OB domain, much of what we believe to be theoretically sound actually depends on the assumptions we bring to our analysis. So how you perceive leadership depends on your (conscious or unconscious) perspective on what leadership consists of. Similarly with topics such as motivation, culture, perception and even 'hard' topics like structure, we are led to arrive at particular conclusions because of our basic assumptions.

HOW DO WE ATTAIN AND USE POWER?

Those individuals and groups seeking to exercise power have several strategies at their disposal. They can act on the whole system, or they can act on individuals and small groups.

- **Fulfilment of contract terms:** When we are employed, we have a contract which governs what is expected of us and of our employer. If we (or our employer) do not abide by the terms of that contract, then we (or they) can be subject to sanctions.[15] Part of an employment contract is the requirement for the employee to carry out their responsibilities at work and to comply with reasonable instructions of management. Various sanctions are available to the employer if an employee fails to carry out their contractual obligations, from informal warnings through to dismissal. The contract of employment gives the employer certain rights over the activities of the employee. These arise from what is referred to as 'legitimate' power and apply to every employee. Part of legitimate power is the ability to set terms and conditions of the employment contract. In the UK, the decline in influence of the trades unions has meant that many more employees have to negotiate their own pay and terms and conditions with employers. This means that people doing similar jobs may be on different pay scales, or have different conditions. Consequently any manager who wants to use a 'divide and rule' approach to managing the workforce is ideally placed to do so in such a context.

- **Using the formal system:** All organisations have rules and regulations, formal practices and procedures. In even small organisations, these can be complex. In highly bureaucratic organisations, these can mushroom, as every inconsistency in the regulatory system is dealt with by developing even more rules. Such a system is very difficult to keep abreast of and most people don't keep up. Consequently, those who do keep up find that they can control the system and ensure that their points of view are the ones that get discussed, whilst those of others, who are much less adept at manipulating the system, can be ignored or dealt with summarily and inadequately.

- **Managing meaning:** This is one of the more subtle ways of imposing your influence on the system. This happens through the uses of symbols, such as slogans, logos and management of public relations and internal communications. We are unconsciously influenced in many ways through the use of symbols, language and images. What those who manipulate systems in this way do is to establish and reinforce important assumptions so that they become internalised and thought of as 'natural' and so beyond critical discussion. The development of language specific to an organisation or profession, work uniforms and badges, mission statements and officially encouraged rituals are all part of this process. Anyone who fails to conform to these conventions can risk isolation.

- **Controlling how decisions are made:** All the activities of any organisation are the result of decisions being taken and communicated to staff.

This may be at the strategic level, where the future direction of the organisation is decided, right down to decisions about the routines of everyday functions. If you have control of how those decisions are made, then you have great power over what people do and how they do it. If decision making is highly formalised, then manipulating the system as described above will provide you with opportunities to control decision making. Some organisations, however, like to work on the basis of consensus decision making. This means that it is rare for groups to vote on decisions until a sense of the group's collective will emerges. The time taken in this process provides an opportunity for people to influence others towards their way of thinking. Clever operators will use tactics like lobbying, bargaining, formation of temporary or more permanent coalitions and even bullying. So if, say, you are hoping for a promotion or some other reward, then you may be reluctant to challenge those who are in a position to influence the outcome of what you want.

- **Giving or withholding resources (including knowledge and information):** This is probably one of the most widely used tactics to exercise power and influence. Those who will support an initiative or way of working will often get the resources to carry it out; those who are more resistant may well struggle to get the minimum they need. As well as resources like finance, staff or equipment, modern organisations use knowledge and expertise as a resource. The more important to an organisation that knowledge is, the greater its value, and consequently, the greater the opportunity to use it as a lever of influence. Within this category we can include professional knowledge, as well as knowledge of, and access to, customers and important social networks like professional bodies, trade associations, chambers of commerce and many others.

- **Proximity to the centre:** Being in frequent contact with those at the top of an organisation can often bring its own possibilities of power. For example, a PA to a senior manager can control access to that person, or may give the impression that when they act, they do so with the approval and support of that person. Even without an official position, daily contact with powerful people in the organisation can provide an opportunity to have you voice heard. So you may well find that in an organisation which has a headquarters with geographically dispersed branches or units, the person from 'head office' can have an aura of power.

- **Alliances and coalitions:** Power is rarely exercised alone. There are always the points of view and activities of others to take into account. If you want people to act on your decisions with commitment, then you have to find strategies that fulfil their wants and needs. Powerful actors often use alliances and coalitions to achieve this. In this context, we can think of alliances as tending to be more long lasting and comprising people and groups who broadly support your point of view. We can see coalitions, on the other hand, as consisting of partners who would not generally share the same perspective, but who are willing to combine their efforts to achieve a certain goal provided that their own cherished goals will be supported in return. In many countries in the world governments are often (if not always) coalitions. This is because no single party can gain complete control of the legislature, so there is a system of bargaining to establish which policies from each participating party will be made priorities.

This is not a comprehensive list of strategies, but it contains most of those we see in our everyday organisational lives. Of course experienced power players will use many of these strategies at once. They will learn which to use in which situation: where an alliance is possible, how to bargain with potential coalition partners, who can be coerced and who needs to be to be handled gently.

Many of us find discussion of power in this way distasteful. However, if we accept Foucault's view that power comes into existence in every human system, then it would seem better to confront and understand it rather than ignore it.

EMPOWERMENT

In the generally accepted use of the word, empowerment is used across a wide range of situations. It is often used to address people who are marginalised in a society by proposing processes and rights which enable them to find and take opportunities otherwise denied them. Empowerment movements have arisen in western countries over the status of women or ethnic minorities, for example. They have been designed to enable individuals and groups to have access to opportunities hitherto denied them and to have a voice in society where previously they went unheard.

In contrast, empowerment processes in organisations are addressing something rather different. They are a part of the human relations approach to managing organisations and can be seen as contrasting with scientific management approaches to organising work. We can broadly define empowerment in organisations as allocating support, authority and resources to workers to achieve specific goals. This is a much more restricted use of the word. It is the granting of power to achieve the goals of management. When we use the term in its broader sociological sense, we are referring to the need to empower people to achieve *their own* goals.

Empowerment of employees in the work place has divided opinion. On the one hand it can be seen as a process which delivers high level performance at the same time as providing staff with motivation, satisfaction and growth.[16]

Others, however, disagree. Harley,[17] researching empowerment initiatives in Australian organisations, shows that there is no correlation between what organisations call empowerment and increased experience of autonomy by staff. In other words, although jobs may have been expanded and the employees given more responsibility and decision-making power, the level of employee autonomy remains the same.

Hales,[18] researching a range of organisations in different sectors of the UK economy, concludes that empowerment initiatives focused on staff at the operational level often masks the disempowerment of junior managers since the latter are traditionally responsible and accountable for the achievement of local operational goals When this is removed, their *raison d'être* is lost.

Nonetheless, the idea of empowerment persists. A quick web search will bring up innumerable publications and other resources showing managers how to implement empowerment programmes.

It would intuitively appear that empowerment is only possible in unitarist organisations. If you find your work uncongenial, or even morally challenging, or overly stressful, then you are unlikely to welcome being given more accountability and responsibility for it, let alone be energised and motivated by it. If, however, you are at one with the organisation and its aims, then empowerment could well be a liberating opportunity.

CONCLUSIONS

If we regard power in organisations as the ability to influence others to act in the way we want them to act, then it is clear that power will be an inherent property in any human system. It may emerge over time as members of that system interact and decide what needs to be done and how they should go about it. Or it may be already designed into the system as a hierarchy of authority, with power devolved from the top of the hierarchy to lower levels. In the latter case, power will be constrained by such things as job descriptions, operational and decision-making norms and other bureaucratic processes.

How (and whether) we try to achieve power in an organisation is what we mean by the word politics, and the political behaviour we exhibit will depend on our assumptions about the people in the organisation. If we take a unitarist perspective, then we will assume that anyone in opposition is dysfunctional and must, if possible, be removed. If our perspective is more pluralist, we will expect opposition and devise strategies to outmanoeuvre our opponents. If we face more radical opposition, then our strategies will be different again.

The resources we have at our disposal arise from the overt sources of power identified by French and Raven as well as from more arcane sources such as the control of the organisational agenda where the powerful are able to dictate what is discussed and the terms of reference under which that discussion takes place. Such power as this, as Lukes and others have shown, can have the effect of forcing the disempowered to accept and internalise the fact of their disempowerment. These are the hidden sources of power, and arguably the more potent.

Those who seek power have a number of strategies at their disposal, some formal, such as their ability to give instructions and expect to have them carried out because of their position. Some are informal, like using relationships and networks to form alliances and coalitions.

There is a wide range of literature on *empowerment*. This involves giving staff at the operational level of the organisation authority, resources and support to make decisions and carry out tasks with greater autonomy than workers who are not so empowered. The notion of empowerment is, however, contested. In a wider societal context, empowerment is seen as giving marginalised groups more power to have their voice heard and to achieve their goals. Empowerment in the organisational sense is different. It involves the delegation of more power, certainly, but in a limited context and in the service of achieving organisational goals.

Art Vault Revisited

When you read Chapter 5, you will have looked at the Art Vault case study. To refresh your memory, here is a recap of the scenario.

Art Vault is an adult community arts and education centre. It is run as a co-operative. That is, all employees are also members of the co-operative and have an equal say in how it is to be run. Policy is made by the Board, which consists of an elected chairman and five other Board members and the centre staff. Members of the public can also become members of the co-op, and are entitled to come to twice-yearly members' meetings and to elect Board members and officers from their number annually. Paula had become a member of the co-op a few years earlier, knowing that her membership money was crucial to keeping the centre afloat. However, she had not been an active participant.

Art Vault has two functions: it is a venue for music, drama and other performances, for which it has a growing reputation; and it is a centre for adult education in arts and related subjects. It has several classrooms, a large and a smaller performance space and a restaurant selling organic food. The restaurant is a franchise run by two partners who are not part of the co-operative. Instead, they pay a rent for the restaurant.

CASE STUDY

It is a registered charity and is funded by the income it receives from putting on performances, course fees and the rent for the restaurant. It is independent of the local education department, though it does receive grants from the Arts and Culture Department of the City Council, as well as charitable grants from some local businesses. Financially, the centre is always on a knife-edge and recent events in the world economy bode ill for the future.

The centre has four full-time staff: the administrator, in overall charge of the day-to-day running of its activities; an assistant, responsible for booking performers and dealing with managing the education activities of the centre; a staff member who takes care of the maintenance and cleaning of the building; and a book-keeper. In addition, there are several part-time and casual staff who are taken on for teaching, bar work, cleaning, helping out at performances and other occasional tasks. As the Art Vault is a co-operative, everyone is paid the same hourly rate, except for the administrator who is paid one third more. There are also several volunteers who can be relied on to step in if extra staff are needed.

Paula was offered, and accepted, the job as Centre Administrator at Art Vault. She began the job almost immediately and has now been in the post for nine months. It soon became clear that the centre could not continue working at the same level unless it could generate, or be given, more income. Its biggest funder, the local authority Art and Culture Department, was under enormous pressure to cut its expenditure and it is by no means certain that any money at all will be forthcoming from that source for the next financial year. Among the full-time staff, there is a feeling of helplessness. They had backgrounds in education and arts administration and were out of their depth when it came to thinking about new sources of income. In particular, Paula's deputy, Lenny, seemed to be very demoralised and at a loss to come up with any ideas. However, working with money was meat and drink to Paula, given her background in banking.

She began by carrying out an audit of the centre's activities and financial situation. When she carefully examined the workload of the four part-timers on the payroll, she became convinced that their numbers could be reduced to three, if not two. The financial control could be done part-time, as could the management of the centre's bookings. The three remaining full-time staff could spread the workload about. They needed to keep a full-time member to maintain the building, since there were health and safety and cleanliness issues which could not be ignored.

She also noticed that many of the classes, especially the various yoga and exercise classes, although starting with healthy numbers, found attendances tailing off about three to four weeks into an eight week course.

Although this did not seem to bother the staff who had been at the centre a long time, it did bother Laura, who thought that the under use of expensive spaces was unacceptable.

Once Paula had carried out her audit, she realised that the centre would have to become much more efficient. For the current financial year the centre would show a surplus of about £1,000. However, the bulk of the income of the centre was from the local authority (about £110,000). She knew that this would be cut by two thirds next year and dwindle to nothing in the following year. More income would have to be generated from somewhere.

Using her experience of the financial services sector (remember, she had been made redundant from a high powered banking job before joining Art Vault), she decided that the Centre would try to find alternative donors. She knew that all the major companies gave grants to charities of various kinds. They generally tried to spread their donations across a wide range of causes. The problem with Art Vault was that it was very local. Any profile raising for a donor would be quite limited. Nevertheless, Paula believed that there were several companies with whom she had contacts who could be persuaded to give money. In return, any business donor would want to know that the centre was being run efficiently. She quickly took soundings from some of her contacts and discovered that, with a group of about ten to twelve donors, the shortfall from the local authority grant could be made good.

There were a number of obstacles, though. Some of the companies she had contacted were suspicious of the centre being run as a co-operative. To them it smacked of socialism. They would also want to appoint their own members on to the centre board so as to monitor (they called it supporting) the centre's activities.

However, from her time in business, these stipulations didn't surprise or perturb Paula, so she drafted a report on the finances of the centre and her proposed response to it and put the matter on the agenda of the next Board meeting. She sent copies round to all the Board members and emailed a copy to the co-operative members. When she went to the Board meeting to discuss the matter, she found a wall of opposition. The Chairman of the Board was the only person in the room who seemed remotely sympathetic and whispered to her that he would not call a vote but suggested that the matter needed more time to investigate. The Board agreed to this. When the meeting broke up, the Chairman took Paula to one side. He seemed quite angry and suggested to her that she should have handled the issue a bit more intelligently.

Your Task

What mistakes had Paula made?
What sources of power might she call upon to turn this situation round?

GLOSSARY OF TERMS

Coercive power Power based on force or the threat of force.

Pluralism The assumption that different groups and individuals pursue different interests in an organisation.

Politics The strategies used to implement or attain power.

Power The capacity to influence others to do what you want them to do.

Power sources Where power in organisations comes from.

Radicalism The assumption that the conflicts within society are reflected in the power differences in organisations.

Referent power A source of power based on a follower's desire to want to be like, or be seen as a follower of a particular person or grouping, or the ideas they represent.

Social paradigms Assumptions about how social relations work which lead to the beliefs we hold about how we perceive organisations.

Unitarism The assumption that the interests of management and employees in an organisation coincide.

KEY POINTS

- Power is the capacity to influence or direct people and events to achieve the goals of the organisation or of those in power. This may be a use of legitimate authority or one of the subtler means of exercising power.

- Politics is the tactics and methods used by those in power, or seeking power, to achieve their goals.

- Unitarism is a view of organisations which assumes that every member of the organisation agrees with its purpose and its ways of achieving them. Such an assumption regards opposition or the proposal of alternatives as dysfunctional and a problem to be eliminated.

- Pluralism accepts that there will be disagreements about ends and means. Consequently, opposition is not regarded as endangering the organisation and there will be a readiness to consult and negotiate.

- A radicalist perspective assumes that the divisions and antipathies which exist in society at large will inevitably also exist in organisations which are part of that society.

- Morgan and Burrell identified and developed a model of four sociological paradigms in a quadrant of two continua: regulation/stability to radical change as one paradigm, subjective theories to objective theories as the other. These paradigms will lead people to have differing assumptions about how societies and communities work.

- Managers and leaders get their power from several sources. French and Raven identified a number of these sources of power.

- Those in power can often control the agenda in an organisation, influencing not only what can and can't be discussed but also the boundaries of any discussion. This is referred to as 'hidden power'.

- The invisible face of power is what Lukes calls the phenomenon where individuals come to accept as unchallengeable that they are disempowered so that they believe that there is nothing they can do about it.

- Empowerment is a process which has become popular in organisations in the last twenty years or so. It involves giving individuals and groups greater authority over resources, decision making and working methods in order to achieve the organisation's goals more effectively.

REVISION QUESTIONS

- Is political behaviour in an organisation inevitably damaging to it?
- Which of the three assumptions about organisations – unitarist, pluralist or radicalist – do you think best represents the reality? Why do you think that?
- In any organisation you know, can you identify who controls the agenda? Who decides what is discussable or not? How do they do this?
- To what extent do empowerment programmes really give more power to operational staff?
- Why might junior managers be reluctant to support empowerment initiatives?

GOING FURTHER

Without doubt the most influential book on power is Machiavelli's *The Prince*. Published in the sixteenth century, this book has been the primer for many of the most powerful people in the world, from Mao Zedong to

Margaret Thatcher. An interesting perspective comes from Tom Spears, who has written a book based on personal experience of corporate power and politics, aimed at those who are new to, or put off by, the idea of politicking. Spears also has a website and blog containing useful material based on his own experiences. The third book gives some useful strategies and tactics on how to recognise, cope with and participate in the inevitable politics of the workplace. Finally, the book by Buchanan and Badham presents a valuable set of case studies in organisational power and politics.

- Machiavelli, N. (2003) *The Prince*, New York, Penguin Classics.

- Spears, T. (2012) *Navigating Corporate Politics*. Published in ebook form by Tom Spears. Available for download from: https://tomspears.squarespace.com/navigating-corporate-politics/.

- Ranker, G., Phipps, M. and Gautrey, C. (2008) *Political Dilemmas at Work: How to Maintain Your Integrity and Further Your Career*, Hoboken, NJ, John Wiley & Sons.

- Buchanan, D. and Badham, R. (2008) *Power Politics and Organisational Change*, Thousand Oaks, CA, Sage Publications.

NOTES

1. Total quality management is an approach to achieving and maintaining high quality by devolving the power and responsibility for quality to the operational level. Staff at this level are encouraged to share ideas and solve quality problems in groups (sometimes called quality circles)

2. For a fuller discussion on empowerment, see later in this chapter.

3. Foucault developed the idea of 'discourse analysis' where you examine what is said, how it is said and the topics which are (and are not) dicussed.

4. Burrell, G., and Morgan, G., 1979, *Sociological Paradigms and Organizational Analysis: Elements of the Sociology of Corporate Life*, London: Heinemann.

5. At least until recently, when many millions of people are now able to travel long distances in a short time. We can now all experience circum-navigating the Earth.

6. A fact in itself a consequence of the use of power?

7. French and Raven and Raven etc.

8. Though for a critique of this view, see http://www.newunionism. net/library/workplace%20democracy/Cradden%20-%20Beyond%20 Hierarchy%20-%20Managing%20Without%20the%20Right%20 to%20Manage%20-%202009.htm, accessed 21August 2013.

9. Bachrach, Peter and Baratz, Morton, 1962, 'Two Faces of Power', *American Political Science Review,* vol. 56, pp. 947–952.

10. Lukes, 1974, *Power: A Radical View,* London, MacMillan (reprinted 2005, Basingstoke, Palgrave MacMillan).

11. Foucault's ideas about discourse are difficult to unpick. However, you might find this link helpful: http://patthomson.wordpress. com/2011/07/10/a-foucualdian-approach-to-discourse-analysis/, accessed 23 August 2013.

12. This is not to tar all professionals with the same brush! Most make strenuous and successful efforts to include clients and other non-professionals in understanding what is happening.

13. 'Truth' in this context is not an observable, measurable, factual truth, but the creation of 'regimes of truth' through their adoption by powerful elites and institutions. In essence, it represents the manipulation of ideologies and value systems, so that things are accepted as being 'true'. See, for example: http://www.powercube.net/other-forms-of-power/ foucault-power-is-everywhere/, para. 5.

14. Hinson, Sandra and Healey, Richard, 2003, 'Building Political Power', prepared for the State Strategies Fund Convening, Grassroots Policy Project. Cited in http://www.powercube.net/analyse-power/forms-of-power/academic-debate-on-forms/lukes-invisible-power/, accessed 28 August 2013.

15. This is Weber's 'rational-legal' authority model.

16. Martin Beirne, 2007, *Empowerment and Innovation: Managers, Principles and Reflective Practice*, Cheltenham, Edward Elgar Publishing.

17. Harley, Bill, 1999, 'The Myth of Empowerment: Work Organisation, Hierarchy and Employee Autonomy in Contemporary Australian Workplaces', *Work Employment & Society,* vol. 13, no. 1, pp. 41–66.

18. Hales, Colin, September 2000, 'Management and Empowerment Programmes', *Work Employment & Society,* vol. 14, no. 3, pp. 501–519.

INTRODUCTION

Almost 50 years ago in 1964, the singer Bob Dylan caught the mood of a generation when he sang 'the times they are a changin'. For those of us who were young then, it signalled a rejection of the stodgily conventional world of our parents and the creation of a world of new and different thinking. The need to radically rethink our world has cropped up more and more frequently since and is now a given in the world of organisations. In fact, things like the world financial crisis, the emergence of new, dynamic economic powers, as well as the seemingly unending development of new technologies keep reminding us that change is constantly with us. We are continually called on to try to solve new problems and to see old problems in a new light. We have to produce different goods and services for new markets against a backdrop of global political uncertainties.

This is the context in which modern organisations have to survive. However, we have seen throughout this book that human systems are not rational, or are, at best, only partly rational. Consequently, although the management of change must be approached using rational analysis of a situation, followed by a calm, considered selection of a strategy to cope with it, there are other, more 'human', less rational matters to consider. Organisational change also involves important psychological and emotional changes for the individuals involved. Changes which require us to work with different technologies, different people, in different ways and with different relationships can be very threatening. Moreover, when those changes threaten our economic or emotional well being, even our livelihoods and our sense of self, then we have to accept that these threats are very real. In addition, when we consider that change can threaten people's ambitions, their power bases, the plans they have made for the future, it should come as no surprise to see that very few change programmes will be carried out without resistance.

There are various ways in which we look at organisational change. The first is a contrast between planned and emergent change. In a mechanistic view of organisations, everything is planned and relatively predictable. It is this conception of the organisation that lies behind the notion of planned change. Emergent change, on the other hand, seems to have more of a feel of the organic perception of organisations, where the organisation, or its parts, react and adapt to external pressures to change. The truth probably lies somewhere between the two extremes. If we want our organisations to be able to live in a changing world, then management needs to be able to scan the environment and plan its responses to any threats or opportunities. No organisation wishes to be seen as merely reactive to events, they want to be able to exert some control where they can. At the same time, most change involves individuals and groups having to make changes at the local or operational level. We know from our understanding of human systems that people's responses cannot be reliably predicted. However, people will and can change when they are confronted with a real need to do so.

Sometimes we differentiate change by describing it as 'top-down' and contrasting that with 'bottom-up' change. What this means is that change can be driven in a directive and possibly authoritarian way by management, or it can be allowed to emerge through processes of guidance, consultation and participation. More often than not the truth probably lies somewhere between the two poles. Management will not want any change to occur outside of their ability to control it and to ensure that it is implemented in the interests of the organisation.[1] At the same time, managers cannot ignore demands from staff to play an important part in changes which have a direct impact on their daily work.

Deciding how to manage change is much more like choosing horses for courses than always taking the same approach. Change comes in many guises: it can be a necessary strategic change involving the whole organisation. It can be as a consequence of financial or other resource constraints. Or it might be an attempt to make the organisation more efficient by restructuring. As we saw in Chapter 8, management often wants to change the attitudes and values of the members of the organisation.[2]

DRIVERS OF CHANGE

When it comes to deciding on and managing the change process, organisations need to know what is driving the change in order to decide on what can be done about it. Perhaps the best known approach to this is the PESTEL analysis. This is an acronym which stands for:

- **Political:** This deals with things like, the form of government operating in an economy, the kind of tax system, what activities it wishes to encourage or discourage, the degree of intervention in business activities it carries out.

- **Economic:** This category covers things like interest rates, economic growth in the relevant markets, levels of competition, wage levels and commodity prices.

- **Social (or sometimes Societal):** Societies are complex, so any organisation needs to understand the social structures applicable in the market or social grouping with which it is concerned. They need to understand demographic changes, socio-economic differentiations; they need to be sensitive to cultural preferences and variations within a society.

- **Technological:** The rapidity of technological change means that all organisations need to understand what the impact of any of those changes may be for its effective running. Almost all organisations now use social media, a trend almost impossible to predict ten years ago.

- **Environmental:** The fact of climate change is now largely uncontested. Consequently, many countries have signed up to worldwide or regional agreements on things like carbon emissions. Organisations consequently have to pay attention to environmental factors when they carry out their operations. Moreover, there are strong interest groups which are set up to protect local areas. There is also greater attention paid to ecological factors when new building or industrial activities are planned.[3]

Fracking is a method of releasing natural gas from underground deposits of shale. We do this by forcing water and chemicals into the shale beds to 'fracture' them and release the gas. There are believed to be enormous deposits of gas stored underground in this way and the energy companies and national governments are keen to exploit this new source of energy. However, there is a great deal of opposition to this on environmental grounds. Environmentalists are concerned that the chemicals used will migrate into the water systems and contaminate them. The companies which want to carry out the fracking operations claim that they can do it safely; their opponents are unconvinced.

VIGNETTE

- **Legislative (or Legal):** All governments pass legislation which affects how organisations are allowed to operate. Some countries, for example, will only allow foreign companies to set up provided they partner with a domestic organisation, others will accept foreign ownership of domestic organisations. Governments also legislate on things like unfair discrimination, basic employment rights, minimum wage rates and a whole range of other issues which any organisation needs to be aware of.

Some of these categories can have porous boundaries, so that it may be difficult to place any given factor in one single category. However, that is much less important than recognising that the factor concerned is something that may provoke the need for a change. Moreover, not all changes will be driven by all factors; it is important to recognise what influences any given factor is likely to have, or, more importantly, the relative importance of each of the factors.[4]

Once the drivers for change are understood organisations need to try to understand the impact they are likely to have on their activities and implement the necessary changes to confront a threat or to exploit an opportunity.

In order to do this, organisations will use a SWOT analysis. SWOT is an acronym for:

- **Strengths** – The features of the organisation which enable it to thrive and which are seen as being superior to similar features in similar organisations.
- **Weaknesses** – Those features of the organisation which are known to be less effective than the same features in similar organisations.
- **Opportunities** – Those things happening outside the organisation which could enable it to be more successful, more competitive or more innovative.
- **Threats** – Things happening outside of the organisation which the organisation (or significant parts of it) is not presently set up to confront successfully, and which will need radical change if the organisation is to survive those threats.

Such an analysis clearly requires accurate and insightful scanning of the organisation's operating environment, the wider, potentially global, context in which it operates and a way of understanding the internal processes and systems within the organisation.

We must also take into account the timescales in which changes need to be made. A sudden crisis will require an urgent reaction in which there may be little time for planning and consultation. Many such changes threaten the very existence of the organisation, so we could expect such a change to be managerially driven and potentially autocratic in style. In contrast, a change which comes about as a result of a careful analysis of how the organisation needs to develop would give management an opportunity to involve and consult throughout the organisation, as well as to support staff through the change process.

RESISTANCE AND DEFENCES TO CHANGE

In any organisation there will be a varied response to any change process. Some will welcome it, seeing it as an opportunity, perhaps because it confirms their own opinions about what should be done, or simply because they have a personality type which thrives in periods of uncertainty and change.

Others, however, will be less welcoming to it and there are many and varied reasons for this. It may be helpful to look at the reasons for resisting change as both individual and collective, though there will inevitably be an overlap between the two in many instances.

Individual defensiveness can be caused by:

- **Insecurity** when facing an unknown future. Many change processes, particularly those involving changes in structure, can lead to strong feelings of insecurity. Workgroups may be broken up and new ones created, staff may need to work in a different location. However, the most potent source of insecurity is any real or perceived threat to continued employment – an all too real threat in difficult economic times.

- **Changes to working methods or processes.** Change often requires staff to learn to use new technologies or adapt to new working methods. This can pose a threat for several reasons, not least a worry that it will be difficult to learn new ways of working.

- **Restriction of opportunities.** Opportunities for advancement may exist in the present system but may not exist in a changed one. For example, a restructuring may well take out layers of management and consequently make the next step up the ladder much more difficult.

- **The breaking up of informal networks.** Work is often made easier and more pleasurable through the informal contacts and friendships individuals form. If a change process removes these networks, then, until new groupings can emerge, individuals will feel uncomfortable.

- **Threats to leadership.** If an individual has developed a leadership role, whether formal or informal, this may be threatened by changes.

Collective or organisational defences to change can be brought about by:

- **Those who traditionally exercise power within the organisation.** These may be groups whose own prescription for change was not adopted, or who wanted to retain the status quo.
- **Rules, procedures and norms changing.** This can lead to confusion about what is done and who does it. It can lead to instability, itself leading to loss of productivity and efficiency.
- **The change process itself.** Most change processes do not achieve the outcomes they are designed to bring about.[5]
- **Reluctance to give up old practices and procedures.** Change will often require a period where old working practices have to run alongside the new ones. For example, where contractual terms need to be honoured or where products which are being discontinued still need to be produced to fulfil past orders. This can be expensive and it can slow down the change process.

Almost any change process will encounter some of these kinds of resistance. They are part and parcel of any complex human system. In large measure the success of a change process may depend on how they are accommodated.

HARD VERSUS SOFT CONTEXTS OF CHANGE

Senior and Fleming[6] describe two contrasting change contexts: 'hard complexity' and 'soft complexity'. They describe hard complexity change problems as 'difficult', while situations of soft complexity are 'messy'. Put simply, these contexts reflect the degree of certainty and predictability of the change context. Hard problems are encountered in situations of certainty and predictability, while soft problems are encountered in conditions of uncertainty and unpredictability. In reality, all change situations are likely to have elements of both hard and soft uncertainty.

VIGNETTE

Imagine an organisation wants to roll out a new intranet. The hard elements of the situation will be: the specification of the system, the levels of access and functionality, the costs involved, the maintenance process, the internal and external support systems. All of these things are predictable and quantifiable – there is a high degree of certainty in these elements of the change.

In contrast, there will also be less certain elements, many of which will not arise until the implementation phase, such as: acceptance of the new system by all users, the quality of any training and support, the ease of use of the new system, the ability of the new system to effectively replace all elements of the previous system in all cases.

So far, what we have discussed is the problem of trying to understand the need for and the nature of a change process. When it comes to carrying out change, we can identify several approaches.

LEWIN'S FIELD THEORY APPROACH

Kurt Lewin was a German social psychologist who migrated to the USA in the 1940s. He is probably best known for his field theory. Lewin proposed that the behaviour of individuals is influenced by the context of a given situation, which he refers to as the 'field'. All of us operate in different fields at any given time. The individual's behaviour is influenced by forces within the field which favour a particular set of behaviours, and inhibited by countervailing forces which set up obstacles to that behaviour. The emergent behaviour is an equilibrium between those opposing forces. In order to bring about the desired behaviours in, say, an organisational change process, then the forces which favour the desired behaviour will be promoted and the forces opposing it will be reduced.

VIGNETTE

An English university had campuses in two towns in its county about ten miles apart. The management of the university decided to close the campus in one town and consolidate its premises in the other. They agreed to sell the land they wanted to vacate to a supermarket chain and use the money to fund expansion of the other campuses in the other town.

This change was proceeding well until the local residents and their political representatives discovered what was planned and mounted such strong opposition that the university and the supermarket could not get planning permission to change the use of the land. Consequently, the university had to change its premises strategy and remain on sites in two separate towns.

The usefulness of this model is, firstly, its simplicity, and, secondly, that it can encompass the change process from the perspective of management driving top-down change, to groups and individuals owning the change process themselves. Consequently, we see this model used in both planned change processes instigated by managers' perceptions of the need to change, as well as prescribing exactly what those changes should be, as well as with the more transformational types of change process that see in processes like organisation development. It is therefore valuable in both hard and soft change contexts.

However, whenever we try to convert a model into a prescription for action, we inevitably find the devil in the detail. So, for example, while the model tells us to identify the driving and resisting forces of change, how can we be sure that everyone will agree as to what they are, or what their relative strengths are?[7] There may very likely be disagreement, moreover, on what the desired state may be. Even where such agreement exists (or emerges), events may intervene which change not only the destination but also the means and direction of travel.

Lewin also models the way individuals, groups and whole organisations change. He uses the metaphor of freezing and unfreezing (Figure 10.1).

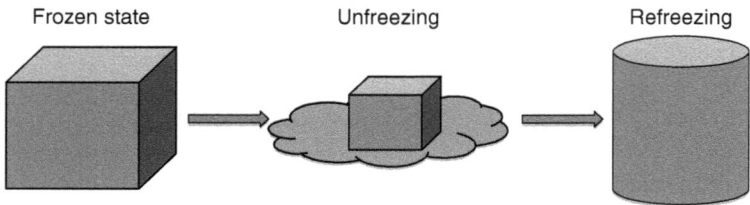

Figure 10.1 Lewin's change process

When we are in a situation we are familiar and comfortable with we are said to be 'frozen'. In order to change we need first of all to 'unfreeze'; that is, we have to move out of the situation we find comfortable into a much less familiar state which seems to have little form or context. Eventually, we begin to internalise the new situation, learn to operate effectively within it and slowly, we begin to 'refreeze'. It is easy to see this model as an exclusively top-down model, where managers unfreeze and refreeze a compliant workforce.

However, Lewin's work was primarily descriptive rather than prescriptive and his model of change was an attempt to *describe* the process human beings go through when change is necessary. He did not see the process as one imposed by authority on others. Like his force field analysis, it is a metaphor which simplifies a complex process and we should always remain aware of that. Nevertheless, his model is frequently cited as a paradigm for 'planned change'.

Using Lewin as a starting point several theoretical approaches have been developed. Some are prescriptive, outlining what managers have to do to implement a successful change process. Others focus on using the staff as a key resource in the development of change. In reality the approach taken will depend on several of the contextual features of the organisation in question, such as:

- The cultural norms of the organisation. Since culture is a key determinant of how members of the organisation will behave, then it will clearly have an impact on how management plans to implement change.

- Management style, itself a component of an organisation's culture, will play a key part in selecting the approach to planned change. We would expect to see an authoritarian management style take a much more directive approach than in an organisation which has a more consultative style of management.

- The time constraints within which change needs to be achieved will be critical to the approach used. An organisation faced with an urgent need to change will adopt a different approach to one where the timescale for change is longer.

- The nature of the change will also be important. A change involving only a small part of the organisation, or just a few of its staff will require a different approach from one where the whole organisation is likely to be involved.

Other features may also be important, but again we can see that change has to be a contingent process. That is, change processes have to take into account the unique characteristics of the organisation and managers will tailor their approach to those contingencies. There is no overall prescription that will fit all circumstances.

However, theorists and practitioners have attempted to distil the important features of change management processes to suggest what is important for achieving success. Kotter emphasises the need for staff to be convinced of the need for change and to be as involved as possible in moving change forward.[8] He prefers people to talk about 'leading change' rather than 'managing change', and to embed that idea into change processes he developed an eight-stage approach, each part of which is essentially about engaging with the staff of the organisation.

1. **Establish a sense of urgency.** It is important that all those involved understand and recognise the need for change. If that does not happen, then there will be yet one more obstacle to successful implementation.

2. **Create a guiding coalition.** There needs to be a cohesive team with enough power and resources to bring about the desired change.

3. **Develop a change vision.** Those charged with leading the change must develop a vision of the change which can inspire and attract people.

4. **Communicate the vision for buy-in.** It is one thing to create a vision, but another to make sure it is communicated in such a way as to enable people to commit to it.

5. **Empower broad-based action.** Try to remove obstacles to change. These could be structures, embedded working practices, resource bottlenecks and many others. At the same time try to encourage creative thinking and risk-taking.

6. **Generate 'short-term wins'.** When people can see that their actions have resulted in a successful conclusion, they will be motivated to look for more success. Therefore it is important to ensure that short timescale goals can be met and celebrated.

7. **Never let up.** Use the credibility won by short-term wins to bring about more and more change to structures, procedures and policies that inhibit the achievement of the vision. Also incentivise those who embrace and work towards the vision.

8. **Incorporate the changes gained into the organisation's culture.** Culture usually changes by embedding behaviours until they become internalised. This can be done in a change process by continually linking actions to desired outcomes and by rewarding and supporting those actions consistently and across the board.[9]

Kanter suggests that there are two main kinds of change:[10]

- **Bold strokes:** these are major changes of strategy due to changing market or general economic issues. They tend to have a big impact on the organisation in a short space of time. These changes are thought to be so important that the co-operation of staff throughout the organisation is not considered critical to the implementation of the change.

- **Long marches:** these tend to be longer term and may consist of smaller change initiatives. However, this type of change needs the wider support and participation of members of the organisation at all levels if it is to succeed.

In spite of identifying two (almost opposing) types of change, Kanter nevertheless proposes a ten-stage guide to implementing change. She called it the 'Ten commandments for executing change'. In listing these ten stages, we can see that they bear an obvious similarity to many of the stages of Kotter's eight-point plan:

1. Analyse the organisation and the need for change
2. Create a shared vision and a common direction
3. Separate from the past
4. Create a sense of urgency
5. Support a strong leader role
6. Line up political sponsorship
7. Craft an implementation plan
8. Develop enabling structures
9. Communicate, involve people and be honest
10. Reinforce and institutionalize change.

Todnem provides a comparison of Kotter and Kanter (as well as the work of Luecke) in his review of change management.[11]

ORGANISATIONAL DEVELOPMENT

Organisational development (OD) is an approach to bringing about change in an organisation. It has been (and continues to be) interpreted in a variety of ways, from seeing it as a tool in the training and development armoury of human resource specialists, to a kind of organisational psychotherapy. For the purposes of this chapter, we are going to locate it firmly in the context of managing organisational change. Although he did not coin the term, Kurt Lewin is generally thought to be the founder of OD through his work on group dynamics and, especially, his development of action research (which will be discussed in more detail below).

Perhaps the most immediately striking thing about OD is that, while it is carried out at the behest of management, it is not done *by* managers. Managers commission and resource OD interventions, but they are themselves a participant group, either as a management team, or as functional managers along with their respective workgroups.

OD is often said to be a 'bottom-up' approach to managing change in the sense that it engages directly with groups within the organisation to help them find ways to solve their problems, though we need to qualify that by observing that management sets the strategic direction of change.

We should also point out that the core values of OD are located squarely in the human relations movement of organisational thinking. OD carries the underlying assumption that workers find satisfaction in being challenged and will be more motivated and effective if they themselves identify problems and find their own solutions to those problems. It is also arguable that the founding theorists and practitioners of OD saw organisations as pluralist in nature.[12] That is to say they recognised that the interests of all the groups in the organisation will not necessarily coincide. Consequently, one of the key tasks of the OD process is to reconcile inherent differences within the organisation.

In addition, OD takes a systems approach to working with organisations. It works with the whole organisation system, as well as with its sub-systems, looking at the fit between the various components of the system.

So how can we define OD? For Wendel and French, two of the earliest researchers and practitioners of OD, it is:

> A long-range effort to improve an organisation's problem-solving capabilities and its ability to cope with changes in its external environment with the help of external or internal behavioural-scientist consultants, or change agents as they are sometimes called.[13]

In this definition we see that OD is carried out:

- over the longer term, and
- that it is concerned with not only solving problems facing the organisation from the outside, but also
- improving its problem-solving capability overall, and
- it does this with the support of behavioural scientists.

Beer's definition fleshes out the OD process in a little more detail:[14]

A system-wide process of data collection, diagnosis, action planning, intervention, and evaluation aimed at

1. enhancing congruence among organisational structure, process, strategy, people and culture,

2. developing new and creative organisational solutions, and

3. developing the organisation's self-renewing capacity.

It occurs through the collaboration of organisational members working with a change agent using behavioural science theory, research and technology.

The Beer definition recognises the 'system-wide' nature of OD interventions. It also recognises the role of OD in developing 'new and creative' solutions to the issues confronting the organisation. The last key point of this definition is that OD develops 'the self-renewing' capacity of the organisation, in other words, its overall ability to learn.

Both definitions make clear the debt OD has to the behavioural sciences. The change agents referred to are usually (though not exclusively) external to the organisation and it is their task to support the OD process at all levels.

The guiding principles behind OD are:

- Groups are the main drivers of change.
- Decision making should take place where the relevant information is, not at some level of hierarchy distanced from the problem.
- All components of the system should monitor their activities against goals. However, goals are for providing feedback on progress, not rigid strategic aims. By this we mean that if it is proving problematic to achieve a goal, then it is legitimate to alter the goal.
- OD should foster open communication, mutual trust and confidence between groups laterally and vertically through the organisation.
- People will support what they are involved in creating, therefore those affected by change should be able to own and participate in the change process.[15]

HOW OD WORKS

The OD process is based on action research, a concept developed by Lewin. The original concept of action research was about working collaboratively with social groups and communities to help them solve problems and bring about systemic change, but from the beginning was also used by Lewin in work organisations. The research element of action research is so-called because it has similarities to research in academic contexts. First we have to identify the problem or issue which we believe needs changing. Next we need to collect data and then formulate a plan of action. The plan is then implemented and its results are reviewed. The process is referred to as the action research 'cycle,' or 'spiral' (see Figure 10.2).

The cycle consists of four stages:

1. **Plan:** The group needs to decide on the nature of the problem that needs fixing and create a plan through the development of goals. In this process the planning needs to take account not only of the impact of the problem on the group trying to solve it, but also the potential impact on other groups in the system.
2. **Act:** The group will then carry out its plan, and
3. **Collect information** on whether the plan has achieved its intended goals. The group then has to
4. **Reflect:** This is critical to the success of action research initiatives since it involves evaluating not only the success of the plan, but often whether it was the appropriate plan in the first place. As a consequence of its reflection the group may need to re-enter the cycle with a modified plan.

We can identify two key points about the action research process:

1. First, action research is not linear, it is iterative. At each stage there has to be the opportunity for feedback and the potential to modify the

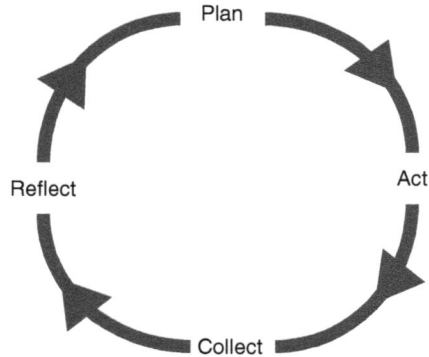

Figure 10.2 The action research cycle

plan based on the feedback. So, at the first stage (and at all subsequent stages), a consensus needs to emerge about the nature of the problem being tackled and about the means to achieve a solution.

When data is collected to find a solution, we again have an iterative process to test whether the data addresses the problem, or whether the problem really is the one the group have identified. Similarly, the formulation of a plan to solve the problem may require several reviews even as it is put into practice. In other words, all stages are subject to review and change. Moreover, any solution found is not necessarily definitive, since in a dynamic organisational context today's solution can itself bring unintended consequences. In fact, because of the complexity of human systems, almost any initiative in an organisation will have consequences that were not anticipated. Action research is, therefore, a continuing process, it doesn't have a point where the job is complete.[16] An organisation may well solve the problems the change agent was brought in to help with, but the solution is not the main point. The main point is the degree to which the community has learnt to deal with new issues which arise and can confront those issues effectively in the future.

2. The second point is that the researchers are the same people who will implement the solution. In other words action research is carried out by practitioners who are researching their own organisational lives. They are not researched *on* as is the case with traditional research processes. This is an important difference, since action research theory is wedded to the idea that those who experience the problem will be more motivated to accept the solution if they have found it for themselves.

While OD and its methodology, action research can be, and have been, used as a vehicle for introducing change in response to outside pressures, their intention is to promote an organisation's ability to be constantly ready for and active in achieving change. Where OD is embedded in an organisation's culture, the organisation can be likened to what Peter Senge has called the 'learning organisation'.[17]

According to Senge, an organisation aspiring to be a learning organisation needs to develop five disciplines:

1. **Systems thinking:** This requires that people in the organisation understand how the component parts of the system integrate and how their acts and omissions affect those other component parts. This enables them to analyse the impact any changes will have on their own work groups and on others.

2. **Personal mastery:** This discipline implies a commitment by the individual and by management to develop skills and understanding as far as possible, not only to carry out job tasks but also to be able to take on new or a greater range of tasks in the future.

3. **Mental models:** These are the *schemata* which were discussed in Chapter 2. They are the internal mental frameworks we use to build a coherent picture of our world. In a learning organisation it is important that everyone shares a similar view of the organisation and that they also share similar values about the organisation.

4. **Shared vision:** There must be a vision of what the organisation wants to achieve which must be shared by its members. Moreover, the goals of each individual need to consistent with the overall values and direction of the organisation. It is important that the individual sees achievement of his or her goals in the context of achieving the organisation's goals.

5. **Team learning:** Individual learning needs to be shared with the team, so dialogue, trust and openness are crucial.

Clearly there are many shared characteristics between OD and the ideal of the learning organisation. However, one arguable distinction is that the latter presupposes a unitarist perspective. In contrast OD understands that differences and competing visions may exist and works to develop consensus so that effective change can be brought about.

CONCLUSIONS

We have seen that the organisation's environment is dynamic and that many of the changes happening outside of it will have a direct or indirect effect on it. How change is managed will often determine the success or otherwise of the organisation.

Change can come in many shapes: there can be market changes, changes to legislation, and the price of commodities may fluctuate and create instability. As well as these large-scale dynamics, we may see change generated from within; a new manager may want to stamp his identity on the organisation, some of the players in the organisation may become very powerful and control the agenda. There is a near infinite number of ways in which change can come about.

> In 1982 Peters and Waterman produced their book *In Search of Excellence* in which they identified the eight principles which enabled major companies to be 'excellent'. If any companies were to prosper in uncertain times, these were the companies.
>
> However some of those major corporations no longer exist. Most of the others have been the subject of takeovers or mergers. Once household names like Pan Am no longer exist, while others, like IBM have come very close to closing. Yet others, like Atari, exist in unrecognisable form from their heyday.
>
> The moral of the story is that however effective you may be in one period of time, you will need to change radically to meet new challenges.

VIGNETTE

Consequently, management have to recognise that things will change and that there is no longer the stability that a well-run organisation can count on to see them through periods of turbulence. Change will come anyway, so we might as well bite the bullet and try to manage it.

But how is this to be achieved? How can we approach dealing with this persistent challenge? We can, of course ignore it and hope that it won't have an impact. Not really a very intelligent response. Or, we can try to understand the environment in which we operate and respond as well as we can to the challenges that arise. Or we can try to pre-empt the changes by organising so that we are able to respond effectively and creatively to whatever problems confront us. The theory and practice of managing change deals with the last two of these possibilities.

Above we have discussed two main approaches to managing change: top down versus bottom-up, or change that is led and controlled by managers contrasted to change where all members of the organisation are involved, and take responsibility for the changes that affect them. However, the choice between the two is unlikely to be clear-cut. It is probably better to see these alternatives as two ends of a continuum. A very authoritarian management might well take an entirely manager-driven approach; most would want to work with the consent and contribution of those staff affected by the changes. At the other extreme of the continuum we can see that there may be the risk of managers losing control if too much of the change was owned by staff.

If we look at the possibilities as existing on a continuum, then we can see how, at different points of the continuum, there will be a different mix of management and staff involvement.

The final point to make is that change rarely visits us in one complete, obvious form. It can be very messy, and you may well find your organisation embarking on a significant change process only to be confronted by another challenge which demands yet another change process be initiated, or which threatens the cohesiveness of the original process. Organisations and their members seem to be at the mercy of events which can alter quickly and radically. This appears to be the only constant we can count on.

North Haverton Advice Centre

North Haverton Advice Centre has been in existence since the early 1980s. It was set up to offer advice on opportunities for the unemployed in the recession of the 80s. Over time, its activities expanded, so that it became a well used local resource offering advice on benefits, family problems, debt, immigration, housing and employment. Funding has been mainly through grants from the local council and some of the legal work carried out from the centre was funded by legal aid, a government fund set up to pay for legal representation for those who could not otherwise afford it.

When the centre was first set up, it was established as a co-operative; that is, it was not set up to make a profit. Everyone who worked there was a member of the cooperative and they set their own objectives and pay levels. The management of the centre was in the hands of a Steering Committee who were answerable to the members of the co-operative. From the outset, the centre paid all its staff the same rates of pay, no matter if you were a qualified lawyer, an advisor or a cleaner. Part-time workers were paid at the same hourly rate as full time workers. The centre also had several volunteers who were not paid but who wanted to participate in the centre's work. The volunteers usually consisted of people with time to spare in the week, especially if they had useful expertise in one of the advice areas such as employment law or debt counselling. There were also volunteers from the law school of the local university, whose students could gain valuable hands-on experience of the law in action.

The centre steering group had one member from each of the areas the centre specialised in, along with an officer of the local council. There was also a representative of the local Law Society, the professional body for solicitors, though they rarely attended the regular Steering Group meetings.

Although the pay levels were very low for professionally qualified lawyers and other qualified people, this was an attractive job for young professionals committed to working in areas of the law dealing with social deprivation. Usually, they stayed for a few years before moving on to other, better paid jobs. A chart of the structure of the centre is presented in Figure 10.3.

In recent years, however, there have been some serious challenges to the very existence of the centre. Severe cuts to the funding of local government by central government have meant that the funding local groups like the centre have been drastically cut. Without further sources of finance the centre would have had to close, like many

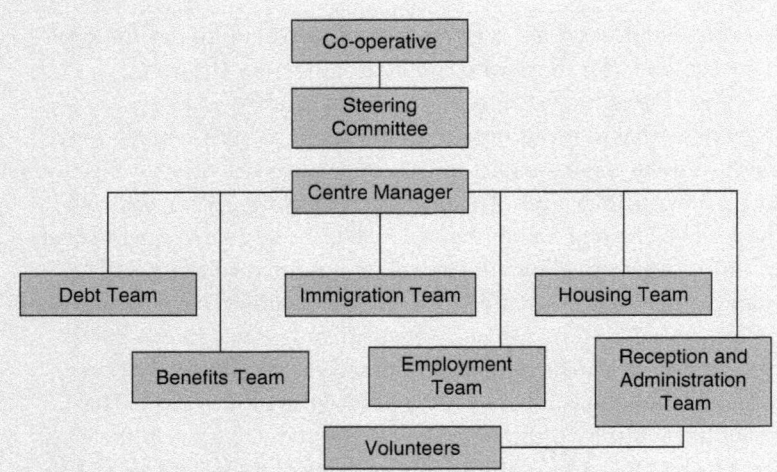

Figure 10.3 Haverton Advice Centre Organisation Chart 1

others throughout the country have closed. Moreover the cuts to legal aid money have also meant that many of the legal services the Centre has become expert in can no longer be offered.

When these cuts and their implications became apparent to the Steering Committee, the co-operative urged them to seek alternative funding streams urgently. After a great deal of networking and negotiation, additional money was found, though it still did not reach the levels previously enjoyed. The local Chamber of Commerce agreed to provide funds for two years, with the grant to be reviewed after that time. A similar arrangement was made with some of the larger Solicitors' firms. Haverton is also a regional centre for banking and financial services and there are continuing discussions with two of the largest to provide funding from their Social Responsibility budgets.

It looks as though these negotiations will bear fruit, albeit with funding on an annual review basis making long term planning impossible.

The new funding sources are, however, adamant that the centre can no longer be run in the same way. The consensus among them is that the co-operative will have to go, to be replaced with a Board of

Trustees containing representatives of the organisations providing the funding. This, of course, will mean that the employees will no longer be part of the overall strategic planning process of the centre as they were as members of the co-operative, although, as a concession, they will be allowed to elect one member to sit on the Board of Trustees. They have furthermore decided that pay will henceforth reflect labour market values, so the professional workers will get more, while the non-professional staff will face a pay cut. Moreover, there will be fewer professional staff, since many of the activities formerly carried out by the centre can no longer be funded. The staff at the centre will henceforth limit their involvement to referring many of their clients to other agencies to deal with their problems, even if these agencies are located many miles away from Haverton.

Legal advice and representation will only be provided for those areas and cases where legal aid is still available, otherwise clients will be advised to go elsewhere. There is also to be a greater emphasis on taking on and training volunteers, especially to deal with debt and benefits while the links with the University Law School are to be reinforced if possible to encourage law students to get involved with the Centre and provide support for the existing lawyers.

The new structure is given in Figure 10.4.

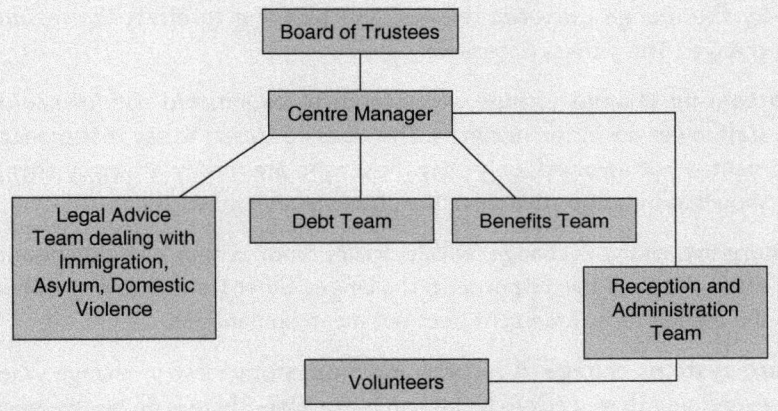

Figure 10.4 Haverton Advice Centre Organisation Chart 2

It is no exaggeration to say that Matthew, the current Centre Manager, is less than committed to these changes. He is very wedded to the ideal of co-operative working and providing direct help to the local community, which has serious social problems. However, he has been tasked with implementing these changes. In the next month he has to come up with a plan to implement the changes. It is envisaged that the changes will be made gradually, over the next six to eight months.

Your Task

1. As far as you can with limited information, carry out a PESTEL analysis. What conclusions can you draw about Matthew's priorities?

2. How would you advise him to carry out the required changes?

GLOSSARY OF TERMS

Action research The methodology of OD. Those most closely affected by the change carry out research and planning to effect the required changes. The process is iterative.

Bottom-up change Change which tends to be initiated and 'owned' by staff lower down the hierarchy. This does not mean to say that management is not involved, only that those who are mainly affect by change should as far as possible solve the problems that affect them.

Emergent change Change which occurs from within the organisation often as an organic response to challenges either from within or outside the organisation. Emergent does not mean unmanaged.

Hard systems change A rational and mechanistic view of change where everything that needs to be known is available. There is no disagreement about the problem or about how it is to be solved. Often fine for short-term, relatively easy change processes.

Iterative processes Processes which are repeated to incorporate new information or to refine a plan.

Organisational development A soft systems approach to organisation-wide changes over a fairly long term. Its aim is not only to manage change but also to ready the organisation to face similar challenges in the future

PESTEL An acronym for analysing the drivers of change from the external environment. It stands for: political, economic, social (or societal), technological, environmental, legal.

Planned change Change which is decided upon and implemented according to an prepared plan.

Soft systems change Change where there is insufficient information available to all those who need it and where there is little agreement about the nature of the problem or about the way to solve it.

SWOT An acronym for examining the internal fitness of the organisation to meet the need for change. It stands for: strengths, weaknesses, opportunities, threats.

Top-down change Change processes which are initiated and controlled from the top of the hierarchy.

KEY POINTS

Change is constant Because of the pace of political, technological and other global an local factors we have to expect that we will constantly be confronted with the need to change. Failure to adapt can easily lead to organisational failure.

Kurt Lewin's field theory Lewin is probably the most influential writer on the management of change. Most of the modern theories about change are influenced by his work. He saw the change process as finding an equilibrium between forces driving change and forces opposing it.

Lewin's 'unfreezing' model Lewin used the metaphor of freezing and unfreezing to illustrate the process of (a) moving people from their comfort zone (unfreezing), (b) learning about the new situation (changing) and (c) internalising the new context so that they became comfortable in it.

Organisational development An approach to change which recognises that organisations are complex human systems. There will be a plurality of views about change and it is necessary to engage with these and, as far as practicable, empower people to manage their own change. OD tends to take place when there is large scale systemic change needed over a longer term period of time. OD uses action research as its main methodology.

Resistance to change This can arise from many sources, both from individuals and from the inertia of current organisational features. In order for change to succeed, resistance needs to be removed or managed.

The change process Essentially this is the identification of the current state of the organisation with a perceived state. By examining the difference a plan is drawn up to move from the present state to the desired future state.

Top-down versus bottom-up change Change is often seen as *either* driven from the top *or* emerging from pressures lower down the organisation. All of the writers and practitioners of change agree about the need for those affected by change to have a say in how it is carried out. The issue is really the degree to which management is comfortable with delegating important decision making lower down the organisation. The issue is best thought of as a continuum.

REVISION QUESTIONS

1. How useful for planning change are PESTEL and SWOT analyses?
2. When might a 'hard systems' approach to change be appropriate? Give examples?

3. How helpful are planned change theories based on a unitarist view of organisations in a period of economic recession and financial constraints? What alternatives are there?

4. In what circumstances would you be reluctant to use an OD approach to managing change?

GOING FURTHER

As with all the topics relating to OB there is a vast range of material, both in book form and online. The reason is that all of our organisations are having to change, sometimes merely to survive, so managers are keen to find good answers as to how to manage the change process. Below is a range of books which will help reinforce the content of this chapter and show how we might develop the management of change process in the future.

- Harvard Business Review (2011) *HBR's 10 Must Reads on Change Management* (including featured article 'Leading Change', by John P. Kotter), Boston, Harvard Business Press.
  This is part of a series produced by Harvard Business Review which sets out the main points of theory and practice in the management of change and in other areas of management.

- Winter, R. (1989) *Learning From Experience. Principles and Practice in Action Research*, London and New York, Falmer Press.
  This book introduces the principles and practices of action research.

- Sarah, L., Passmore, J. and Cantore, S. (2011) *Appreciative Inquiry for Change Management: Using AI to Facilitate Organizational Development*, London and Philadelphia, Kogan Page.
  This book is a guide to using appreciative inquiry to facilitate change. AI is in some ways a development of action research, though it purports to go beyond the problem solving process of action research and engage with the process of personal transition.

- Kotter, J. and Rathgeber, H. (2013) *Our Iceberg is Melting: Changing and Succeeding Under Any Conditions*, Basingstoke, Macmillan.
  This is an imaginative fable about change in the face of great danger.

• Cameron, E. and Green, M. (2012) *Making Sense of Change Management: A Complete Guide to the Models Tools and Techniques of Organizational Change,* London and Philadelphia, Kogan Page.
A very useful 'how-to' guide.

NOTES

1. Although as we saw in Chapter 9, the claim to be acting in the interests of 'the organisation' can be contested.

2. However, we saw in that chapter that culture may not be susceptible to being 'managed'.

3. The example of fracking given in the vignette is a good example of a current environmental debate. For brief summaries of the positions taken by both sides see http://www.dangersoffracking.com/ for the anti-fracking argument and http://www.chevron.com/deliveringenergy/naturalgas/shalegas/responsibleshalegasdevelopment/ for arguments in favour of and reassurances about the dangers of fracking.

4. Wilfredo Pareto, is known for his development of the 'Pareto principle'. This is sometimes also referred to as the '80:20 rule'. The Pareto principle suggests that in many situations, we have to concentrate on the 20% of things which have a big impact, rather than on the other 80% which have much less impact. So, in carrying out a PESTEL analysis, we need to focus on the drivers of change which are likely to have the biggest effect.

5. Up to 70% according to Balogun, J. and Hope Haily, V., 2004, *Exploring Strategic Change, Second Edition,* London: Prentice Hall, p. 1.

6. Barbara Senior, Jocelyne Fleming, 2005, *Organizational Change (Third Edition),* Harlow and New York, Prentice Hall, Financial Times.

7. This kind of difficulty points up the distinction between hard complexity change, where there is general agreement about what the problem is, what is causing it and how it should be solved, with soft system approaches, where none of these issues is uncontested.

8. Kotter, John P., 2012, *Leading Change,* Harvard Business Review Press

9. The eight-stage approach is presented in further detail on John Kotter's website, which can be found at www.kotterinternational.com.

10. From Simms, 2005, Helen, 'Organisational Behaviour and Change Management', *Cambridge International Diploma in Management,* vol. 21, pp. 127–128.

11. Todnem, R., 2005, 'Organisational Change Management: A Critical Review', *Journal of Change Management,* vol. 5, no. 4, pp. 369–380.

12. For a discussion on pluralism and other assumptions about the nature of organisations, see Chapter 9.

13. Wendell L. French, Cecil H. Bell, 1998, *Organization Development: Behavioral Science Interventions for Organization Improvement, Sixth Edition,* New York, Prentice Hall.

14. Beer, Michael, 1980, *Organization Change and Development: A Systems View,* Santa Monica, Goodyear Publishing Co.

15. Adapted from Beckhard, Richard, 1969, *Organization Development: Strategies and Models,* Reading, MA, Addison-Wesley.

16. Hence why some people prefer to see the process as a spiral, indicating a progression rather than a repetition of the process.

17. Senge, P. M., 1990, *The Fifth Discipline,* New York, Century Business.

11

THE FUTURE FOR ORGANISATIONAL BEHAVIOUR

LEARNING OBJECTIVES

- Identify trends in the development of OB
- Discuss these trends in the light of global economies and geo-political developments
- Identify the main themes in critiques of OB
- Use a variety of perspectives to understand the forms and functions of modern organisations.

INTRODUCTION

The study of organisations has constantly developed. It has developed both as an area of rigorous academic study and as a body of knowledge which can be applied in organisations to make them more effective. We can see examples from the earliest days of the subject. The mechanistic efficiency of scientific management was challenged by the more people-centred human relations movement. That itself has been followed by an interest in systems thinking and contingency. More recently, researchers and practitioners have examined the role of technology on organisational structures and patterns of work.

However, it would be completely wrong to suggest that each new approach replaces what went before. The progression of theory and approach is not linear. Rather, new ideas have to co-exist with what went before. New perspectives provide us with more choice about how to think about and examine organisational life.

It is worth noting that no subject proceeds and develops in a linear way. It would be easy, for example, to produce a timeline showing when various novel views arose in OB. However, a brief observation will show that novel theoretical perspectives, however influential, did not displace those which came before. Scientific management has remained central to mass production and can be seen in contemporary forms in fast food retailers or call centres as well as in more traditional manufacturing. This is in spite of the work done to show the psychological and emotional aspects of how work is designed which can determine how satisfied, motivated and engaged we are with our jobs. Similarly, although we can discern a growth in, for example, virtual organisation forms and in distributed networks, not all organisations are becoming networks or virtual. The bureaucratic, hierarchical model is still alive and well.

Moreover, we need to remember that none of the approaches to OB is value-free. That is to say that any perspective is premised on a set of values, assumptions and ideologies which influence how we approach the subject. For example, scientific management (and many of the classical theories and perspectives) was based, as we have seen, on the notion of the 'rational-economic man'. This is a way of perceiving human nature which says that in the workplace we primarily calculate the economic benefits we will receive from applying our effort and skill to our work. All other considerations are secondary. Such a perspective enables managers to organise work using pay as the only reward factor without having to consider the emotional or psychological effect that work has on those who carry it out. It massively simplifies (or over-simplifies) the relationship of the individual with the organisation.[1]

Similarly, we have seen in the contrasts of radicalist, pluralist and unitarist perspectives on organisations that there is a very real difference in how you would manage an organisation depending on your assumptions about people, organisations and their management.[2]

Consequently, when we look at how OB is developing, we can identify two parallel areas of interest.

The first is the more traditional one which tries to understand what organisations are like, how they are changing and the quality of the relationship of their members to the organisation as a whole. As in this book, OB at the introductory stage mainly tends to focus on understanding organisational life at three interconnected levels: the individual, where we focus on the relationship of the individual to the organisations; the group level, where we consider the relationship of collectives of workers to the organisation and to each other within the collective; and, finally, the perspective of the whole organisation, its purpose, its functional arrangements and its culture. All of the chapters in this book (except this one) deal with topics at one or more of these three levels. Research into these areas is designed to better understand how organisations work and to develop models and theories which can be applied in the running of organisations. It examines trends in the way work is organised and carried out as well as trying to identify changing organisational forms. It is also interested in understanding how people can become motivated and gains satisfaction from their work.

The second area where the subject of OB is developing engages with issues of values and ideologies. All academic subjects need to examine themselves in order to identify and understand the underlying (and often unspoken) assumptions and ideological perspectives which drive both research into the topic and implementation of the theories which the research develops. OB is no different. Indeed, if no-one was asking these questions, we would have to doubt the authenticity of OB as an area for valid academic study.

This second area has come to be known as critical management studies (CMS). It is important that we distinguish CMS from simply being critical! We would expect anyone studying any subject to apply a critical mind to the topic they are studying. This kind of criticality is about trying to ensure that arguments developed are valid and logical, or at least persuasive, that sources used are properly relevant to the area being researched and that there is a proper academic rigour in the subject. CMS, however is at a different level of criticality; it investigates, identifies and challenges the underlying assumptions behind the subject. It confronts the premises (explicit or tacit) which drive its theoretical basis. We can see a parallel here with single

– and double-loop learning.[3] 'Single-loop' research attempts to try to understand and improve on existing knowledge and understanding of the topic. The 'double-loop' approach (taken by CMS) addresses questions like: why is research carried out in the way that it is? In whose interests is it carried out? What alternative assumptions and values could we be investigating?

In this chapter we will try to look at both the 'single-loop' and 'double-loop' work that is being carried out. However, we should also remember that there is very little that is new. Human nature does not change, it continues to exist in all its variety just as it has done for thousands of years. What changes is the context in which we express our nature and how we adapt to those changes. The main drivers of these changes are technology and the increasingly global nature of business. We can add to this the exciting work being done in the fields of genetics, psychology and other sciences and social sciences which are having, or could have, an impact on how we understand and run organisations. So, even if we humans are not changing the organisational world is. It is not the same as it was even 20 years ago and will almost certainly be very different 20 years hence, so we need to look at how OB and the disciplines that feed into it are helping us to understand and cope with those changes.

DEVELOPMENT OF OB THEORY: HOW IS OB CHANGING?

OB has always been ready to embrace new ideas. From F. W. Taylor's rationalising of the principles of division of labour in his development of scientific management, through the more humanist approach of the human relations movement trying to find satisfaction and motivation in the carrying out of work, to the later systems approach which tries to understand the working of the organisation as a set of interrelated parts connecting with he world outside of the organisation, change has been a constant accompaniment to the subject.

Perhaps the reason for this acceptance of (even enthusiasm for) change is that organisations are complex systems and it is difficult, if not impossible to get any kind of overview of an organisation without models and theories which to some extent are obliged to simplify that complexity. So if we had managed to find convincing, overarching theories which reliably explained and predicted what was needed for organisational effectiveness, then we could leave it at that. There would not be any need for new theories, merely fine tuning of those that already existed. Consequently, anyone running an organisation is likely to be open to new ideas that better explain how it works. Moreover, we all recognise that the world is rapidly changing, and new problems demand new solutions. The place where we learn about organisations must recognise this and develop more contemporary insights and solutions.

THE GLOBAL ECONOMY

In Taylor's day (and right up to fairly recently) the Western (American and, to a lesser extent the British and European) view of how things should be done was the one that dominated. In the 1960s, 70s and 80s the status quo was shaken by the success of the Japanese model. Western organisations tried to emulate this, without entirely managing to understand it. In Europe, the German economy has grown in strength from the post-war economic miracle. Its manufacturing prowess, its apprenticeship system of training and its high levels of worker input into corporate governance have largely passed the Anglo-American business school based system by. Since then in recent years we have seen the rise of new economies like China, India, Russia and Brazil. These economies provide competition which Western organisations struggle to match.

So we can expect the world economy to continue its global expansion and Western organisations will need to adapt to all the challenges this throws up. These will include greater competition for markets and resources. Organisations will need to pay even more attention to their costs in order to compete. They will have to develop ever more innovative products to sell in the new markets and they will need to try to outthink their rivals.

THE KNOWLEDGE ECONOMY IS ALSO GLOBAL

From this we can see that organisations will need structures and forms which enable them to not only to think innovatively, but to be able to make those innovations a marketable reality. This process has come to be known as knowledge management,[4] and organisations which need to use knowledge as a competitive asset have come to be known as knowledge companies.

Such a need changes the traditional relationship between managers and workers. Workers are no longer paid for their time and labour, but are paid also to develop and share their knowledge. Many workers, in other words, potentially possess a marketable asset. They are no longer merely contributors to the production of an already known output. Secondly, a knowledge management approach often means that workers will often have knowledge and expertise which outstrips that of their managers. So the role of the manager may need to change from a supervisory one to that of facilitator and provider of a working environment that will encourage knowledge development. Moreover, organisations will need to have processes through which new ideas can by generated, developed and brought to market.

Along with this there may need to be changes in reward systems. Will staff at all levels of the organisation be willing to share knowledge which could have an important monetary value to the organisation for a predictable salary which does not recognise that? Might they want to share in the financial benefits that their knowledge had helped deliver? Where organisations fail to address issues of reward, they may find that they lose key staff to competitors who have a more flexible system. Those staff who realise that they have knowledge and skill which the market values may well decide to work independently and reap more of the benefits of their knowledge themselves.

The nature of the global economy means that independent experts are not confined to working within a national economy, but can sell their expertise throughout the world and can command a price for their work that they may not get if they were employees.

WORKING ACROSS CULTURES

Nor is it only independent workers who will need to adapt to the global nature of work. Many of our organisations have spread throughout the world and workers in one country will need to communicate and collaborate with workers all over the world. This calls for the ability to operate cross-culturally, to be open to differences of perspective, values and motivations. As well as working remotely with people of other cultures, many staff will find themselves moving geographically to work with colleagues of different cultures. Not only does this present a challenge to individual staff in this position, it also begs the question of how (or indeed whether) a corporate culture can be imposed on staff working in a different national culture.[5]

CHANGES IN TECHNOLOGY

Accompanying globalisation, indeed largely enabling it, we have seen unbelievable developments in new technologies, thanks almost entirely to the invention of the micro-chip. From communications, through medical technologies to robotic production techniques, the organisation of today looks nothing like the organisation of even 20 years ago. Organisations have had to confront these changes and find ways of incorporating them into their structures and work patterns.

> The author of this book began his working life many years ago. Organisations looked very different then. Computers existed, but they were nothing like the ones we are used to. They were operated by roomfuls of staff (mainly young women) using keyboards to produce cards with punched holes in them. These were then fed into the machine (taking up almost as much room!) and printouts of data were produced. The main form of remote communication was by telephone. If the person you were calling was not near the phone, you had to wait and try again. If you were late for a meeting, say because there was a traffic hold up, there was no way you could let anyone know until you found a working telephone and could call them. If you needed to produce a document, it had to go to a typing pool (also staffed by very skilled young women), so had to be drafted in longhand, placed in a filing tray which someone would

VIGNETTE

collect at certain times of the day, taken to the typing pool and left with all the other longhand documents until a typist was free. It would be returned, probably the next day, hopefully completed and correct.

In contrast to the situation painted here, we can now transmit information, images, links to other computers very quickly. If we need to find information, we can do it straight away. If we want to speak to another person (or even more than one) we can do that no matter where we are. The only constraints are signal strength and the availability of the other person.

As well as the astonishing immediacy of global communication, we also see an increase in automated production. This often means that many production lines are virtually devoid of human presence. The noisy, dangerous and often dirty factory floor can be replaced by an almost clinically clean environment where the drudgery of repetitive work is taken on by programmed machines, able to work without breaks (other than for maintenance) and without complaints about working conditions or pay. In such factories, labour costs are reduced, though the set-up costs of the machinery are high and need the equipment to be operating at near capacity most of the time. Staff working in these facilities tend to be skilled technicians, rather than the more traditional unskilled and semi-skilled workforce of the older industrial period.

THE STRUCTURE OF ORGANISATIONS

We have already seen[6] the rise of the network structure in its various forms. Are we likely to see an increase in this kind of structure? The answer, on the face of it, is yes. It makes sense for managements to contract with independent workers to deliver an agreed output. From the perspective of management, this gives the organisation flexibility and enables them to respond to market and other changes. So we are likely to see more and more of this kind of working. Does this development mean the end of the bureaucratic structure? This is very unlikely. The organisational functions of operations, finance, marketing and managing people will remain since goods and services still need to be funded, produced and marketed over very varied timescales. Many outputs, such as aerospace products and pharmaceuticals, need a long lead time before they are ready for the market. So tried and tested stable organisational forms will still be needed. In order to achieve flexibility where flexibility is required, we can see hybrid forms in large organisations. There is no reason why organisations cannot be part bureaucracy, part matrix, part network and part virtual.

DEVELOPMENTS IN THE HUMAN SCIENCES

In addition to developments in global business and technological innovation, work in other areas such as the study of genetics and research into the human brain[7] is likely to affect organisational life, though the nature of these changes is largely unpredictable. Though we now know much more about the workings of the human brain than we did even ten years ago, thanks to developments in scanning technology and painstaking neuro-scientific research, the consequences of our new knowledge are still very uncertain. What is likely is that in the future we will have a greater understanding about things like learning, perception, intelligence[8] and how we form our understanding of the world.[9]

Accompanying this is work done by psychologists and philosophers on our emotions, an understanding of which has implications for the design of work, our motivational processes and our relationships with other people. In *Managing the Human Animal*, Nigel Nicholson has tried to identify the implications of evolutionary psychology (EP)[10] on how we function in the workplace.[11] However, none of this work goes unchallenged. EP is often criticised for being too deterministic – for claiming that all our actions are the consequence of evolutionary adaptation. Stephen J. Gould suggested, for example, that not all of our mental and emotional processes have an evolutionary function, but rather are the result of mutations which occurred which serve no adaptive purpose, but neither have any deleterious effect.[12]

The more we can know about the workings of the human mind, its resilience, its motivational processes and how it learns and adapts, the more likely it is that those who manage work can make jobs more satisfying and those who carry it out can find greater uses for their creativity.

THE ENVIRONMENT

We are also becoming increasingly familiar with the existence of threats from the planet itself which we must also confront. Growth in world consumer demand means even greater need for dwindling energy and material resources. Climate change may render many populated parts of the Earth uninhabitable in a few generations whilst other regions, hitherto unpopulated, will be available for settlement. On the face of it this seems an easy problem to solve – allow people to move from one part of the world to the other. However, the problems associated with migration, and the social, economic and cultural impact of such changes, can leave us with little confidence that any such population movement will be without serious problems.[13] The effect this will have on markets, national economies and political institutions is impossible to predict except to say that this single issue will probably affect all our organisations and is likely to test the resilience and creativity of everyone.

Accompanying climate change is population growth. Life expectancy is increasing almost everywhere (with some notable exceptions in areas of the world where there is agricultural failure or chaotic and violent political activities). A bigger population means a greater pressure on resources and greater competition on how those resources should be shared out. The consequences of this are enormous. The challenge is principally to politicians throughout the world, though the impact on the goods and services produced will necessarily be felt by our organisations.

So, there are certain things we can say about the impact of globalisation on our organisations because they are already happening. For example, much of the world's manufacturing is now done in the Far East, especially China. Many Western manufacturing organisations have moved the actual making of their goods eastwards, while retaining research and design in the 'home' country. An example of this happening in the UK is the Dyson company, which makes vacuum cleaners, fan heaters and driers. In 2002 the owner, James Dyson, moved the manufacturing of his goods to Malaysia, where it remains. Dyson claims that the cost savings of manufacturing enabled him to carry out essential research and development in the UK.

The interconnectedness of the world is laid bare by globalisation and the impact of geo-political events is immediate and often far-reaching. Consequently, we can say that organisations must now be aware of their relationship to the world at large and need people who can understand and react effectively to events.

We can see that old certainties are constantly under threat. The classical approach to management tended to simplify and focus its attention within the organisation. Greater complexity was introduced with the work of human relations and the systems approach that focused on the relationship of the organisation to the outside world. Perhaps it is best to say that we are now in an era where the happenings in the world beyond the boundaries of the organisation are the key drivers of the kind of organisations we need and that flexibility and rapidity of response are the keywords for the present and the immediate future. We can see for ourselves the complex, even chaotic environment we have to contend with.

CRITICAL MANAGEMENT STUDIES

We usually trace the beginnings of CMS back to the early 1990s, though there were certainly critiques of management before that time.[14] Indeed, some of the schools of thought that we now see as mainstream began as dissatisfaction with contemporaneous thinking about business and business organisations and were attempts to critique that thinking and find alternatives theories.[15] However, by the early 90s there was a significant number of thinkers who were critical of the pre-eminence of what we can call the 'business school model' of organisation and management. They saw it as promoting and supporting economic neo-liberalism and a managerialist ideology. These are the two themes which have received much of the attention of CMS theorists, so it is worth trying to encapsulate what is being discussed and critiqued.

NEO-LIBERAL ECONOMICS

The term neo-liberalism refers to a collection of economic ideas. In the social and political sphere, we have come to regard the word liberal as meaning open to or respectful of others' opinions, promoting the freedom of the individual within the bounds of social responsibility. In Europe, we tend to see liberalism as being politically a little left of centre. Economic liberalism, in its modern sense (hence *neo*-liberalism) is a set of economic ideas whose proponents see themselves as being the very opposite of left ideologies. For them, the primacy of the market is unquestioned.[16] We can identify a number of key ideas which contribute to our overall concept of today's neo-liberalism:

- **Markets must be free to operate untrammelled by regulation or state intervention**. This applies to the labour market, too. Since many organisations operate globally, they should be able to take advantages of lower labour costs where they find them in any part of the world. Moreover, national economies should not regulate markets through subsidies or statutes. The neo-liberals argue that laissez-faire economic activity will enable organisations to find their own level of activity and that if an organisation needs subsidy or regulation to sustain it it is inefficient and should be allowed to wither away. Additional costs on organisations from government and law will reduce profit and that is not in the long-term interest of the organisations or of the economy in general.

- **Public expenditure should be cut and the size of the state drastically reduced.** The state should only provide services at the most basic level, the market can take care of all other requirements. Consequently, as much of the state as possible should be privatised and left to market forces to determine.

- **The 'public good' is best served by the free operations of markets.** Margaret Thatcher (a confirmed neo-liberal) once famously announced that 'There is no such thing as society'. By these words she articulated a key theme of neo-liberalism, that of taking personal responsibility for all aspects of an individual's life. By implication (and often through more explicit statements) neo-liberals shift responsibility – and consequently blame – on to those who for lots of reasons can't thrive in a free for all market economy. The idea behind shifting the emphasis from the public to the private is that wealth accumulated by private organisations or individuals will be invested and provide work throughout the less wealthy sectors of the population.

• **Managerialism:** Managerialism is a term often used pejoratively, and it is easy to see why. Broadly speaking, the term is used for the emergence of a cadre of senior workers trained in the theories and techniques of the Western business schools. Whilst different people used slightly differently nuanced definitions of the term, we can distill the concept into a few key points:

• **Organisations are more similar than different**, so there can be a generic set of theories and techniques which can be applied in any management situation.

• **Managerialism takes little account of the nature of the organisation's purpose or of the professional status of its workers.** The knowledge base and techniques of management can be applied as effectively to running a circus as to a supermarket.

• **Everyone in the organisation can be subjected to the same reporting procedures no matter what their professional status.**

• **Managerialism empowers management over workers and even owners.** Because the ownership of commercial organisations is often diffuse through the structure of shareholding, owners find it difficult to act concertedly. Consequently, management is often left to make key decisions about strategy and its implementation, as well as about its own pay and conditions. Its accountability is often limited to annual reports and shareholder meetings. Since the major shareholders of public companies are often themselves large organisations, they tend to share the managerialist perspective.

• **Managerialism relies on two main bases for its legitimation:**

   a. 'Legal-rational authority' as described by Weber. This view proposes that any organisation, just by coming into existence, generates a system of authority and legitimately confers that authority on those who control and manage the organisation. In the case of commercial organisations, that authority is deemed to be delegated by owners. In the case of public organisations, it arises from government.

b. Professional managers have a knowledge base and set of techniques which makes them uniquely and professionally capable of exercising the roles of management

- **Management purports to be rational, though in practice that rationality is *bounded*.** Bounded rationality suggests that our rational decision-making is in fact limited by three important constraints: the quantity and quality of information available to the decision-maker, the cognitive capability of the decision-maker and the time available in which the decision has to be made. In practice, many decisions are *satisficing* rather than *optimising*, in other words we often have to accept a decision that will be just about acceptable for our purposes rather than an ideal solution.

- **This ethos has been translated into the public sector.**

- **Training of managers is largely the role of the business schools.** The theories and techniques taught in the business schools have cascaded into the management training industry beyond the business schools.

Although managerialism shares few of the values of neo-liberalism – the primacy of the individual, autonomy to act in one's self-interest and trust that the market, or market-like interactions, will ultimately benefit all, for example – it nevertheless puts itself in the service of a neo-liberal control of the economy.

And herein lies an irony. Neo-liberal rhetoric propounds the freedom of the individual to pursue his or her economic interests with the least possible interference from governmental or other kinds of regulation. Yet the whole thrust of managerialism is the development and application of metrics of control, from the setting of targets and performance indicators to the control of language and discourse, even of workplace 'play' events.[17]

Because of this apparent contradiction, both of these phenomena have received scrutiny from CMS thinkers, even when they come from different ideological perspectives.

The critical analysis comes mainly from two philosophical traditions: critical theory and post-structuralism, though there are other traditions, often from within these two overarching approaches, such as feminism, queer theory and neo-Marxism.

CRITICAL THEORY

Critical theory (CT) is mainly associated with the Frankfurt School which was founded at the Institute for Social Research in Frankfurt in the 1920s. Its members were Marxists who wanted to apply Marxism beyond the narrow prescriptions which had come to dominate it under the Soviet Union. Since that time some key thinkers have developed this line of thought over several generations. We can identify several strands of CT up to the present.

CT is not limited to analysing and understanding society, its purpose according to one of its founders, Horkheimer, is to liberate human beings from the circumstances that enslave them. CT embraces any philosophical approach if it has this aim. So more modern thinkers from this tradition have focused on things like communication, power, control of institutions and the concept of hegemony as areas which need to be uncovered and challenged. It has provided a theoretical basis for radicals confronting prejudice on race, gender and sexual orientation as well as on class. That theoretical basis needs to have three criteria to make it 'critical':

- It must be explanatory; that is, it has to say what is wrong with the social reality experienced by categories of people who see themselves as oppressed or disadvantaged.
- It must propose how it can be changed and by whom.
- It must be normative. It must provide norms which those carrying out the critique agree on and which can be used to set practical goals for transforming capitalism.

Almost by definition, analysts in this tradition find themselves in opposition to the dominant social order and work to undermine and transform it. They are working to challenge the prevailing hegemony, or the process of domination by one set of ideas which subverts or dominates another. If we go back to the discussion on power in Chapter 9, we saw how management sought to control not only what was done but also what was discussed and the terms on which those discussions took place. Certain topics and modes of discussion were off limits. This, at a societal level is what is meant by hegemony.

In the case of organisations critical management theorists examine how the hegemony of neo-liberalism oppresses and marginalises interests it sees as hostile and proposes alternative modes of organising which are more democratic and more psychologically liberating.[18] The work of CMS is very wide in scope and touches on every area of OB.

POST–STRUCTURALISM

The influence that this has had on CMS is the light that it sheds on the limits of objectivity and rationality. So the individual is shaped by their individual psychology, their social context and their language and culture. The individual has no control over these factors, though they can be uncovered using specialised investigative techniques (such as psycho-analysis for example). The post-structuralists, among whom Foucault is one of the pre-eminent thinkers, agreed that there were important underlying causal factors which gave us our sense of being, but considered them impossible to uncover since they are complex and dynamic. Moreover, it would be impossible for the individual to step outside of him- or herself to objectively examine these factors.

Critical management thinkers use the techniques of post-structuralist research to challenge the notions of organisational culture, the management of individual differences, motivations and reward and other managerial initiatives. They attempt to uncover the processes by which management apply and exploit power and advance ideas for the liberations of individuals from these oppressive structures.

CRITICISM FROM THE OB COMMUNITY

Criticism does not come only from the perspectives of left-leaning schools of philosophy, however. There is plenty of criticism from within the OB community itself. This criticism mainly centres around the role and effectiveness of the business schools, the content of their curriculum and its applicability to the practice of running organisations. Examination of business school effectiveness is not new. In the early 1950s a study by Zimmerman[19] criticised business schools for being a collection of trade schools and consequently lacking any real academic credibility. This criticism spurred the business schools to develop this aspect of their work. So much so, in fact, that many now criticise them for being too much like other academic departments and failing to teach (or research) applicable areas of management.

In the UK a potential alternative to the business school route was developed. Because there was concern at the standard of management practice, the British Institute of Management along with the Confederation of British Industry sponsored two key reports: the first, *The Making of British Managers*[20] and the second, by Charles Handy,[21] made the case for the importance of effective management to the national economic performance and the need for the professionalisation of British management. The competence standards that were produced as a result of these reports led to the first workplace, competence-based management qualifications in the world. The Institute of Management validates these programmes and runs a professional management membership scheme. So we see in the UK a potential competitor for traditional, university-based management learning, located within the workplace and founded upon day-to-day real world management work. However, for aspiring executive level managers, the MBA remains the preferred route.

The problem that has been highlighted here is that of the separation of the academic from the workplace experience of management. Often the careers of business school staff are much more closely tied in with the number and status of peer reviewed papers than they are with how valuable to the understanding and running of organisations those papers are.

Work done by Schön and Argyris, for example, has pointed out the stark differences between the technical rationality of academic enquiry and the formless nature of professional practice.[22] In the former, problems are presented to elicit knowledge and understanding of the theoretical perspectives taught in the lecture hall. In the latter, problems arise unformed and first have to be identified and contextualised before any attempt to solve them can be sought. Even then, it is unlikely that any problem arising will bear any similarity to the problems identified in the academic context. Moreover, different individuals can see the same issue from different perspectives and will bring a different approach to dealing with the issue.[23]

Petriglieri, blogging on the *Harvard Business Review* website[24] recognises the role that business schools play in developing what amounts to a managerial class, whose members are international and who share the same approach to running organisations no matter where those organisations are or what their purpose may be. In his blog he claims that:

> In short, business school courses serve as rites of passage – shaping the values, commitments, habits and mores of aspiring leaders. Let me be clear. I am not saying they should. I am saying that they already do. The questions are: how mindfully? How skilfully? On whose behalf?

He goes on to suggest that the business school curriculum needs to be both technical *and* humanistic and that schools' alumni should make the case for 'authenticity, service, equality, concern for the planet just as fervently as the case for shareholder value maximization'.

Other criticisms of business schools focus on the career success of MBA graduates. The findings tend to suggest that positive correlation between possession of an MBA and career success in terms of income level achieved is very small indeed, if the case for it can be made at all.[25] More pithily, Scott McNealy, the founder of Sun Microsystems, in an interview for Compassion in Politics says:

> Every other graduate school you do something. If you're a chemist, a graduate in chemistry, you go in and you do doctor beaker stuff and you make chemicals. If you're a physicist, you smash atoms. If you're a doctor, you get the rubber glove on and you cut and poke and prod in med school. If you're an English major, you read English and write English. And every other profession that you're going to go study graduate [sic], when you go to graduate school of business, you don't buy anything, you don't sell anything, you don't make anything, you don't hire anybody, you don't review anybody, you don't fire anybody, you don't do anything that you do when you get into the real world.[26]

CONCLUSION

What is taught in the business school is overtly vocational, so the reputations of the business school model will stand or fall on how effectively the learning achieved in an academic context will be put into operation in the workplace. OB sits a little uneasily here. Whilst its outputs are expected to contribute to organisational effectiveness, its roots in psychology, sociology and anthropology, as well as its scrutiny from various philosophical and ideological perspectives lie firmly in the scope of academic critique. Academics owe loyalty to a much wider concept of truth than the purely practical or vocational, so there is a tension within the OB community between its economic, value-adding function and what is owed to a wider constituency.

Moreover, OB engages with a key human activity – work and wealth creation. In whose interests should it work, that of capital, which is largely what happens now, or should it be infused with a more democratic, humanistic ethic?

GLOSSARY OF TERMS

Critical theory Based on the work of the Frankfurt School, CT sees organisations as vehicles of oppression and tries to find alternative paradigms.

Evolutionary psychology This is an area of study which is premised on the fact that we have inherited our minds from our ancient forebears, whose living circumstances were radically different from our own. In the 10–20,000 years since agriculture was developed and the 200 years since the start of the industrial age, our minds have not had time to make any evolutionary adaptations; consequently we have to live in a post-industrial world using the minds of hunter-gatherers.

Globalisation The trend that we have increasingly seen over the last 30 years of productive activities being carried out worldwide, not just within a national economy.

Knowledge companies Companies for whom the development of knowledge is a primary function.

Knowledge management Where knowledge is an important asset for an organisation, it has to be able to organise so that it can create market value from the knowledge that its staff develop.

Managerialism The technocratic application of knowledge and techniques to the running of organisations. The growth of a managerial class.

Neo-liberalism An economic theory which claims that free, unregulated markets will create and distribute wealth more efficiently than centralised planning.

Post-structuralism A philosophical school which challenges the notion of an objective world which can be known to us through research and analysis.

KEY POINTS

- OB continues to develop its current research base by examining how organisations and jobs are changing.
- The two main drivers of change in our perception of organisations are:
  - Globalisation and
  - Developments in technology.
- In addition, breakthroughs in our understanding of human emotion and brain physiology will probably inform our understanding of issues like motivation, perception, leadership and learning.
- As an academic subject, OB is also under scrutiny form a variety of perspectives. These include:
  - Post-structuralism – this is a philosophical perspective (a reaction to structuralism) which challenges the concept of an objective world where causality can be discerned by analysis. Its adherents take the view that while there is probably an objective structure underlying all things, it is impossible to uncover or analyse it because our subjectivity prevents us. As social entities, organisations are as subject to a post-structural analysis as any other social entity.

- Critical theory – this school of thought goes back to the foundation of the Frankfurt School in the 1920s. Over the generations, critical theory has developed its fundamental premise that societal structures, including (sometimes especially) work organisations, are sources of oppression and that the purpose of critical theory is liberation. Movements like feminism and gay liberation, and anti-racist and anti-colonial movements have arisen from this perspective.

- The critical management theorists come largely from the post-structuralist and critical theory perspectives. They have two main areas of critique:

  - The neo-liberal economic agenda which they believe that mainstream OB serves to the exclusion and detriment of a more humanistic version of business and organisation, and

  - The growth of managerialism. When we use the term managerialism we are thinking about the growth of a managerial technocracy, possessing the knowledge and skills taught in the business schools. Managerialists take the view that management is a technical activity to be carried out by those qualified to do so. The purpose or activity of the particular organisation is irrelevant, they are all subject to the same management techniques. In managerialism, managers run the organisations, decide its strategy and implement its plans largely without reference to a dispersed ownership.

- Criticism also comes from within the OB community. This criticism focuses largely on the business schools and the effectiveness of the OB curriculum and its applicability to real world management.

GOING FURTHER

The impact that global capitalism is having on Western societies is growing. Key moments like the banking crash of 2008, and before that the collapse of Enron have fuelled criticism of modern global capitalism. Consequently, we can expect that critiques of how businesses are run will increase. Moreover, the widening of the wealth gap, along with decreasing wage value, will see a continued interest in corporate governance to control remuneration of top executives and possibly greater regulation of certain industries, in particular the financial services industry.

All of this will certainly have an impact on research and practice in OB. Hopefully this chapter has given a flavour of the ways in which OB is developing and is being challenged from outside and from within. Below is a range of material which will be of value to anyone wanting to pursue some of the ideas in the chapter:

- Alvesson, M., Bridgman, T. and Willmott, H. (2011) *The Oxford Handbook of Critical Management Studies*, Oxford, Oxford University Press. *A very useful collection of the ideas and trends in critical management studies.*

- Thompson, P. (1989) *The Nature of Work: An Introduction to Debates on the Labour Process*, Basingstoke, Palgrave Macmillan.
  An early examination from a neo-Marxist perspective of issues like deskilling, control, Taylorism and others.

- Clegg, S., Kornberger, M. and Pitsis, T. (2005) *Managing and Organizations: An Introduction to Theory and Practice,* Thousand Oaks, CA, Sage.
  An insightful work using various sources and giving a view on how organisations and management need to change.

- Alvesson, M. and Willmott, H. (1996) *Making Sense of Management: A Critical Introduction*, Thousand Oaks, CA, Sage.
  A critique of management from a critical theory perspective by arguably the leading writers in critical management studies.

- Clarke, T. (2009) 'A Critique of the Anglo-American Model of Corporate Governance', *CLPE Research Paper* No. 15/09, Osgoode-Hall Law School, Toronto.
  An article examining how types of capitalism in different parts of the world produce different levels of inequality.

- Bronner, S. E. (2011) *Critical Theory: A Very Short Introduction*, New York, Oxford University Press.
  Short but informative and knowledgeable.

- Belsey, C. (2002) *Poststructuralism: A Very Short Introduction*, Oxford, Oxford University Press.
  Again interesting and informative for the lay reader.

NOTES

1. See Chapter 1.
2. See Chapter 9.
3. See Chapter 2 for an explanation of these terms.
4. For an overview of knowledge management see http://www.km world.com/Articles/Editorial/What-Is-.../What-is-KM-Knowledge-Management-Explained-82405.aspx, accessed 18 March 2014.
5. For an overview of this issue, take a look at this article published in Forbes, the American business magazine in 2010: http://www.forbes.com/2010/08/27/global-corporate-culture-multinational-leadership-managing-mitsloan.html, accessed18 March 2014.
6. In Chapter 7.
7. Antonio Damasio, 2005, *Descartes' Error: Emotion, Reason and the Human Brain*, London and New York, Penguin Books.
8. See, for example, ideas on intelligence like those of Howard Gardner, who challenges the still powerful notion of general intelligence; Gardner, H., 2011, *Frames of Mind: The Theory of Multiple Intelligences*, New York, Basic Books.
9. See the discussion on schemata in Chapter 3.
10. Evolutionary psychology (EP) attempts to study the human mind as a legacy of our evolutionary past. Agriculture only began about 10,000 years ago, industrialisation a mere 200 years ago and the post-industrial world we now inhabit has happened within the lifetimes of many of the readers of this book. Evolutionary psychologists argue that our minds and bodies evolved primarily for a hunter-gatherer society, so our adaptations to modern living have been a challenge to our minds and bodies. To put it crudely, we still have stone-age brains.
11. Nicholson, Nigel, 2000, *Managing the Human Animal*, London, Texere Publishing.
12. Gould, Stephen Jay, 2007, *The Richness of Life: The Essential Stephen Jay Gould*, New York, W. W. Norton and Company, especially Parts III, VI and VII.

13. For a useful overview of this issue, and others involving climate change and population, see http://www.ipcc-wg2.gov/publications/SAR/SAR_Chapter%2012.pdf, accessed 17 March 2014. See also the Intergovernmental Panel on Climate Change website, http://www.ipcc.ch.

14. We tend to date modern CMS from the date of publication of Alvesson, M. and Willmott, H. (eds), 1992, *Critical Management Studies*, London, Sage.

15. We have already seen how the human relations movement arose as a counter theory to classical management theories, especially to scientific management, and systems thinking forces organisations to examine the environment and context in which they operated rather than focusing just on the organisation and its internal workings.

16. The term neo-liberalism was used rather differently between the two world wars and in post-war Germany.

17. See Hunter, C., 2012, 'Child's play and corporate culture', accessible online at http://criticalmanagement.org/play.

18. For a useful portal providing resources and links to issues in critical management, see http://criticalmanagement.org/.

19. Zimmerman, J. L., 2001, *Can American Business Schools Survive?*, unpublished manuscript, Simon Graduate School of Business Administration, cited in Pfeffer, Jeffrey and Fong, Christina T., 2002, 'The End of Business Schools? Less Success Than Meets the Eye', *Academy of Management Learning & Education*, vol. 1, no. 1, accessible online at http://www.aomonline.org/Publications/Articles/BSchools.asp, accessed 31 March 2014.

20. Constable, John and McCormick, Roger, 1987, *The Making of British Managers: A Report for the BIM and CBI Into Management Training, Education and Development*, Corby, British Institute of Management.

21. Handy, Charles, 1987, *The Making of Managers*, A Report for the BIM and CBI

22. Schön, D., 1987, 'Educating the Reflective Practitioner', in Schön, D. and Argyris, C. (eds), 1996, *Organizational Learning II: Theory, Method and Practice*, Reading, MA, Addison Wesley.

23. Schön calls real world professional practice operating in 'the swamp', while he refers to the techniques developed in the academic context as belonging on 'the high ground'.

24. Accessible online at http://blogs.hbr.org/2012/11/are-business-schools-clueless/

25. See Pfeffer, Jeffrey and Fong, Christina T., 2002, 'Less Success Than Meets the Eye', accessible online at http://www.aomonline.org/Publications/Articles/BSchools.asp, accessed 28 March 2013.

26. For the full text, see http://compassioninpolitics.wordpress.com/2011/01/24/criticism-of-business-schools-mba-degrees/.

INDEX

acculturation, 295
achievement-oriented leadership, 205
action centred leadership, 208–9
action learning, 61
action research, 325–7, 336
action research cycle, 326
Adam Smith, 7, 8, 184
Adams, JS, 127
adjourning, 164
aesthetic needs, 118
Alderfer, 120, 144, 145, 148
Argyris, C, 356
artifacts, 253
attitudes, 96, 148, 162, 182, 313
authority, 210
autonomy, 25, 136, 146, 150, 168, 188, 192, 300, 353

Bamforth, 21
Barach, P and Baratz, S, 294
Beer, M, 324
behaviourism, 55
Belbin, MR, 169
benefits of group working, 152
benevolent authoritative system of leadership, 193
benevolents, 128
Bentall, 47
bet-the-company culture, 258
Binet, 52
Blake, R and Mouton, J, 196
body language, 86

Brech, 13, 39
bureaucracy, 13, 14, 39, 40, 225, 265, 348
Burns, T and Stalker, GM, 29, 221
Burns, JM, 209
Burrell, G and Morgan, G, 289
business schools, 352, 353, 356

cafeteria benefits, 133
Cattell, R, 45
centralisation, 12, 246
Challenger space shuttle, 173
change agents, 324
charismatic leadership, 210
Chartered Institute, of Management, 66
classical approach, 6–15
classical conditioning, 56
coalitions, 270, 298, 299, 301
coercive power, 293
cognitive dissonance, 97
cognitive learning, 57
cognitive needs, 118
collaborative working, 157
command groups, 154
Compassion in politics, 357
complex system, 22, 24, 25, 35
complexity, 188, 226, 247, 251, 267, 278, 317, 327, 343, 350
consciousness, 80
consideration, 192
consultative system of leadership, 193

content theories of motivation, 116
the contingency approach, 7
co-operative working, 157
core job dimensions, 135
core-periphery structures, 234
Country Club management, 196
critical management studies, 342, 350–7
critical theory, 354–5
Cropanzano, R and Mitchell, MS, 161
Cross, R et al., 239
cross-functional groups, 156
Cuba, 173
cultural web, 258, 259
culture, definitions, 250–1
culture, stories, 261
Cuseo, J, 158

Deal, T and Kennedy, A, 255
deficit needs, 118
definitions of leadership, 189
deprivation-satiation proposition, 160
differentiation, 29, 196, 223, 225, 226, 227, 243, 247
dimension of the organisational context, 2
dimension of the whole organisation, 2
dimensions of the organisation, 1
directive leadership, 205

discourse, 288, 294, 295, 309, 353
discrimination, 41, 65, 66, 69, 99
dissatisfiers, 121
division of labour, 8, 35, 150, 153, 158, 159, 175, 343
Dyson, 349

elements of management, 11
emergence, 24
emergent change, 311, 312
emotional intelligence, 73
emotional stability, 44
emotions, 188, 215, 252, 348
employment contract, 296
empowerment, 299–301
entitleds, 128
equity, 12
equity theory, 127
ERG theory, 120
Erikson, E, 47
ethnicity, 63–6
evolutionary psychology, 348
existence needs, 120
expectancy, 123
expectancy theories, 123
experienced meaningfulness of work, 136
experiential learning, 59
expert power, 293
exploitative authoritative system of leadership, 193
extroversion, 44, 48

Fayol, H, 11, 13, 15, 39, 233
feminism, 354
Festinger. L, 97
Fiedler, FE, 201
field theory, 318–20
force field analysis, 320
formal groups, 153, 154, 163, 180, 182

forming, 163
Foucault, M, 295, 355
fracking, 314
Frankfurt School, 354
Frankfurt, Institute for Social Research, 354
French, J and Raven, B, 292
frustration-aggression proposition, 160
functional flexibility, 235
functional relationships, 224
functionalist paradigm, 290
fundamental attributional error, 91

Gale, EAM, 18
Gardner, H, 52
gender, 66–8
Gestalt, 58
Gilbreth, FB and LM, 10
Gillespie, R., 18
globalisation, 41, 63, 66, 227, 238, 280, 346, 349, 350
goal conflict, 132
goal-setting theory, 130–5
Goleman, D, 53
Gould, SJ, 348
group dimension, 2
group cohesiveness, 165
groupthink, 172
growth needs, 118, 120

Hackman and Oldham, 135
Hakim, C, 68
Hales, C, 300
halo effect, 91
Handy, C, 263, 281, 356, 363
hard complexity, 317
Harley, B, 300
Harrison, R, 263
Harvard Business Review, 357
Hawthorne Effect, 16, 18

Hawthorne studies, 15, 18, 19, 153, 165, 184
hegemony, 354
Henry Ford, 9
Hersey, P and Blanchard, KH, 207
Herzberg, F, 121, 122, 126, 129, 134, 135, 144, 145
heuristics, 90
hidden power, 294–5
hierarchical structure, 223–7
hierarchy, 187, 223, 224, 230, 232, 247, 301
hierarchy of needs, 117, 120, 138
Hinson, S and Healey, R, 296
Hofstede, G, 65
Homans, GC, 160
homeostasis, 24, 35
Horkheimer, M, 354
Human Relations approach, 17, 18, 36
human relations, 15
humanist psychology, 119
Huseman, 128
Hygiene Factors, 121
hypothesis, 4

idealised influence, 211
idiographic, 43, 47, 50, 55
illusion of unanimity, 173
impoverished management, 196
inattentional blindness, 89
individual differences, 42, 69, 76, 199
individual dimension, 1
indoctrination, 295
inequity, 128, 129
informal groups, 25, 153, 154
informal organisation, 17, 222, 238
informational power, 292

initiating str, 192
Institute of Management, 356
instrumentality, 123
integration, 29, 222, 225
intellectual capital, 54
intelligence, 41, 51, 53, 74, 362
interpretive paradigm, 290
invisible power, 295–6
IQ, 52

Janis, I, 173
Japanese economy, 231
Jensen, MA, 164
job design, 42, 114, 146
Johnson, G and Scholes, K, 258

Kanter, RM, 322
Kirkpatrick, SA and Locke, EA, 190
knowledge management, 345
Kohler, 58
Kotter, J, 321
Kurt Lewin, 318

Latham, G and Locke, E, 130
Lawrence and Lorsch, J, 29
leadership, contingency theories, 200
leadership, authoritarian, 191
leadership, democratic, 192
leadership, functional theories, 191–200
leadership, laissez-faire, 192
leadership, trait theories, 190–1
leadership, see Chapter 6
learning, 4, 43, 54–63, 57, 58, 61, 69, 138, 142, 178, 269, 356, 359
learning cycle, 60
learning organisation, 327

learning sets, 61
Least Preferred Co-worker questionnaire, 201
legal-rational authority, 352
Legge,K, 237
legitimate power, 297
Likert, R, 193
line relationships, 224
Locke, E, 130
locus of control, 124

MacGregor, D, 193
macho/tough-guy culture, 258
Mack, A, 89
Making of British Managers, The, 356
maintenance dimension, 192
maintenance roles, 169
Management Information Systems, 230
management of change, see Chapter 10
management style, 168
management levels, see Scalar chain
managerialism, 352, 359
Margaret Thatcher, 351
Marxism, 291, 354
Maslow, A, 117, 135, 138, 144, 147
matrix, 188, 233, 234, 238, 243, 244, 265, 348
matrix structure, 232–4
Mayo, E., 18
McNealy, S, 357
Mead, GH, 47
mechanistic, 16, 28, 29, 221, 222, 242, 269, 312, 334, 340
Middle of the Road management, 196
Miller, K, 161
misaligned goals, 174

mission statement, 253
Morgan, G, 268
motivation, see Chapter 4
motivation, definition of, 122–7
motivators, 121
multiple intelligences, 53
Myers Briggs, 47

Nazis, 173
neo-liberalism, 350, 351, 353, 355, 363
neo-Marxism, 354
network organisation, 238–41
networking, 26, 239
Nicholson, N, 348
nomothetic, 43, 47, 49, 50, 55, 74
norming, 163
norms, 21, 44, 48, 159, 162, 164, 165, 185, 251, 301, 317, 320, 354
numerical flexibility, 235

OB and the social sciences, 4
OCEAN, 46
Ohio State University leadership studies, 192
open system, 20
operant conditioning, 56
operations research, 10
organic, 28, 29, 177, 221, 242, 312, 334
organisation chart, 221, 228, 239, 240, 247, 256, 275
organisation theory, 23, 27
organisational culture, see Chapter 8
organisational development, 323–8
organisational politics, 282
organisational power, see Chapter 9
out-groups, 173

paradigm, 259, 281, 288, 290
participative system of
    leadership, 193
path–goal theory, 205–8
Pavlov, IP, 56
pay flexibility, 236
people culture, 266
perception, see Chapter 3
perceptual set, 85
performance-related pay,
    133
performing, 164
Personal Construct Theory,
    47
personality, 43–51, 50, 55,
    68, 125, 170, 200, 204,
    316
PESTEL, 27, 29, 313, 334,
    335
Peters, T and Waterman,
    J, 234
Petriglieri, G, 357
physiological needs, 119
piece working, 133
planned change, 213, 282,
    311, 312, 314, 319, 320
pluralism, 285
politics, definition of, 284
Porter and Lawler, 126
post-structuralism, 354, 355
power culture, 263
power distance, 64
power, definition of, 283–4
power, strategies for using,
    296–9
participative leadership, 205
priests, 257
primacy effect, 91
principles of management,
    11
problem-solving, 22, 101
process culture, 257
process thories of
    motivation, 122

productivity, 8, 15, 21, 25,
    35, 116, 164, 196, 231,
    317
prosody, 86
psychic prisons, 270
public service ethos, 255

qualitative research, 4
quantitative research, 4
queer theory, 354

Race Relations Act, 65
radical humanist paradigm,
    291
radical structuralist
    paradigm, 291
radicalism, 286
rational-economic man, 11,
    137
rationality, 17, 187, 210, 290,
    353, 355
recency effect, 91
reference groups, 157
referent power, 293
reflection in action, 60
reflection on action, 60
reflective practice, 60–1
reinforcement, 56
relatedness needs, 120
reliability, 46, 47, 53, 129
reward, 115, 123, 124, 126,
    127, 144
reward power, 292
risky shift, 174
rituals, 250, 251, 256,
    261–2
Rogers, C, 47
role, 1, 9, 18, 26, 32, 42,
    45, 49, 51, 63, 68, 71, 77,
    80, 89, 94, 104, 149,
    168, 172, 191, 209, 211,
    213, 253, 256, 264, 294,
    323
role culture, 264

satisficing, 353
scalar chain, 12
Schein, E, 252
schemata, 84, 86, 94, 108,
    254, 255, 328, 362
Schmidt, 9
Schön, D, 356, 363, 364
scientific management, 5,
    8–11, 10, 16, 18, 135, 290
self-actualisation, 118
self-censorship, 173
self-efficacy, 124, 131
self-managed work groups,
    155
self-organisation, 24
Semler, R, 291
Senge, P, 327
sensitives, 128
sensory thresholds, 83
16PF, 45
skill variety, 135
social categorisation, 161
social comparison, 162
social identification, 162
social exchange theory, 159–61
social identity theory, 161–3
social learning, 58
social loafing, 158
socialisation, 295
socio-technical systems, 21,
    35, 155
soft complexity, 317
sources of power, 292–3
span of control, 28, 151, 231
spatial ability, 52
Spearman, 52
spies, 257
staff relationships, 225
stereotyping, 90
stimuli, 81
stimulus proposition, 160
Stogdill, RM, 190
Stoner, JAF, 174
storming, 163

storytellers, 256
sub-systems, 21, 183
success proposition, 160
Sun Microsystems, 357
supportive leadership, 205
synergy, 152, 166, 174
systems approach, 7, 19–26, 335

tacit knowledge, 60
Tajfel, H and Turner, JC, 161
Tannenbaum and Schmidt, 197
task groups, 156
task identity, 136
task culture, 265
task dimension, 192
task management, 196
task roles, 169
task significance, 136
Tavistock Institute, 21
Taylor, WM, 5, 8, 10, 13, 35, 39, 133, 137, 240, 343

Team Roles Inventory, 170
team style management, 196
technical rationality, 356
Terman, L, 52
Theory X, 194, 195, 196, 215
Theory Y, 194, 195, 215
Thorndike, E, 91
Thurstone, LL, 52
trades unions, 297
transactional leadership, 209
transcendence needs, 118
transformational leadership, 209–12
Trist, EL, 21, 155
Trompenaars, L, 65
Tuckman, B, 163
two-factor theory, 121

ultimate attributional bias, 92
uncertainty avoidance, 64
unitarism, 285, 290
Unity of Command, 12
Ure, A, 66

USSR, 173

valency, 123
validity, 18, 47, 52, 53, 118, 129, 190, 206
values, 199, 209, 215, 250, 253, 263, 270, 278, 281, 294, 313, 342, 346, 353
verbal ability, 52
virtual organisation, 241–2
Vroom, V, 123
Vroom, V and Jago, A, 204

Weber, M, 13, 14, 39, 225, 352
whisperers, 256
Woodward, Joan, 28, 40
work group, 25, 149, 150, 151, 152, 159, 175, 184
work hard, play hard culture, 257

Yang, LR et al., 168